DO NOT QUENCH THE SPIRIT

OTHER BOOKS BY THE SAME AUTHOR

Matthew's Messiah: a Guide to Matthew's Gospel

The Most Amazing Prophecy in the Bible: Daniel's Prophecy of the Seventy Sevens

Is the Bible Really the Word of God? The Doctrine of Scripture

DO NOT QUENCH THE SPIRIT

A Biblical and Practical Guide To Participatory Church Gatherings

Andrew W. Wilson

Do Not Quench the Spirit: A Biblical and Practical Guide to Participatory Church Gatherings

Copyright © 2016 Andrew W. Wilson

Believers Publications, P. O. Box 485, North Lakes, Queensland, 4509, Australia

All rights reserved. No part of this publication may be reproduced or transmitted in any form or by any means, electronic or mechanical, including photocopy, recording or otherwise, except for brief quotations in printed reviews, without the written permission of the publisher.

Scripture quotations, unless otherwise noted, are taken from the New King James Version, copyright © 1979, 1980, 1982 by Thomas Nelson, Inc. Used by permission. All rights reserved.

Scripture quotations marked (KJV) are taken from The Holy Bible, Authorized King James Version

Scripture quotations marked (ESV) are taken from The Holy Bible, English Standard Version® (ESV®), copyright © 2001 by Crossway Bibles, a publishing ministry of Good News Publishers. Used by permission. All rights reserved.

Scripture quotations marked (NIV) are taken from the Holy Bible, New International Version®, NIV®, copyright © 1973, 1978, 1984, 2011 by Biblica, Inc.™ Used by permission of Zondervan. All rights reserved worldwide. www.zondervan.com The "NIV" and "New International Version" are registered in the United States Patent and Trademark Office by Biblica, Inc.™.

ISBN: 978-0-9943977-2-0

CONTENTS

1	Participatory Church Gatherings	1

SECTION ONE: BIBLICAL

2	1 Corinthians 14:26-40: Early Church Gatherings	29
3	1 Thessalonians 5:19-21: Do Not Quench the Spirit	49
4	Participatory Church Gatherings in the Pastoral Epistles	62
5	If Any Man Speaks: 1 Peter 4:10-11 and James 3:1	89
6	Ephesians 4:7-16: Mutual Edification	103
7	Participatory Church Gatherings in Acts	122
8	Biblical Principles behind Participatory Church Gatherings	140

The Work of the Holy Spirit • Spiritual Gifts • Mutual Edification • The Priesthood of All Believers • Church Government • Body Life • The Lordship of Jesus Christ

9	Objections to Participatory Church Gatherings	163

Didn't Paul preach till Midnight at Troas? • Paul was Criticizing the Corinthians, not Commending them • 1 Cor. 14 is Descriptive not Prescriptive • 1 Cor. 14 only Mandates Edification, not a Model of Church • Since Charismatic Gifts have Ceased, Participatory Church Gatherings no longer Apply • It is Inconsistent to have Participatory Church Gatherings and not have Speaking in Tongues • The New Testament Evidence is Confused and Contradictory • 'Principles, not Patterns' • Just because they did it in NT times, does this mean that we have to? • 'I'm not Convinced'

CONTENTS

SECTION TWO: PRACTICAL

10 Practical Reasons for Participatory Church Gatherings 200
Church as a Performance • The Pragmatic Approach is not Working • Consumer Convenience Culture • Poor Results in Producing Disciples • Why Christian Growth Stalls • Christians are not Experiencing God in Worship • Pastoral Burnout • People Learn and Grow Best by Participating • Participation Increases Productivity

11 Participatory Church Gatherings and the Lord's Supper 221

12 Women's Participation 244

13 How NOT to have Participatory Church Gatherings 258
Devaluing the Lord's Supper • No Time for Teaching • Picked Speakers • Only a Token Time of Teaching • Special Occasions • No Questions or Discussion • Small Group Bible Studies • Sharing Groups • The Church Business Meeting

14 Practical Objections, Problems, and Questions 281
Wouldn't it be Easier to Organize Church? • "I don't get it" • The Danger of Adding Man-Made Traditions • "I don't get anything out of it" • What about Strangers Speaking and Causing Confusion? • Majoring on Minors • The Danger of Division • How to Get Quiet People to Speak • The Problem of Silences • The Problem of Poor Quality Preaching • The Problem of Meetings becoming Stale • What to do in Big Churches

15 Steps to Implementing Participatory Church Gatherings 302

Index 310

CHAPTER 1

Participatory Church Gatherings

How is it then, brethren? Whenever you come together, each of you has a psalm, has a teaching, has a tongue, has a revelation, has an interpretation. Let all things be done for edification (1 Cor. 14:26)

A Midweek Bible Study

When I was a young Christian in my late teens, our church had a midweek Bible study in which we used to work through a Bible book, chapter by chapter, verse by verse. We usually had one person give a fifteen-minute introduction and overview, and then different people would comment as we made our way down through the passage, sharing thoughts, offering different viewpoints, asking questions, or suggesting practical applications. We did not use any 'study guides', so we went at our own pace and sometimes took nearly a year to get through a longer book, like a Gospel. I used to spend one evening a week doing my own study of the passage, in preparation for Wednesday night's Bible study.

One of the books we studied was 1 Corinthians and one of the things I noticed as I did my study was that chapter 14 (particularly from verse 26 onwards), seemed to provide detailed instructions about the way that the early church conducted its main weekly gathering. These church gatherings seemed to be participatory – a little bit like our midweek Bible study. Church for the early Christians was not a case of one person preaching a sermon while everyone else sat and listened. Instead, multiple members of the congregation were able to teach or to give a word of encouragement, or to ask a question, or to use a variety of other different spiritual gifts, all for the mutual building-up of God's people.

Up until this point in my life, I had simply accepted the *status quo*, the way we did things in church. I did not think to question it or look to compare it with what the New Testament taught about church life. I had always been taught that the Bible, as God's inspired Word, was what we must follow – not human traditions or trendy new fads or clever-sounding ideas. But here in 1 Corinthians 14, I had come face to face with what church life was like in the Bible. I found the picture of participatory church gatherings it presented quite intriguing.

Let me try and summarize what I mean by 'participatory church gatherings'. When the church gathered in New Testament times, all of the brothers had the opportunity to contribute to the meeting by using their spiritual gifts (not just by saying amen or acting as ushers or stacking chairs or singing). Church in the New Testament was interactive; each member had a part to play (just like in a human body). Church in the New Testament involved a gathering which included the Lord's Supper, or Communion, and also included opportunity for the believers to use their spiritual gifts to build up each other. Church was not a 'service' put on by a few for the benefit of the many, but a gathering to which all the church contributed.

Part of the reason for my interest was that our church had another meeting (the Lord's Supper) that resembled in many respects what the passage in 1 Cor. 14 described (although it differed in a number of ways too). The key idea, however, was the same: there was opportunity and freedom for multiple members of the congregation to participate in the service, according to their gifts, as led by God's Spirit.

Two Surprising Reactions

Over the following years, however, I noticed two surprising things. Firstly, I discovered how dismissive some people were about the idea. When I mentioned this subject to some of my Christian friends, they were very reluctant to consider the concept. Virtually every person to whom I mentioned this New Testament picture of church reacted negatively.

I spoke about this picture of church life in 1 Corinthians 14 to one friend, a Pastor who had been through Bible college. Without even opening the Bible, he brushed off the suggestion that 1 Cor. 14 was describing a participatory style of church with the words, "perhaps the imperatives are indicatives". He was suggesting that Paul was simply describing the situation in Corinth without commanding us to do things the same way. I had enough New Testament Greek under my belt by this stage to know my friend's grammatical argument was a bluff, and that translating the imperatives (i.e. commands) in 1 Corinthians 14 as indicatives (i.e. statements) didn't really work, which is why no Bible version has ever translated the passage this way. However, I did not debate the point; I was so surprised by the attempt to 'blind me with science' that I kept quiet, and let the matter slide.

Another friend, a church leader who had been through Bible college, responded by saying something similar: "perhaps Paul was criticizing the Corinthians rather than encouraging such behaviour". Now it is true that a small minority of commentators down through the centuries have suggested this idea, and it is also true that Paul had to correct some disorders in the church gatherings at Corinth. However, we only have to open the Bible and read the passage to see that my friend's argument does not hold water. Paul is laying out detailed directions about how church gatherings should be organized, and in verse 31 he specifically encourages free and open participation, saying, 'you can all prophesy one by one, that all may learn and all may be encouraged'. In verse 37, after having given guidelines governing how various gifts are able to be freely used he insists that 'the things which I write to you are the commandments of the Lord'.

Again, I did not want to get into an argument, but what surprised me was the dismissive manner in which the response was made and the conversation shut down without even looking at what the Bible said. Both of these friends seemed very reluctant to consider the issue, but were happy to grab at any reason, however flawed, to evade the conclusions that the passage suggested.

The second surprising thing I noticed over the years was how many Bible commentators and theologians agreed that 1 Corinthians 14 (and other New Testament passages) described a participatory style of church gatherings in New Testament times. These commentators showed that participatory church gatherings were not some strange or eccentric personal idea that I had picked up from 1 Corinthians 14 and other passages, but the mainstream, majority view of Bible scholars. Here are quotes from five respected commentators.

Leon Morris, commentating on 1 Corinthians 14:26-40, writes: 'this little paragraph is very important as giving us the most intimate glimpse we have of the early church at worship ... it is our earliest account of a service and it enables us to see something of what the first Christians actually did when they assembled to worship God. Clearly their services were more spontaneous and less structured than was normally the case in later days. We have no way of knowing how typical of the whole church worship at Corinth was, but it cannot have been very far from the norm, else Paul would have said so'[1].

John Drane, author of the best-selling *Introducing the New Testament*, concurs, 'In the earliest days ... their worship was spontaneous. This seems to have been regarded as the ideal, for when Paul describes how a church meeting should proceed he depicts a Spirit-led participation by many, if not all ... There was the fact that anyone had the freedom to participate in such worship. In the ideal situation, when everyone was inspired by the Holy Spirit, this was the perfect expression of Christian freedom'[2].

William MacDonald in his *Believer's Bible Commentary* writes: 'What happened when the early church came together? It appears from [1 Cor. 14] verse 26 that the meetings were very informal and free. There was liberty for the Spirit of God to use the various gifts which He had given to the Church. One man, for instance, would read a psalm and then another would set forth some teaching ... Paul gives tacit approval to this "open meeting" where there was liberty for the Spirit of God to speak through different brothers. But having stated this, he sets forth the first

---

[1] Leon Morris, *1 Corinthians*, TNTC, Nottingham: IVP, 1985, p190
[2] John Drane, *Introducing the New Testament*, Lion, 1999 Revised Edition, p402

control in the exercise of these gifts. Everything must be done with a view to edification'³.

Howard Marshall, writing about a similar passage in 1 Thessalonians 5:19-21 (*Do not quench the Spirit. Do not despise prophecies. Test all things; hold fast what is good*), argues that what was happening in church in Corinth was found also in Thessalonica: 'What is set out in detail in 1 Cor. 12-14 is stated here summarily. The Spirit is powerful and active like fire in the congregation (cf. Rom. 12:11, 2 Tim. 1:6 for the metaphor). Gifts for ministry were being exercised, but some people were trying to suppress them (we don't know just how), but it is wrong to do so'⁴.

Scottish theologian James Denney went so far as to say, commenting on the passage in 1 Thess. 5:19-21, 'An open meeting, a liberty of prophesying, a gathering in which any one could speak as the Spirit gave him utterance is one of the crying needs of the modern Church'⁵.

These are just a few of many commentators, from a wide variety of church backgrounds, who agree that participatory church gatherings were practised in Corinth and other New Testament churches. As this book will seek to show, the evidence from various passages of Scripture is clear and consistent: participatory gatherings were not only normal in the New Testament, but were endorsed by the apostles as divinely ordained.

Why the Objections?

Why were my friends so quick to dismiss the possibility of participatory church gatherings? Why such half-baked objections? The reason was not biblical interpretation, even if they dressed up their criticisms as such. I don't know the motives for different individuals' defensive attitudes, but from the similar reactions of a range of people, I believe there are two underlying reasons for the negative responses. Firstly, virtually all

---

[3] William MacDonald, *Believers Bible Commentary*, Nashville, TN: Thomas Nelson, 1995, p1801

[4] I. H. Marshall, "1 Thessalonians", *New Bible Commentary*, 4th Ed., Leicester: IVP, 1994, p1284

[5] James Denney, "The Epistles to the Thessalonians", in *The Expositor's Bible*, ed. W. Robertson Nicoll, Baker Books 1982 reprint of 1903 US edition, p357

Christians have strong personal feelings about church life. Most of us are involved in churches and owe a great debt to them. We also have personal preferences about all sorts of church-related issues. As a result, we naturally adopt a defensive attitude – or even feel hurt – when our church tradition is called in question. On the other hand, we know that all our churches are imperfect, in practice if not in theory. We realise that we must be prepared to hold our church life up against the test of Scripture. God's Word must be the ultimate foundation for church life, not human traditions or cleverness. In the first half of this book we will look at a number of passages about church services in the Bible. Many Christians have never been shown what church meetings were like in New Testament times, and are unaware that one of the central features was the participatory nature of congregational life. Now, of course, participation is not the most important feature of church life; other things like love, evangelism, teaching and worship are more important. Nevertheless, participatory gatherings make up part of the New Testament picture of church life, and if we want to be faithful to God's Word then we must face up to this fact. Even though we find it difficult, we need to allow our church life to be measured up against and corrected by what the New Testament teaches.

The truth is that participatory church services have good biblical support. There are far more Bible references to participatory meetings than there are for Sunday worship, deacons, or a weekly collection[6], let alone some modern evangelical church practices for which there is no biblical basis. As we will see, there are as many Bible references describing participatory church gatherings[7] as there are verses describing church government by elders[8].

The second reason for the reluctance to consider participatory church gatherings stems from doubts that the idea would work in the real world.

---

[6] Sunday worship: Acts 20:7; deacons: Acts 6:1-6, Phil. 1:1, 1 Tim. 3:8-13; weekly collection: 1 Cor. 16:2

[7] Acts 11:28, 15:6-7, 12-13, 1 Cor. 14:26-40, Eph. 4:7, 11-16, 1 Thess. 5:19-21, 1 Tim. 1:3-7, 6:3-5, 2 Tim. 2:14-17, Titus 1:9-11, Jam. 3:1, 1 Pet. 4:10-11

[8] Acts 11:30, 14:23, 15:2, 4, 6, 22, 23, 20: 17, 28-35, Phil. 1:1, 1 Tim. 3:1-7, 4:14, 5:17-20, Titus 1:5-9, James 5:13-14, 1 Peter 5:1-5

Personally, I think that people wondering whether or not participatory church gatherings are practical have got their priorities wrong. As followers of Christ, our first question should not be whether something is practical (or traditional, or reasonable, or politically possible). Instead, we should think like Christ, and ask ourselves His opening question: 'What is written in the law? How do you read it?' (Luke 10:26). He challenged His critics, 'Have you not read ...' (Matt. 12:3, 5, 19:4, 21:16, 42, 22:31, etc.). He commonly replied with the simple words, 'It is written' (Matt. 4:4, 7, 10, 21:13, 26:31, etc.) and constantly quoted Scripture as the authoritative basis for faith and practice. If we claim to be Christ's followers, then before we start worrying about whether something is practical, we must consider whether it is scriptural. Are we genuinely open to what the Bible says, and ready to do what it teaches, or do we practice a sort of 'cafeteria' Christianity that picks and chooses certain parts of the Bible that we find more palatable?

This is not to say that we cannot ask questions about whether something is practical. A. W. Tozer wrote, 'Facts are glorious, tough, stubborn things, and they are fine criteria against which to measure our beliefs. Wesley taught that any doctrine which was found untenable in practice should come under suspicion of being erroneous and should be carefully re-examined in the light of Scripture. If it would not *work* in real life it was not likely to be the true teaching of the Bible'[9]. The second half of this book will explore practical issues related to participatory church gatherings. But notice that, even so, pragmatic questions are not the final judge of what is true for a Christian; they merely prompt us to carefully re-examine Scripture and refine our practices in its light. We should not 'lean on [our] own understanding' (Prov. 3:5), but trust and obey God's Word. If we believe that Scripture is inspired then we must also accept that it is profitable, i.e. it works (2 Tim. 3:16).

I once spoke to a Christian friend who was broadly sympathetic to the idea of participatory church gatherings but who wondered whether the idea had any real potential. This friend's question was not just

---

[9] A. W. Tozer, *Wingspread: A. B. Simpson, a Study in Spiritual Altitude*, Camp Hill: PA, Christian Publications, 1943, p80, emphasis in original

whether participatory gatherings would work in the life of a modern church. His question was even more basic: would anyone even listen to an idea so radically different to the way most church services are run? This friend was sceptical that many churches would adopt anything like this picture because it was so different to what they already did.

Maybe my friend was right: perhaps there are few churches that would re-evaluate their church services in the light of the New Testament. But the reality is that many Christians have a completely wrong idea of the church. John Stott writes: 'What model of the church, then, should we keep in our minds? The traditional model is that of the pyramid, with the pastor perched precariously on its pinnacle, like a little pope in his own church, while the laity are arrayed beneath him in serried ranks of inferiority. It is a totally unbiblical image, because the New Testament envisages not a single pastor with a docile flock but both a plural oversight and an every-member ministry'[10].

Even in those evangelical churches that claim to believe in 'every-member ministry', the reality usually amounts to little more than menial, semi-administrative jobs like going on the cleaning roster, or being car park attendants. Here is a typical church invitation for people to get involved in serving God: 'We are always looking for volunteers to help bring our Sunday services to life. Everyone is crucial, and without you they would not happen. There are many different ways to serve: from sound, visuals, music, singing, welcoming, ushering, making coffee and tea, and managing the building on the day. If you think any of the above sounds like you, or want to know of other ways to get involved, please contact the church office'. From the increasing frequency that one hears such advertisements for help, it would seem that people are becoming more reluctant to do these menial jobs. God created us to be more than cogs in a machine.

The New Testament envisages all the members of the church being involved in *spiritual* ministry – not just getting involved in the machinery of an organization. Of course there are mundane jobs to be done, which

---

[10] John R. W. Stott, *The Message of Ephesians*, BST, Nottingham: IVP, 1979, 1989, p167

come under the gift of 'helps' (1 Cor. 12:28). But they are not the spiritual ministries Paul was thinking of in Ephesians 4, (the passage that Stott was commenting upon), where Paul pictures the church growing as every part of the body works together, using their spiritual gifts. Paul wrote that every Christian has a spiritual gift (Eph. 4:7), so that 'speaking the truth in love, (we) may grow up in all things into Him who is the head, Christ, from whom the *whole* body, joined and knit together by what *every* joint supplies, according to the effective working by which *every* part does its share, causes growth of the body for the edifying of itself in love' (Eph. 4:15-16).

Martyn Lloyd-Jones asked, 'Are we giving the members of the church an adequate opportunity to exercise their gifts? Are our churches corresponding to the life of the New Testament church? Or is there too much concentration in the hands of ministers and clergy? You say, "We provide opportunity for the gifts of others in week-night activities." But I still ask, Do we manifest the freedom of the New Testament church? . . . When one looks at the New Testament church and contrasts the church today, even our churches, with that church, one is appalled at the difference. In the New Testament church one sees vigour and activity; one sees a living community, conscious of its glory and of its responsibility, with the whole church, as it were, an evangelistic force. The notion of people belonging to the church in order to come to sit down and fold their arms and listen, with just two or three doing everything, is quite foreign to the New Testament, and it seems to me it is foreign to what has always been the characteristic of the church in times of revival and of reawakening'[11].

The Three Discoveries of Dublin Univerity Students

In early 19th century Ireland, Edward Cronin, a medical student recently converted from Catholicism, was dismayed at the divisions amongst Protestants. Holding that all true believers were members of the one Church of God, he was reluctant to join any particular denomination.

---

[11] D. M. Lloyd-Jones, *Knowing the Times*, Edinburgh: Banner of Truth Trust, 1989, pp195-196

After being publicly denounced for this by one of the Independent churches, he started meeting together with some other Christians, welcoming any who were truly Christ's. Faced with the opposition of Catholicism all around, they believed strongly in unity in Christ, irrespective of secondary differences. Having started meeting in such a humble way, they also came to see that no minister was needed to lead their meetings or to officiate at the Lord's Supper. Anthony Norris Groves was a theology student hoping to become a missionary, which meant he had to be ordained. But he discovered that ordination to preach the gospel at home or abroad is no requirement of Scripture. The New Testament does not teach a division of believers into clergy and laity any more than it teaches division into denominations. But this left them with a problem. How should they organise their meetings? When they first met together, they left the order of service to the person in whose house they met. However, as they continued studying Scripture, they came to realise that 'we should come together in all simplicity as disciples, not waiting on any pulpit or ministry, but trusting that the Lord would edify us together by ministering as He pleased and saw good from the midst of ourselves' (Groves). In other words, they discovered the New Testament format of participatory church gatherings. The Brethren movement (as it was later called) with its vision of evangelical unity, the authority of Scripture over tradition, and a desire to put God's Word into practice, went on to become a major missionary movement (with more missionaries than any British denominational mission). Its rapid spread was not only a testament to the power of the Holy Spirit, but also to the principle of every-member ministry.

Some Practical Objections

I remember being in the office of a Pastor of a medium-sized church (a few hundred people) who was in the middle of preaching a series of Sunday sermons on the subject of the church, when I happened to notice on his desk a book called *Life in His Body*, by Gary Inrig. I was surprised to see the book, and recommended it, particularly the chapter about participatory church gatherings (called 'The Meeting of the Church'). I explained briefly what I meant by participatory church gatherings and (as

I should have expected) he responded negatively, with words to the effect: "Sounds like a recipe for disaster. Surely, a bit of organisation is going to work better than that". Had I been more quick-witted, I might have replied by picking up Inrig's book and reading out a passage where he describes one participatory church gathering.

Inrig writes: 'On one occasion, some Christians who had heard me preach elsewhere came to our assembly meeting. They sat down and waited for the service to begin. They were somewhat startled when someone from the congregation arose to start the meeting. There was no one sitting on the platform and so the man leaned over and said to his wife, "Gary must be late and they're starting without him". Several others participated, and she leaned over and said, "They're doing pretty well, aren't they" expecting my appearance on the platform at any moment. But slowly they realized that this diversity wasn't just an accident. This was the way it was meant to be. Yet it was very new to them, and they concluded that the meeting really had been organised and various people had been appointed to participate. They were surprised to discover, as they talked with friends, that there had been no planning or arranging, but that various men had participated under the leading of the Holy Spirit, out of a desire to edify the body of believers and to glorify the Lord Jesus'[12].

Or consider what Dr. William McRae wrote: 'Following the pattern of the New Testament church, in our Sunday evening meeting at Believers Chapel there is just such freedom [for the Spirit-led exercise of gifts]. There is always opportunity for the discovery and continuing development of spiritual gifts. Just a few weeks ago, one of the highlights of our Sunday evening meeting was when a high school lad read the first three verses of Psalm 1 and shared with us some thoughts from the Psalm. We must be very careful about our perspective. Sometimes we can become just a little resentful when we look at a young person speaking and think of him as practicing on us. Our attitude toward that situation should be like the track coach who is used to seeing men speed down the

---

[12] Gary Inrig, *Life in His Body*, Wheaton, IL: Harold Shaw Publishers, 1975, pp71-72

hundred-yard track in nine seconds flat, and then sits in his own living room and watches his first son take his first two or three toddling steps. Which is more thrilling to him? It depends on his perspective. If he is looking as a track coach only, the living room scene is kid stuff. But if he is looking as a father and sees that young lad starting to grow and mature, taking his first couple of steps, he is the most elated man on the face of the earth! Sometimes I leave the Sunday evening service almost that elated. I see a man who has become a Christian and then he stands up and he gives out a hymn or he prays. It thrills my heart because here I see a man who is growing. He has taken his first public step and it is a sign of spiritual growth. Men talk to men about wanting to discover their spiritual gift, wondering how to discover it and how to develop it. My response is: in the meeting of the church. One major purpose of it is for the Spirit led exercise of spiritual gifts'[13].

But the criticism of participatory church gatherings by the Pastor of the medium-sized church is one for which I have some sympathy. It is true that participatory church gatherings can sometimes be far less polished than the average evangelical church service. One person described one such meeting as 'amateur night at church'. Sadly, there have been churches which practised participatory church gatherings in certain (unbiblical) ways which, rather than being spiritually fruitful, have instead produced spiritual barrenness and decline. Others, ignoring the guidelines in God's Word, have had services which have been chaotic (as we see in Corinth) and disastrous. It is also true that unless there are substantial, good-quality contributions to the meeting by Spirit-filled Christians, it can be unedifying.

There is no denying the fact that there are plenty of potential problems with participatory church gatherings. We see these difficulties in 1 Corinthians and other New Testament letters. However, instead of telling the early Christians to abandon such meetings, these letters present 'trouble-shooting' solutions to these problems, particularly by encouraging the believers to participate in spiritually edifying ways.

---

[13] William McRae, *The Meeting of the Church*, Dallas: Believers Chapel, 1974, 2001

Someone might say that it would be better for us to ignore participatory church gatherings, lest we suffer from the same sort of problems we see in various New Testament letters. But do we have the right to reject biblical truths because they may involve potential difficulties? Since when was Christianity about taking the easy path? Often it is in the difficulties of life that we grow the most as Christians. Instead, we need to be aware of the potential problems, and adopt the precautions and solutions that the New Testament itself provides, so that church gatherings are both biblical and also profitable and edifying.

I remember once speaking to a missionary serving God in a southern European country who laughed off the idea of participatory church gatherings by saying, "If we did this in our church, the Christians would be standing up and attacking each other". I'm pretty sure that this was just another case of someone trying to ridicule the idea, in this case by exaggerating the spiritual immaturity of his own church. From all reports, the Christians in his congregation seemed to be quite zealous in their evangelism, a sure sign of spiritual development and progress. In addition, I had visited another church in the same country which practised interactive church gatherings, and their worship did not consist of people abusing each other at all, but was respectful and beneficial.

But I can imagine many other pastors thinking something similar to the Mediterranean missionary: "participatory meetings would not work in my church". Here's a question for such pastors: would this be a reflection of the shallow spirituality, laziness, lack of maturity, and limited gift-development of your church members? And if so, should the blame for this spiritually-stunted state of affairs rest with the pastor's preaching, or with the current style of church services? The current church services obviously must not be very spiritually effective if they are not developing mature disciples able to teach others.

Paul's congregations were composed of people from Mediterranean cultures, and these churches seemed to have their fair share of disputes, both doctrinal and personal. Yet Paul evidently considered participatory church gatherings up to the job of producing spiritual maturity and maintaining doctrinal orthodoxy, for he established their patterns of worship, and sent letters reinforcing and regulating this style of gathering. If they practiced participatory church services (as the evidence seems to show), and they managed to take the gospel to the furthest reaches of their world, fulfilling the Great Commission in their lifetime, then we can hardly object that the idea of participatory church gatherings won't work. These were the most successful churches in the history of Christianity.

On purely practical grounds the great German biblical scholar J. A. Bengel (1687 – 1752), argued that participatory church gatherings are to be preferred. Writing in *Gnomon*, his New Testament commentary, on 1 Cor. 14:26, he said, 'At that day the assembly was more fruitful than in our own, when one man, whatever his state of mind, is expected to fill up the time with a sermon'[14]. Bengel was surely correct in this: New Testament Christianity was far more fruitful than our modern Western evangelical version, and not just in its evangelism. Consider how quickly the early Christians grew: within a year of conversion the Galatians had elders appointed in every church (Acts 14:23), who had presumably developed well beyond spiritual babyhood, while the Thessalonians and Colossians had letters sent to them with advanced teaching about the Person of Christ and His return.

Three Practical Reasons for Participatory Church Gatherings

Participatory church gatherings are not without their challenges. Are there any good reasons why we should adopt such a form of church worship? We will look at a number of practical reasons for participatory church gatherings in a later chapter, but here I want to suggest three reasons why the benefits outweigh the challenges they bring.

Firstly, the modern 'church growth movement' is not working. There are not many Christians opposed to the idea of the church growing, or unbelievers coming to Christ, but for all the talk of church growth, there is not much happening. Despite our seeker-sensitive services, celebrity

---

[14] Bengel's quote comes from his *Gnomon*, p660; the translation here is taken from *The Critical English Testament*, by Rev. W. L. Blackley and Rev. James Hawes, London: Daldy, Isbister and Co, 1877, 3rd. Ed., Vol. 2, p468

preachers, technology, and contemporary music, the percentage of evangelical Christians in the West continues to drop.

George Barna, the foremost analyst of trends in the American evangelical scene, wrote in his 1990 book *Marketing the Church*[15]: 'Since 1980, there has been 'no growth' in the proportion of the adult population that can be classified as 'born again' Christian. The proportion of 'born again' Christians has remained constant at 32%, despite the fact that churches and para-church organisations have spent billions of dollars on evangelism. More than 10,000 hours of evangelistic television programming have been broadcast, in excess of 5,000 new Christian books have been published, and more than 1,000 radio stations carry Christian programming. Yet despite such widespread opportunities for exposure to the gospel, there has been no discernable growth in the size of the Christian body'[16].

Worse still, in his 2014 book, *Churchless*, Barna documents how the numbers of people attending church have dramatically dropped in the intervening decades: in the 1990's the unchurched (those never, or no longer, attending church) represented 30% of the American population, but this proportion had risen to 43% by 2014. Over the last twenty years about 3,500 churches have closed every year in the United States, and 80-90% of churches that remain are declining and dying[17].

Worst of all, even though hundreds of mega-churches have sprung up during this period, giving the appearance of explosive growth, the reality is that eighty percent of modern Western church growth is simply transfer growth. Use whatever metaphor you will, but in a day of increasing numbers of church hoppers and shoppers, the sad truth is that most 'success-story' churches are just better at sheep stealing, shuffling the pack or musical chairs.

---

[15] George Barna, *Marketing the Church*, Colorado Springs, CO: Navpress, 1990

[16] In the Australian edition, Barna's statistics reflect the Australian, New Zealand and United Kingdom situation, which also shows 'no growth in the proportion of the adult population that can be classified as committed Christians'; *Marketing the Church*, Sutherland: Albatross Books, 1988, pp21-2

[17] See Brian Croft, *Biblical Church Revitalization: Solutions for Dying and Divided Churches*, Fearn: Christian Focus Publications, 2016

In 2001, Barna wrote: 'Claims of prolific church growth have been grossly exaggerated; not only are most churches not increasing in size, but those that are expanding are doing so at the expense of other churches. More than 80 percent of the adults who get counted as new adherents and thus as part of the growth statistic are really just transplants from other churches – religious consumers in search of the perfect, or at least more exciting or enjoyable, church experience. Disturbingly little church growth is attributable to new converts. All in all, it was not a good decade for church growth'[18].

We cannot build God's church by our worldly sophistication and human wisdom (2 Cor. 1:12). Here is John Piper: 'Everybody knows that with the right personality, the right music, the right location, and the right schedule you can grow a church without anybody really knowing what doctrinal commitments sustain it ... The long-term effect of this ethos is a weakening of the church that is concealed as long as the crowds are large, the band is loud, the tragedies are few ...'[19]. Many big evangelical churches are growing for one simple reason: a crowd draws a crowd – mostly from other churches. But this is not the way that God works. Christianity is about a prayer-answering God not appeals for money, the conviction of sin not catchy tunes, the power of the Holy Spirit not polished pulpit performances (see 1 Cor. 2:1-4).

Compare the modern evangelical scene with the growth of the early church in the book of Acts. Without money, formal education, political influence, natural giftedness or clever strategies, a small group of nobodies – cowardly failures, led by a few fishermen – were given the task by Christ of evangelising the world. What did they do? Did they set up a committee to hold 'brainstorming' sessions, think of a trendy name for their new group, take up a collection and print some advertisements, give out leaflets, or rent a room and start preaching? No, their self-confidence had been completely shattered. Instead of depending on their

---

[18] George Barna and Mark Hatch, *Boiling Point: It only Takes One Degree; Monitoring Cultural Shifts in the Twenty-First Century*, Ventura, CA: Gospel Light/Regal Books, 2001, p236

[19] John Piper, *Counted Righteous in Christ*, Nottingham: IVP, 2002, p22

own cleverness, they prayed for ten days straight until God sent His Spirit to do what all our human abilities will never accomplish.

We need God, not gimmicks or the latest fads. We need the power of the Holy Spirit. If we want to see God's blessing in our day, we should be careful not to quench the Spirit in our churches. Participatory church gatherings which are open to the leading of the Holy Spirit are an important part of God's pattern for church life found in the New Testament for the simple reason that they continually teach us the need for humble dependence upon the Holy Spirit.

A second practical reason for participatory church gatherings relates to spiritual growth. Most evangelical churches believe that one of their most important responsibilities is to produce spiritually mature followers of Christ. What is the most effective way to do this? I suggest that people learn and grow best by participating. The diagram that follows is called the Learning Triangle[20], and it shows how much our brains retain by various learning methods.

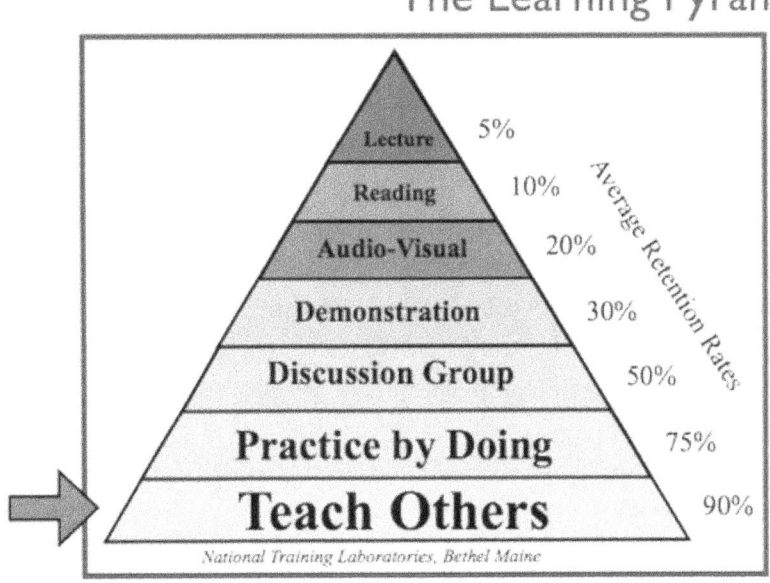

---

[20] National Training Laboratories Institute for Applied Behavioral Sciences (2005), *The Learning Triangle: Retention Rates from Different Ways of Learning*, National Training Laboratories, Bethel, ME

What does the Learning Triangle teach us? Listening to a lecture (or sermon) results in a paltry 5% retention rate, adding written notes or a visual presentation on screen hardly improves this percentage (10-20%), while discussion results in a 50% retention rate (not bad!), and those actually doing the teaching remember 90% of what they said.

Here is how Dr. Ellen Weber sums up the message of the learning triangle: 'Brains require workouts to learn and grow ... while lectures foster a couch potato mentality ... from the brain's perspective, you learn more and better retain it if you talk to your dog ... than if you listen to lectures'[21]. We might almost say that it is better to preach to your pet than sit and listen silently to a sermon.

Now you know why most Christians cannot remember in any detail what was said in any of the (approximately) fifty sermons that they listened to in the last year, apart from some silly joke that a preacher told. This also explains why you hear Christians saying things like, 'Our preacher on Sunday was really great', but when you ask them what the message was about, they can hardly remember. No wonder some Christians seem to make so little spiritual progress – they do little more than listen to sermons. As Charles Spurgeon said in the context of some people's rather shallow Bible reading, 'the Bible has mighty free course among us nowadays, for it goes in at one ear and out at the other'.

The reason why lectures persist, despite the fact that listeners get very little out of them, becomes clear from this triangle too: teachers themselves find that lecturing provides the most stimulation for their own brains. Preachers will tell you this very thing – they feel spiritually exhilarated from studying the Word of God, preparing messages that present the truth of God, and prayerfully depending on the Lord for help in their delivery.

The lesson for church life should be obvious: if we were really interested in getting people in our congregations to develop spiritual maturity and grow more like Christ, we would do two things. Firstly, we would include stimulating discussion straight after our sermons so that God's people would interact and remember a lot more about what was

---

[21] www.brainbasedbusiness.com/2006/08/three_parts_of_your_brain_need.html

taught, and secondly, we would try as quickly as possible to get people involved in teaching the Word of God to others, for that is the very best way for them to grow themselves.

Strangely enough, or sensibly enough, that is precisely what the New Testament picture of the church involves. The New Testament shows a participatory model of church life where individuals are firstly able to interact with the message preached by asking questions, or suggesting additional thoughts, and secondly, they have the freedom to present a message from God's Word that shares something they have learnt themselves, or share a word of wisdom from some personal experience, or a word of encouragement, exhortation or admonition. Like most things in life, we only get out of church what we put into it, so the more we contribute, the more we benefit. As the saying goes, 'A truth taught is interesting, a truth caught is exciting, a truth discovered is life changing'.

A third practical reason for participatory church gatherings flows on from this: the modern evangelical world is failing at the task of discipleship. A. W. Tozer described the terms of true discipleship as 'the willingness to turn our backs on everything worldly for Jesus' sake'[22]. But Christ went further: if anyone wants to follow Him, they must put Him before father and mother, wife and children, lands and houses, even their own life (Luke 9:23, 14:26, Matt. 19:29).

We will look at the evidence in more detail later, but what it shows is that modern Western evangelical Christianity is not producing many disciples. Michael Horton sums up the situation: 'Gallup and Barna hand us survey after survey demonstrating that evangelical Christians are as likely to embrace lifestyles every bit as hedonistic, materialistic, self-centred, and sexually immoral as the world in general'[23]. David Wells put it like this in his 1995 booklet, *The Bleeding of the Evangelical Church*: 'we

---

[22] A. W. Tozer, *Faith Beyond Reason*, Camp Hill, PA, Christian Publications, 1989, p4

[23] Michael Horton, "Beyond Culture Wars", *Modern Reformation* (May-June 1993), p3

have produced a plague of *nominal evangelicalism* which is as trite and as superficial as anything we have seen in Catholic Europe'[24].

Modern evangelicalism has become a religion of consumer convenience Christianity. Church primarily exists to serve and provide for me; in return, I am required to contribute very little.

Is there any connection between the modern discipleship deficit and the way we run church life? Frank Viola argues that, because the 'professionals' carry 'the spiritual workload, the majority of the church becomes passive, lazy, self-seeking ("feed me"), and arrested in their spiritual development'[25]. With ever-increasing numbers of large churches where most people are spectators, we are producing a Christianity that is one mile wide and one inch deep.

Many Christian leaders realise there is a discipleship problem in modern Western evangelical Christianity, and some are trying novel schemes and clever programs to solve it. No doubt some of these plans will yield some results, and for that we should give thanks. But if we are sincerely concerned about the need for developing disciples, the New Testament pattern of church gatherings that are participatory is worth considering. This is not to say that increased involvement in church life alone will result in a dramatic improvement in discipleship. Discipleship also involves personal work, coming alongside individuals and encouraging them in their walk with the Lord.

Participatory church gatherings encourage discipleship and personal spiritual responsibility because followers of Christ are motivated to use their spiritual gifts to build up and encourage others in church. They also find fulfilment in serving God themselves. On the other hand, church gatherings where nobody is ever required to participate except the pastoral staff do little to encourage the development of disciples.

Discipleship involves more than sitting on a seat on Sunday for an hour or so. Discipleship is a total commitment to Jesus Christ as Lord.

---

[24] David Wells, *The Bleeding of the Evangelical Church*, Edinburgh: Banner of Truth, 1995, p8, emphasis in original

[25] Frank Viola, *Reimagining Church*, David C. Cook, Colorado Springs, CO, 2008, p160

Dedicated, growing followers of Christ not only stay healthy by being fed; they also need to exercise by using their spiritual gifts to worship God and serve others. One of the primary venues where this occurred in the New Testament was in the church gatherings. Discipleship requires an outlet, or else it stagnates.

Here then are three practical reasons to consider participatory church gatherings. Firstly, because the Western evangelical church is declining despite all our human cleverness – we need the power of the Holy Spirit. Secondly, because people grow and learn best by participating – we need to adopt the biblical guidelines for how this should happen in church. Thirdly, because the modern evangelical model of church is not producing good enough results in the discipleship department – we are barely distinguishable from the godless.

What About Expository Preaching?

Someone will ask, Is there not a place for expository teaching in the Church? Is there no room for a gifted teacher to systematically expound Scripture? Is it not true that there is great ground to be gained by the consecutive treatment of Christian truths? The answers to all these questions are, of course, Yes.

We see the systematic teaching of believers happening in the New Testament, where the apostles not only preached the gospel, but also instructed the new believers in the faith. We see this multiple times in the book of Acts, where the apostles were teaching daily in the temple courts in Jerusalem or in lecture halls in cities like Ephesus and Corinth (Acts 2:42, 5:21, 42, 11:26, 18:11, 19:9-10). Such preaching fulfils part of Christ's Great Commission: 'teaching them to observe all things that I have commanded you' (Matt. 28:20).

In the New Testament, there was *both* systematic teaching as well as participatory church gatherings. These seem to have occurred separately; systematic teaching occurring either daily (Acts 5:42, 19:9) or in some other intensive fashion (Acts 11:26, 18:11) while participatory church gatherings occurred weekly in conjunction with the Lord's Supper. It is clear that the apostles grounded new disciples in the faith by systematic teaching. Such teaching would have involved some form of consecutive explanation of Christian truth for the simple reason that anyone who aspires to teach others has to be logical and systematic.

The systematic instruction of Christians is still needed today; it sets out a framework of Christian truth. In addition, expository preaching also results in God's people becoming more biblically-literate as they are exposed to preaching from whole books of the Bible, instead of isolated texts or favourite passages, and it trains believers in how to properly read, interpret and apply Scripture in their own lives.

But expository preaching has its downsides too. For many Christians, the exercise involves nothing more than passive listening. Because it is impersonal and there is no interaction, people come to church only to sit and listen. If the preacher is good, the listeners may be impressed, or if he tells lots of illustrations and anecdotes, they may be entertained. In New Testament language, many people come to church today to have their ears tickled (2 Tim. 4:3). Expository preaching has its most powerful effect upon new Christians or those who have not been exposed to good Bible teaching before. A whole new world opens up as they realise the spiritual power of Scripture as it is preached well. But expository preaching obeys the law of diminishing returns; the beneficial effect wears off over time. Prolonged exposure to such preaching does not translate into continued spiritual growth; instead of steadily increasing discipleship, it is possible for people to plateau spiritually and turn into pew-potatoes and sermon-tasters. Expository teaching is often largely informational; it has an intellectual flavour. Participatory church gatherings, on the other hand, are more than food for thought; they are an encounter with God Himself, not only as He speaks to the heart of the listener (1 Cor. 14:23-25), but as church members grow through using their spiritual gifts. By sharing insights that God has taught them and interacting with Bible messages, Christians are prompted to further study of God's Word for themselves. This results in spiritual progress: not only increased knowledge, but because the truth becomes personal, it is more likely to be put into practice and obeyed.

There were two types of gatherings held in the New Testament: what we might call 'the church meeting' and other 'evangelistic or discipleship services'. Watchman Nee calls these two types of gatherings 'the church meeting' and 'the apostolic meeting'. The first was participatory and inward-looking, intended to meet the needs of the Christians, while the second was outward-looking, seeking to explain the Christian faith to outsiders and the newly-converted. Nee writes, 'In the early Church there were meetings which were definitely connected with the churches, and others that were just as definitely connected with the work. In the latter, only one man spoke, and all the others constituted his audience. One stood before the others, and by his preaching directed the thoughts and hearts of those quietly listening'[26].

Not only was evangelistic outreach or intensive systematic instruction a separate activity to participatory church gatherings in the New Testament, it was also the case that the apostles did not continue spoon-feeding new Christians with systematic teaching indefinitely. In many cities, Paul was run out of town very quickly without the opportunity for extensive periods of instruction. The new believers were left with the task of teaching and encouraging one another using their own spiritual gifts. The early Christians were told to 'edify one another' (1 Thess. 5:11, cf. Col. 3:16, Rom. 15:14). Like children in the physical realm, new Christians in apostolic times were expected to quickly grow out of an immature, dependent, baby-stage and develop the ability to feed themselves and others. On the other hand, passages like Hebrews 5:12-14 show us that some Christians regressed, and needed basic truths re-taught: 'though by this time you ought to be teachers, you need someone to teach you again the first principles of the oracles of God'.

This book is not a call for scrapping expository teaching, or replacing it with something else. Systematic preaching and participatory church gatherings are not alternative models but complementary. Both are found in the New Testament and both are needed today for proper Christian growth and healthy church life. In fact, they provide a counter-balance to each other; participatory church gatherings allow for Christians to grow in a more personally-engaged way, while systematic teaching by those

---

[26] Watchman Nee, *The Normal Christian Life*, Washington: International Students Press, 1962, p118

who are the most gifted sets a model for good handling of Scripture and helps to focus on matters of doctrinal substance.

Further, because expository teaching is one of the most beneficial forms of spiritual contribution in church, there is no reason why expository preaching should not occupy a prominent place in participatory church gatherings. Thus, instead of limiting the potential for expository preaching, interactive church services expand its effectiveness, by allowing people to ask questions or suggest added insights after such preaching, and allow the possibility for more than one such message.

Expository preaching is not the only sort of preaching, nor does it meet all the spiritual needs of God's people. Sometimes expository preaching can be very dry, faithful to the text but devoid of the Spirit's power, as dull as ditchwater and irrelevant to the spiritual needs and concerns of God's people. By contrast, a five-minute Spirit-filled exhortation can sometimes be a word from God that has a life-changing effect upon God's people. A short testimony can reinforce a truth and root the wisdom of God's Word in real life. Limiting all contributions to thirty-minute perfectly-polished performances of Scripture exposition also means that many younger Christians are kept back from taking the first steps in developing their spiritual gifts in the church gatherings.

Does 1 Corinthians 14 Still Apply Today?

One objection frequently raised is that 1 Cor. 14 describes the use of two gifts that do not exist today (prophecy and speaking in tongues), and therefore the participatory church gatherings that 1 Cor. 14 describes are not applicable for today's church. This is not the place to wade into the controversy over charismatic gifts, however it is worth saying one thing about the spiritual gifts mentioned in 1 Cor. 14.

It is true that speaking in tongues and prophecy are the two most frequently mentioned gifts in 1 Corinthians 14, but they are hardly the only two gifts described in the chapter. The passage mentions teaching (v6, 19, 26), exhortation (v3), and knowledge (v6), which are elsewhere described as spiritual gifts. In addition, 1 Corinthians 14 also mentions other types of spiritual contributions that can be made to the church gathering, including praying (v15), 'giving of thanks' (v16), suggesting a psalm to sing (v26), singing more generally (v15), critiquing prophecies (v29, 30), and asking questions (v35). Also, in the broader context of 1 Corinthians 12-14, there are other spiritual gifts mentioned like a word of wisdom (12:8), or faith (12:9), which sometimes prompts us to speak ('I believed, and therefore I spoke', 2 Cor. 4:13). Have all these spiritual gifts ceased? The fact that all these ways of speaking are still operative today, means that we cannot dismiss 1 Corinthians 14 as only applying to a charismatic ministry, or to the apostolic era when certain more spectacular gifts were active.

J. B. Watson (writing from a non-charismatic position) says, 'The fourteenth chapter of 1 Corinthians discusses the relative helpfulness of two of the principal gifts possessed by believers in that assembly, tongues and prophecy, and recognizes the superiority of the latter. Though these two gifts are not now found in operation in the churches it does not follow that the chapter is without relevance to present-day conditions. As soon might it be alleged that the Epistle to the Galatians is without a voice to us because it was occasioned by a teaching concerning circumcision which is not now a live issue. The truth is that God used the circumstances and failures of first-century churches as the occasions for giving permanent and authoritative directions to his people. The principles enunciated in 1 Cor. 14 for the guidance of ministry when the assembly is gathered together (v. 26) are of full authority to us: the changed circumstances of our times as compared with those of Corinth in the first century do not diminish their force or applicability'[27].

In many evangelical churches today, there is only room for one sort of spoken spiritual gift: expository teaching. But in the New Testament, we find room given for many varied spiritual contributions to the church gathering. In 1 Corinthians 12:7, Paul tells us that every Christian has a spiritual gift and that these spiritual gifts are manifestations of the Spirit of God: 'the manifestation of the Spirit is given to each one for the profit of all'. If we believe that spiritual gifts still exist today, that they are many and varied, that all believers possess them, and that their use is a

---

[27] J. B. Watson, "Oral Ministry in the Church", *J. B. Watson: a Memoir and Selected Writings*, London: Pickering and Inglis, 1957, p218

manifestation of God's Spirit, then we should be actively encouraging them in the church gathering, not trying to find reasons to suppress them. 1 Corinthians 14 shows that God's people had the right to exercise these gifts, and 1 Corinthians 14 also provides directions for regulating their use in the church gatherings. The idea that 1 Corinthians 14 only deals with prophecy and speaking in tongues is false, and the attempt to dismiss participatory church gatherings on this basis is unwarranted.

Frank Holmes

The Rev. Frank Holmes was a minister in the Free Church of England (a 19th-century evangelical break-away from the Church of England, formed in response to the re-introduction of Roman Catholic practices into the church by the so-called Oxford Movement). In the 1940s and 1950s, Holmes was the minister of Emmanuel Church in Barnstaple in the West Country of England. While still the minister there, he researched and wrote the biography of the godly 19th Century Barnstaple Christian patriarch, evangelist and pastor, Robert Cleaver Chapman, described by Spurgeon as 'the saintliest man I ever knew', who had left such a legacy upon the spiritual life of the town that fifty years after his death, the impact was still felt. In chapter seven of his book *Brother Beloved*, Holmes described the participatory style of church gatherings that Chapman introduced in his church in Barnstaple.

Even though Holmes had by now become acquainted with both the biblical evidence for participatory church gatherings and the practical demonstration of its local effectiveness, he felt comfortable continuing as he had always done in his ministerial position in his church. Holmes' reasoning was: 'It is not commanded'. Then one evening as he sat at his desk preparing for his two Sunday sermons, Holmes was hit by the force of the verse in 1 Cor. 14:37, where towards the end of Paul's instructions about participatory church gatherings, the apostle writes, 'If anyone thinks himself to be a prophet or spiritual, let him acknowledge that the things which I write to you are the commandments of the Lord'. This verse says that the New Testament instructions about church meetings in 1 Cor. 14:26-40 were not simply Paul's suggestions, or the way early Christianity evolved – they were God's directions. As we shall see when we look at this verse, Paul is saying that the Corinthians did not have the right to decide how to organise church gatherings, for the Lord Himself has given commands about how this should be done.

After wrestling with the implications of this verse, Holmes laid his hands on the Bible, bowed his head, and surrendered to the conviction of the Holy Spirit through the Word of God. He preached his two final sermons that Sunday, and resigned his living and comfortable manse to try to put into practice with other believers what the Bible teaches about church gatherings. He knew that, within his denomination, there would be little room or tolerance for any attempt to put the Bible's teaching into practice. So he left.

This is not to suggest that all Christian pastors must quit their positions. R. C. Chapman did not. The New Testament clearly teaches the need for godly leadership in the church, and for the right of some Christian leaders to be financially supported by the church because of the spiritual work they do amongst the flock (1 Cor. 9:3-11, Gal. 6:6, 1 Tim. 5:17-18). Pastoral church leadership and participatory church gatherings are not mutually exclusive. Rather, there is an even greater need for godly, gifted, wise, well-taught, experienced and pastorally-sensitive leadership in a church where the believers have a greater degree of spiritual freedom and responsibility.

What the Bible gives us, however, are divine guidelines for participatory church gatherings. If God in His Word has given us instructions about how His Church should operate, then it is our responsibility to obey what He tells us. It is His Church, not ours.

Many Christians can quote 1 Thessalonians 5:18 by heart: 'in everything give thanks; for this is the will of God in Christ Jesus for you'. We are sometimes reminded that this is a command we should obey. But the next verse also contains a command: 'Do not quench the Spirit'. Both verses 18 and 19 contain commands (in the imperative mood, not the indicative), but while we are regularly reminded to give thanks, few Christians seem concerned about obeying the verse that follows. Why do we feel obliged to obey one biblical command and ignore the next in two consecutive verses? Interpretational consistency would suggest that we either ignore the two verses, or obey them both. In addition to being thankful Christians, we should also give the Holy Spirit His rightful place in the church. We should allow Him room to move and opportunity to work, as believers use their spiritual gifts.

In this book, we are going to cover two main issues related to participatory church gatherings.

1. Section one will consist of expositions of the key passages in the New Testament that deal with participatory church gatherings. We will endeavour to see exactly what the New Testament tells us about the way gatherings for worship were organised in the early church. This section will also consider objections of a biblical and theological, rather than practical, nature.
2. The second part of the book will look at some of the practicalities of participatory church gatherings. It will look at the practical reasons for them, how to deal with some of the problems that arise, and some suggestions for putting into practice what the Bible teaches about participatory church worship.

My prayer is that readers will examine the Bible passages we will look at with the sincerity of the Bereans of Acts 17:11, out of a conviction that God blesses those who not only know what the Scriptures teach, but also start putting God's Word into action (John 13:17, James 1:25).

CHAPTER 2

1 CORINTHIANS 14:26-40 – EARLY CHURCH GATHERINGS

If 1 Corinthians chapters 12 to 14 are the *locus classicus* on spiritual gifts in the New Testament, then 1 Corinthians 14:26-40 correspondingly represents the classic treatment of the use of those gifts in the gatherings of the church. In this passage we have the most detailed picture of what actually went on in a church service in New Testament times.

Professor T. M. Lindsay, Principal of Glasgow College of the United Free Church of Scotland, wrote, 'It is St. Paul, in his First Epistle to the Corinthians, who gives us the most distinct picture of the meetings of the earliest Christian communities'[28].

S. Lewis Johnson (commenting on verses 26-33), says, 'Instruction for the exercise of the gifts is given here. The section is important because it is "the most intimate glimpse we have of the early church at worship" (Morris). What a contrast is found here with the formal and inflexible order of service that prevails in most of Christendom today! … The early believers did not come to the worship meeting to hear a sermon from one man or simply to receive; they came to give. Much has been lost by the renouncement of these privileges'[29].

Notice ten observations from this passage:

---

[28] T. M. Lindsay, *The Church and Ministry in the Early Centuries*, New York: A. C. Armstrong and Son; London: Hodder and Stoughton, 1902, p43

[29] S. Lewis Johnson, *The Wycliffe Bible Commentary*, London: Oliphants, 1963, p1254

1. There is Freedom to Participate ... (verse 26)

How is it, then, brethren? Whenever you come together, each of you has a psalm, has a teaching, has a revelation, has a tongue, has an interpretation. Let all things be done for edification.

Verse 26 teaches the principle of freedom – the freedom of the ordinary believers to use their spiritual gifts in the church meeting.

Craig Blomberg summarizes: 'Verse 26 insists that the Corinthians continue to worship in highly participatory and spontaneous fashion: "Everyone has a hymn, or a word of instruction, a revelation, a tongue, an interpretation." This does not mean that every person present exercises all of the gifts, nor even that all exercise at least one in every service. But opportunity is made available for all whom the Spirit leads on any given occasion to contribute'[30].

Notice that Paul writes to the Corinthians here as '*brethren*'. He does not give instructions to one person (the Minister, the Pastor). Nor does he write to the elders to organize or arrange the church gatherings according to the wisdom given to them. Nor does he write to the Preaching Team, consisting of the nominated, qualified Bible teachers in the church at Corinth. Instead, he addresses the believers generally. This is because the spiritual gifts that Paul is writing about in chapters 12-14 belong to the Christians generally, not to one man, nor to a ministry team, or a governing body.

T. M. Lindsay writes, 'In his description ... the apostle introduces us to an earnest company of men and women full of restrained enthusiasm, which might soon become unrestrained. We hear of no officials appointed to conduct the service'[31].

Paul Barnett in his commentary on 1 Corinthians writes: 'In verse 26 Paul gives us a window into the 'meeting together' of this apostolic congregation ... we are struck by absence of reference to a church leader

---

[30] Craig Blomberg, *The NIV Application Commentary*, Grand Rapids, MI: Zondervan, 1994, p278
[31] Lindsay, *The Church and Ministry in the Early Centuries*, p44

or presbyter. Evidently, Paul looked to a free-flowing movement of the Spirit'[32].

Gordon Fee likewise says, 'What is striking in this entire discussion is the absence of any mention of leadership or of anyone who would be responsible for seeing that these guidelines were generally adhered to. The community appears to be left to itself and to the Holy Spirit'[33]. Fee goes on (in the footnotes) to quote an earlier commentator who says that "these are rules for the chairman"! (the exclamation mark is Fee's, but the rest of the quote comes from R. St. John Parry[34]).

The church services were not planned or scripted beforehand by a ministry team or led from the front by a minister or pastor, but instead there was opportunity for any of the brothers to use their gifts to build up the church. The Holy Spirit was free to speak through who He wished.

Lindsay writes, 'What cannot fail to strike us in this picture is the untrammelled liberty of the worship, the possibility of every male member of the congregation taking part in the prayers and exhortations, and the consequent responsibility laid on the whole community to see that the service was for the edification of all. When we consider the rebukes that the apostle considered it necessary to administer, it is also somewhat surprising to find so few injunctions which take the form of definite rules for public worship, and to observe the confidence which the apostle had that if certain broad principles were laid down and observed, the community was of itself able to conduct all things with that attention to decency and order which ensured edification'[35].

Gary Inrig writes, 'The church meeting is ... an open, spontaneous meeting. There was absolute freedom for men to exercise their spiritual gifts, as we have seen in 1 Corinthians 14:26. In a context discussing spiritual gifts, this verse can only mean that these gifts are to be freely

---

[32] Paul Barnett, *1 Corinthians: Holiness and Hope of a Rescued People*, Fearn, Ross-shire: Christian Focus Publications, 2000, p263

[33] G. D. Fee, *The First Epistle to the Corinthians*, NICNT, Eerdmans, 1987, p691

[34] R. St. John Parry, *The First Epistle of Paul the Apostle to the Corinthians*, CGTSC, Cambridge, 1926, p209

[35] Lindsay, p49

and openly exercised in the church meeting ... The liberty of such a meeting allowed for a multiplicity of ministry and an orderly informality ... It is unfortunately true that this open, free and spontaneous meeting, where joys can be shared and burdens can be borne, is sadly lacking in the contemporary church. There is a great deal of organisation and formality, but little opportunity for open ministry and enthusiastic sharing of God's gifts, and the result is that the majority of Christians have become silent spectators, contributing only the correct liturgical response and singing an occasional hymn'[36].

Again, notice how Paul says '*each of you*' has something to contribute. Paul does not say, 'one of you' (a minister), or 'some of you' (a group appointed to lead the services) - instead, he says 'each of you'.

A. C. Thiselton objects to any weight being placed on the word 'each' here. He writes, 'It is unfortunate that many commentators interpret the meaning of *each* in v. 26 (Gk. *hekastos*) too readily in accordance with their own church traditions ... the Greek alone cannot determine the matter, but a woodenly literalist understanding of *each* strains the text in this context'[37]. Thiselton says that 'each' must not be taken literally, but he does not explain what it does mean.

C. K. Barrett, by contrast, argues that '*each one* must be taken seriously here'[38], going on to reference 1 Cor. 12:7: 'the manifestation of the Spirit is given to *each one* for profit'. That is, just as each one is given spiritual gifts (Ch. 12:7), so each one may participate in the church gathering using these gifts (Ch. 14:26). Leon Morris comments: 'We need not press 'everyone' (or 'each', *hekastos*), as though it meant that every member of the congregation always had something to contribute. But it does mean that any of them might be expected to take part in the service'[39].

---

[36] Gary Inrig, *Life in His Body*, pp70-71

[37] A. C. Thiselton, *1 Corinthians: A Shorter Exegetical and Pastoral Commentary*, Grand Rapids: Eerdmans, 2006, p246

[38] C. K. Barrett, *First Epistle to the Corinthians*, HNTC, 1968, p327

[39] Leon Morris, *1 Corinthians*, p190

Actually, Paul (under the inspiration of the Holy Spirit) has used exactly the right word here: 'each' (not 'one' or 'a few' or 'the pastor' or 'the elders') could potentially contribute in the meeting, but not 'all' could contribute in every meeting due to the guidelines that Paul commands for sake of order ('two or three prophets', etc). 'Each' could potentially contribute, but not 'all' actually.

Paul later in the passage concludes by allowing – as a general principle – that 'you can all prophesy, one by one, that all may learn and all may be encouraged' (verse 31). Similarly, in verses 5 and 24, Paul encourages 'all' to participate in certain ways. But due to the guidelines and limits that Paul lays down in this passage, it is true that it was not possible for 'all' to contribute in every particular meeting. However, 'each one' was potentially able to participate – there are no disqualifications based on nationality, social standing, education, training or spiritual maturity.

Commenting on *every one* (KJV, NIV) or *each one* (most other Bible versions), S. Lewis Johnson writes, '*Every one* points to free participation, but because such freedom might lead to disorder, Paul counsels, *Let all thing be done unto edifying*. The speaking is to be by course (lit., *in turn*)'[40].

The obvious lesson that we learn as we read these instructions is that the responsibility for what a person could contribute rested entirely with the individual. Each one had a spiritual gift (or gifts), and a responsibility to use them. Each one had freedom to use their gifts and an opportunity to contribute in the church gatherings.

2. ... In the Church gathering ...

Secondly, we notice that this passage is talking about the church gatherings. Verse 26 says, '*when you come together*'. These are the same words used five times in connection with the Lord's Supper in 1 Cor. 11:17-34 (verses 17, 18, 20, 33, 34). By putting the references to 'when you come together' in 1 Cor.11:17-34 alongside the references in chapter

---

[40] S. Lewis Johnson, The *Wycliffe Bible Commentary*, London: Oliphants, 1963, p1254

14 (vs 23 and 26), we may conclude that when the church in Corinth met together, their gathering incorporated within it the Lord's Supper as well as the opportunity for the use of spiritual gifts for ministering to the needs of the believers – it was a meeting for worship as well as for edification. Notice that Ch.14 does not specify 'when you come together *to use your spiritual gifts*', as if this were a separate meeting that needed to be distinguished from 'when you come together *for the Lord's Supper*'. The reference in 1 Cor. 14:26 simply says 'when you come together' and there seems to have been one main weekly church gathering, including both the Lord's Supper and the exercise of spiritual gifts. We see the same thing at the institution of the Lord's Supper in John 13-16 (at which Christ also taught His disciples, who interacted with questions and discussion: John 13:36, 14:5, 8, 22, 16:17, 19) and in Acts 20 in Troas, where the meeting involved both the Lord's Supper and general edification.

Gary Inrig writes, 'It is important to recognize that the biblical assembly did not have one meeting ... for teaching, another meeting for worship and the Lord's Supper, and another for testimonies and mutual exhortation. All of these features were a regular part of the church meeting, whenever the assembly came together. Thus the church meeting, as set forth in the Word of God is remarkably diverse. It is diverse in its content, containing such elements as the Lord's Supper, singing, teaching, prayer, the exercise of spiritual gifts and the asking and answering of questions (cf. 1 Cor. 14:35)'[41].

Paul's instructions for the use of spiritual gifts in this passage thus refer to the church gatherings; not to some private or small-group fellowship meeting. Nor is Paul writing here about some occasional or extraordinary meeting of the Church, or some special conference to which people from many churches are invited. What he writes about here refers to the main, normal, weekly gathering of the church.

Verse 33b ('as in all the churches of the saints') suggests that the picture described here was found in all the apostolic churches. T. M Lindsay writes, 'The meeting described by the apostle is not to be taken

---

[41] Inrig, *Life in His Body*, p68

as something which might be seen in Corinth but was peculiar to that city; it may be taken as a type of the Christian meeting throughout the Gentile Christian churches; for the apostle, in his suggestions and criticisms, continually speaks of what took place throughout all the churches. It is to be observed that if the apostle finds fault with some things, he gives the order of the service and expressly approves of every part of it'[42].

1 Cor. 14:26-40 is not describing a situation that was unusual among early churches or simply confined to Corinth. F. F. Bruce suggests that verse 33b 'means that the order prescribed for the church of Corinth is that followed by other churches, especially in Paul's mission field'[43].

3. ... Using a Variety of Gifts and Multiple Participants

Thirdly, variety characterised the early church gatherings. Paul lists a number of spiritual contributions that people made in the service: *each of you has a psalm, has a teaching, has a tongue, has a revelation, has an interpretation.*

Notice: Paul nowhere mentions 'the sermon', one main message, the centrepiece of a church service. This is not because Christians in apostolic times did not believe in preaching. Rather the reverse: they believed in preaching so much that they allowed opportunity for multiple people with different spiritual gifts to preach in the church service. Nor does Paul mention any liturgy, a prescribed and fixed 'order of service', involving set prayers, hymns and ceremonies. He does not even mention someone 'up the front' leading the meeting, from a pulpit or dais. All these ideas are absent from the New Testament.

Paul uses the general word '*has*' five times in this verse to describe the contributions. He could perhaps instead have said that they each *brought* a psalm or a teaching to the meeting, as no doubt some of the contributions required prior preparation, or at least partially depended upon things learnt over a period of time. This would particularly apply to

---

[42] Lindsay, p48
[43] F. F. Bruce, *I & II Corinthians*, NCBC, London: Marshall, Morgan and Scott, 1971, p135

teaching, which would require 'sustained biblical reflection' (Thiselton[44]). In contrast, some contributions (e.g. interpretation of a tongue) would have been more spontaneous. Other contributions fall into either category. For example, a revelation need not refer to something that had been revealed during the church meeting; it could have been something revealed during the week before the church met together, which was then shared during the meeting. Thus, the word *has* is deliberately broad enough to include within it the idea that some have prepared beforehand things to contribute to the meeting, but it also leaves room for a spontaneous and extemporaneous contribution prompted during the gathering.

The list of five spiritual contributions in this verse (psalm, teaching, tongue, revelation, interpretation) is not exhaustive, for Paul mentions over fifteen different types of spiritual gifts or church contributions in chapters 12-14. Nor can we take it as some order of service in which a psalm had to be followed by a teaching, etc. Instead, the list is representative, the point being the plurality and variety of the contributions.

This variety should be reflected in modern church life. For example, Christ the Head of the church gave some of his people the gift of 'exhortation', a short word of challenge or encouragement (Romans 12:8), or a 'word of wisdom', a short word of advice or experience based on lessons learned in a person's life (1 Corinthians 12:8). Surely Christ is saddened that these people, because of our humanly-devised 'Order of Service', are effectively silenced in the church gatherings where their public contributions might benefit all His people?

The variety of gifts, contributed by multiple people interacting with each other, shows that the New Testament church was not a 'one-man show'. How different the New Testament picture is to what we find in most contemporary churches, with our productions and programs, liturgies and set orders of service. Any resemblance between modern churches and the New Testament is entirely coincidental!

---

[44] A. C. Thiselton, *The First Epistle to the Corinthians: A Commentary on the Greek Text*, NIGTC, Grand Rapids, MI: Eerdmans, 2000, p1135

4. The Purpose is Edification

Fourthly, Paul says, *'let all things be done for edification'* (verse 26). The purpose of the use of different gifts in the church gathering was so that the church was edified, that is, built up. Note carefully that the purpose of the church's gathering was not simply remembrance, worship and praise ascending Godward, nor evangelism extending outwards, but encouraging edification through instruction that built up the believers.

William MacDonald says: 'Paul gives tacit approval to this "open meeting" where there was liberty for the Spirit of God to speak through different brothers. But having stated this, he sets forth the first control in the exercise of these gifts. Everything must be done with a view to edification. Just because a thing is sensational or spectacular does not mean that it has any place in the church. In order to be acceptable, ministry must have the effect of building up the people of God. That is what is meant by edification – spiritual growth'[45].

F. F. Bruce neatly summarizes the message of verse 26: 'The upshot of all this is that, when the church meets, it is perfectly proper for each member to contribute to the worship, provided that all things be done for edification'[46].

5. There are Guidelines for Order (verses 27-33)

If anyone speaks in a tongue, let there be two or at the most three, and in turn, and let one interpret. But if there is no interpreter, let him be silent in church, and let him speak to himself and to God. Let two or three prophets speak, and let the others judge. But if something is revealed to another sitting by, let the first be silent. For you are all able to prophesy, one by one, that all may learn and all may be encouraged. And the spirits of the prophets are subject to the prophets. For God is not the God of disorder, but of peace, as in all the churches of the saints.

In verses 27-33 Paul introduces a number of guidelines for order. These verses balance the truth of our freedom to participate in verse 26 by

---

[45] William MacDonald, *Believers Bible Commentary*, p1801
[46] F. F. Bruce, *I & II Corinthians*, New Century Bible Commentary, Marshall, Morgan and Scott, 1971, p134

giving guidelines for order, so that the meeting does not descend into anarchy or become a 'free for all'. Paul does not undermine the freedoms of verse 26 under the guise of 'order', taking back with the left hand what he earlier gave with the right. There is a tension between freedom and order, balancing the requirements of individual participation and collective edification. 'Paul insisted on an orderly meeting, not a fixed order'[47]. He steers a course between the extremes of chaotic disorder and suffocating control that inhibits the working of the Spirit of God.

Notice: the church gathering is not governed by suggested time-limits (the Holy Spirit governs the meeting, not the clock on the wall!), nor does Paul leave matters to the church leaders, so that they have authority or licence to organize whatever order of service they wish. The contrast between Paul's instructions for order and modern churches is stark: in the name of 'doing all things decently and in order', it is possible to rob believers of their right and freedom to exercise their spiritual gifts.

The guidelines for order required that those speaking in tongues must speak one at a time, and at the most two or three (verse 27). Messages in tongues were to be interpreted (verse 28). Likewise, there were only to be two or three prophets speak, one by one (verses 29 and 31). The messages of the prophets were subject to evaluation and critique: 'let the others judge' (v29). There was thus both quantity and quality control. There was also the opportunity for interaction with the speaker if something was revealed to a listener (v30); rather than talking over the top of each other, the speaker is told to allow the listener to share the insight. Paul's directions here seem intended:

a) to make sure that the meeting is not entirely dominated by people using only one gift. In Corinth, Paul's instructions were intended to limit the number of people speaking in tongues or prophesying, to the exclusion of other sorts of contributions. In some churches in our modern situation, we might also limit the number of hymns or songs (or prayers) that can be offered, so that they do not dominate the meeting to the exclusion of other contributions.

---

[47] Robert and Julia Banks, *The Church Comes Home*, Peabody, MA: Hendrickson, 1998, p36

b) to guard against the meeting going on for so long that the congregation becomes exhausted. In the church in which the author grew up, there was a brother who refused to attend our annual conference on the grounds that four invited speakers contravened the limitation in this passage upon 'two or three prophets'. However, 1 Corinthians 14:27-33 is not dealing with a yearly conference but rather the normal, weekly church gathering. While this brother's criticism was somewhat eccentric and misplaced, it is true that four expositions of Scripture every Sunday are probably beyond the ability of most listeners to profitably endure or benefit from.
c) to ensure that the meeting does not descend into chaos as different people speak over the top of each other, and,
d) and most importantly, to guarantee that the messages are intelligible and meaningful (by being translated and interpreted into normal language), so that God's people may derive spiritual benefit from them.

In verse 30 the prophet was to be silent if something was revealed to someone else. We might think that such gifts as speaking in tongues or prophecy were ecstatic, frenzied and uncontrollable gifts, overflows of the Holy Spirit. Instead, the person using these gifts was able to control them and be quiet. Verse 32 says that the spirits of the prophets are subject to the prophets – that is, they can control their spirit, and be silent if need be.

F. F. Bruce says, 'There is no thought here of prophesying under an uncontrollable impulse; the prophets' rational mind is expected to be in command, even in moments of inspiration, so that they can speak or refrain from speaking at will, whichever may be more expedient'[48].

Verse 33 concludes this paragraph by saying *for God is not the author of disorder (*or confusion*) but of peace, as in all the churches of the saints*. Gordon Fee says, 'everything has to do with the character of God and

---

[48] F. F. Bruce, *I & II Corinthians*, 1971, p134

what God has already established to be true of his divine activity in the rest of the churches'[49].

In addition to the divine basis for orderliness, this passage also pays attention to human considerations. Certain factors enhance the effectiveness of church gatherings, the primary one being that spiritual enthusiasm must be balanced against the need for edification. Messages must be communicated in such a way as people can understand what is being said. Meetings that go on for too long are less effective than those which do not extend beyond the endurance of God's people. Instead of a competitive environment, there is a need for Christian courtesy and self-control, in allowing others a chance to participate, in waiting for one's turn patiently.

Thus, if verse 26 teaches the truth of the freedom of God's people to use their spiritual gifts in the church gathering, verses 27-33 balance this truth with the equally important truth of order. Verse 40 similarly says, 'let all things be done decently and in order'.

6. Public Evaluation is Necessary (verse 29)
Let two or three prophets speak, and let the others judge.

Sixthly, we see that contributions to the meeting were to be evaluated and discussed: *'let the prophets speak and let the others judge'*. Note carefully: preaching without public evaluation and comment was as foreign to Paul's thinking as speaking in tongues without interpretation. Paul does not advocate 'roast preacher for Sunday lunch', but rather roast preacher right after he has sat down (in the most courteous and edifying way, of course). Nor is it a case of people talking privately after the meeting finishes; there is public comment, discussion and evaluation on the spot. We find a similar thing in 1 Thessalonians 5:19-21, 'Do not quench the Spirit, do not despise prophecies, test all things, hold fast what is good'. The principle here is that we should not believe everything that someone with a spiritual gift says. Instead, there was opportunity for evaluation and discussion of what had been said.

---

[49] Gordon Fee, *1 Corinthians*, NICNT, p696

Barrett argues that 1 Thessalonians 5:21, 1 John 4:1 and indeed, 'the whole long section on spiritual gifts which began in chapter 12' proceed 'on the assumption that all spiritual manifestations must be tested and the test provided in 12:3 is one that can be applied by any Christian, whether himself a prophet or not'[50]. Thus, we may say that, just as 'all can prophesy' (verse 31), so all can judge too.

A. C. Thiselton argues[51] that the meaning of the word 'judge' (*diakrinetosan*) here is really to 'distinguish between' and refers to the act of discerning between what is 'God-given and coheres with the gospel of Christ and the pastoral situation' and, on the other hand, 'speech which is merely self-generated rhetoric reflecting the speaker's disguised self-interests, self-deceptions, or errors, albeit under the guise of "prophecy"'. This sort of discernment is, of course, what most Christian congregations silently engage in as they listen to preaching and teaching today. Most preachers would probably be a little more careful about what they said if they had to face public cross-examination afterward.

Not all judging necessarily involves correction, criticism or cross-examination. Other types of evaluation include comments that agree with what is being taught, helpfully balance or clarify Biblical truths, suggest other lines of thought or cross-references, or add lessons of personal application based on spiritual experience.

J. B. Watson suggests that those contributing to the meeting need to pay careful attention to the sorts of feedback they receive: 'There is to be submission by the individual to the general judgment of the spiritual as to the value of his ministry. He is not himself competent to assess the worth of his own contribution, and is to accept with good grace the collective judgment of the spiritual among his fellow-saints. If that judgment is favourable let him be encouraged and humble: if it is qualified, let him be wise and speak but seldom: if adverse, let him cease to inflict unprofitable talk on the Lord's people'[52].

---

[50] C. K. Barrett, *1 Corinthians*, New York, 1968, p328

[51] A. C. Thiselton, *The First Epistle to the Corinthians: A Commentary on the Greek Text*, NIGTC, Grand Rapids, MI: Eerdmans, 2000, p1140

[52] J. B. Watson, "Oral Ministry in the Church, *J. B. Watson: A Memoir and Selected Writings*, London: Pickering and Inglis, 1957, p221

7. The Holy Spirit is Active

Seventhly, the Holy Spirit was active in the church gathering. Although the Holy Spirit is not mentioned in this passage or indeed in chapter 14 (the word 'spirit' is used in verses 2, 14, 15 and 16, but it is unlikely that it is the Holy Spirit being referred to), yet the three chapters 12-14 are all about the gifts of the Holy Spirit. 1 Corinthians 12:7 teaches that spiritual gifts are 'a manifestation of the Spirit'. More significantly, at the beginning of chapter 12, we read that no person who speaks by the Holy Spirit can call Jesus accursed, nor can anyone say that Jesus is Lord except by the Holy Spirit. God's Spirit is evidenced in a true Christian by acknowledging (that is, 'speaking out', for 'spirit', *pneuma*, also means 'breath') that Jesus Christ is Lord. Here in chapter 14, which concerns believers 'speaking' (mentioned 23 times in the chapter), we see evidence of the Holy Spirit not only prompting thoughts, but also expressing them through various contributions in the church gathering.

The work of the Holy Spirit is implied in 14:30, where we read about something being 'revealed' to someone sitting in the meeting listening as a prophet speaks. Notice it doesn't say that this person 'thinks' of something and feels compelled to share it. Revelation is the work of the Holy Spirit, according to 1 Corinthians 2:10: 'for God has revealed them [divine truths] to us through His Spirit'.

Paul teaches that the person who believes that the Holy Spirit has revealed something to him has the right to speak in the gathering, while the prophet who was speaking when the revelation was given is told to be silent.

Earlier in the chapter in verses 24-25, we have another reference to the work of the Holy Spirit, as an unbeliever comes into the church gathering. As a prophet speaks, we read that 'the secrets of his heart are revealed', resulting in him being convicted and convinced that 'God is truly among you' (verse 25). Again, we notice the word 'revealed', a pointer to the activity of the Holy Spirit in the gathering, resulting in conviction (which is another work of the Holy Spirit, John 16:8-11).

Thus, the Holy Spirit is working, not in any outward or visible way, but silently and almost imperceptibly, prompting prophets and other gifted people to speak, revealing truth, convicting hearts, and orchestrating the different members of the body to work together in the church gathering.

8. Interaction is Allowed (verse 30)
But if something is revealed to another sitting by, let the first be silent.

Paul allows opportunity for interaction with and even interruption of the preacher. As we have just seen, '*if*' while a prophet was speaking, '*anything is revealed to another who sits by, let the first keep silent*'. This second person to whom something has been revealed was free and had the right to interact with the speaker and share what had been revealed there and then. This was not considered bad manners. Instead, the early church's meeting had about it something of the informality of a group Bible study.

This is not such an unusual or foreign concept as it might at first seem. Still today, while someone is preaching, remarks upon one passage of scripture may spark us to better understand some other passage or doctrine (or our thoughts on other passages of Scripture may help us to better understand what the preacher is speaking about). Here Paul urges that there should be opportunity for such thoughts to be shared with the congregation. There is no need to wait for the end of the prophecy (as in the case of judging) – they can be shared on the spot.

The collaborative approach to spiritual growth (learning in community) advocated here is far more effective in enabling more people to learn and be encouraged than when just one person speaks.

9. Women's Participation (verses 34-35)
Let your women keep silent in the church gatherings, for they are not permitted to speak; but they are to be submissive, as the law also says. And if they want to learn anything, let them ask their own husbands at home; for it is shameful for women to speak in the church.

Should women participate publicly and audibly in church? The subject of women's ministry is very controversial today and we are going to leave it for a later chapter of the book. For the moment, we will just mention two simple observations that all Christians can agree on that we learn about participatory church gatherings from these verses.

First, verses 34 and 35 show that there is opportunity for asking questions. Although this right appears to be denied to certain people (women) in verse 35, it is implied that asking questions was normal in the New Testament church. Verse 30, earlier, refers to someone interrupting a speaker in full-flight, and licenses us to suppose that the right to ask questions was not restricted to the end of a speaker's message. Experience teaches that the best way for people to learn is by engaging publicly with what is being taught: asking questions, testing what is being said against Scripture, and growing by learning from each other. This is true for the speaker as much as for the listener. The speaker has to be ready to have his message challenged, corrected or complemented, while listeners can ask for clarification, assess, interact with and respond to what is being said. Asking questions is an important way to learn, grow and develop in the Christian life.

Notice, secondly, in passing, the curious fact that most evangelicals view these verses about women's participation (however different people interpret them) to still be applicable for church life today, but conversely, the main message of the passage – the participatory nature of church gatherings – is considered to be optional, unimportant or irrelevant to church life today. The inconsistency is odd, to say no more.

10. The Authority is Apostolic, and ultimately Divine (vs 36-40)

Or did the word of God come originally from you? Or was it you only that it reached? If anyone thinks himself to be a prophet or spiritual, let him acknowledge that the things which I write to you are the commandments of the Lord. But if anyone is ignorant, let him be ignorant. Therefore, brethren, desire earnestly to prophesy, and do not forbid to speak in tongues. Let all things be done decently and in order.

A tenth observation (in vs 36-38) deals with the authority for such church gatherings. Paul says that these are not his ideas or instructions about church gatherings – they are the Lord's commandments. Paul did not offer a number of suggestions to produce more profitable church meetings at Corinth, or pass on some ideas that he had heard tried in some other churches, or encourage the Corinthians to experiment on their own initiative. Paul says that the instructions in this chapter were God's directions for how church gatherings should be conducted. Paul's concluding remarks reinforce the authoritative nature of the instructions regarding the operation of gifts in the Church gathering in four ways:

Firstly, in verse 36a, Paul rhetorically asks if the Corinthians are the source of Divine revelation: *'did the word of God come forth from you?'* Any attempt by the Corinthians to chart their own path as far as church practices, would be claiming that they were 'some kind of fountainhead from which the word of God gushed forth' (Paul Barnett[53]). We might paraphrase Paul's argument here as, Do you think you are the source of the Word of God, so that you can make up your own guidelines for how church gatherings should operate? Paul is implying that the instructions for church gatherings he has given here are the very word of God.

Secondly, in verse 36b, Paul continues his rhetorical assault upon the Corinthians: *'or was it you alone that it reached?'* Are the Corinthians the one and only church in the world, with their own authority to decide how to run their church gatherings, free to do as they please irrespective of how the other churches meet? How dare the Corinthians think that they can ignore what all the other apostolic churches practice in their church gatherings! The Corinthians were not to think that they were free to 'march to their own drum' (Fee[54]). Instead, the Corinthians were to conform to the practices of the other apostolic churches. Paul thus returns to the benchmark principle that he touched upon earlier in verse 33b - the uniformity of practice among the apostolic churches.

Thirdly, in verse 37, Paul says that it is the mark of true spirituality to accept what he has written: *'If anyone thinks himself to be a prophet or spiritual, let him acknowledge that the things which I write to you are the commandments of the Lord'*. Paul's instructions in this chapter are to be obeyed because they are the commandments of the Lord. Leon Morris stresses that Paul, by arguing that these are the commands of the Lord, 'could not possibly make a higher claim' (*1 Corinthians*, p194).

---

[53] Paul Barnett, *1 Corinthians*, p267
[54] G. D. Fee, *The First Epistle to the Corinthians*, p710

Fourthly, in verse 38, those who object and dispute over these matters, in addition to being neither prophets nor spiritual (verse 37), are ignorant of the will, truth and knowledge of God: *'but if anyone is ignorant, let him be ignorant'*[55]. Paul says that those who argue against the Word of God have conceited opinions of their own spirituality and learning. If they do not wish to learn God's ways, they are to be left to their own ignorance.

We might summarise Paul's message in this paragraph as follows: anyone who is unwilling to accept the guidelines for church gatherings here in 1 Corinthians 14 is setting themselves above the Word of God (v36), is disobeying the Lord's direct commands (v37b), is unspiritual (v37a) and ignorant (v38). Paul Barnett puts it more politely: 'the written words of the apostle determine what we believe and how we order our lives inside and outside the church throughout this age'[56].

Two Concluding Principles

Paul concludes the chapter by laying down two general principles. Firstly, in verse 39, Paul encourages the use of the gift of prophecy and warns against forbidding anyone speaking in tongues: *'therefore brethren, desire earnestly to prophesy and do not forbid to speak with tongues'*. This would appear to recapitulate his teaching in the first 25 verses of the chapter. It is an encouragement to God's people to participate in the church gathering using the spiritual gifts that God has endowed them with.

Secondly, in verse 40, Paul says, *'let all things be done decently and in order'*. This summarizes Paul's teaching in verses 26-40. Some would take this last verse in isolation (ignoring verse 39), and claim that, in the

---

[55] For the form of Paul's argument here, compare Rev. 22:11. Many English versions prefer to translate this verse in a more mealy-mouthed way: 'if anyone does not recognize this, he is not recognized' (ESV, NASB, etc). But, the ignorance (Gk. *agnoeo*) Paul speaks about in v38 stands in contrast with the knowledge of a prophet or spiritual man of v37, and the imperative ('let him be ignorant') is at least as textually well supported (P^{46}, B, Majority) as the less-clear indicative ('he is not known').

[56] *1 Corinthians*, Christian Focus Publications, 2000, p268

name of doing things decently, we are hereby licensed to impose order (of any description, however restrictive) upon the church gatherings. In fact, someone has rightly said that if decency and order were the most important verse or the only principle in the life of a church, the church would become a spiritual cemetery, for that is the only place where nothing is out of order.

However, the principle of orderly decency is here a second principle that is to be balanced against the principle of opportunity for participation given in verse 39.

In Summary

1 Corinthians 14:26-40 is teaching that the church gathering should be characterised by:
- freedom,
- the opportunity for participation by each one,
- the use of a variety of spiritual gifts by multiple participants,
- prompted by the Holy Spirit,
- for the spiritual growth of the church,
- with opportunity for questions, discussion and assessment,
- yet there are also limits and restrictions for the sake of decency and order.

William Barclay writes, 'Paul comes near to the end of this section with some very practical advice. He is determined that anyone who possessed a gift should receive every chance to exercise that gift; but he is equally determined that the services of the Church should not thereby become a kind of competitive disorder ... There must be liberty but there must be no disorder ...'

Barclay continues: 'It is true to say that there is no more interesting section in the whole letter than this, for it sheds a flood of light on what a Church service was like in the early Church. There was obviously a freedom and an informality about it which is completely strange to our ideas. From this passage two very great questions emerge. (i) Clearly the early Church had no professional ministry. True, the apostles stood out with a very special authority; but at this stage the Church had no professional local ministry. It was open to anyone who had a gift to use that gift ... it must remain true that if a man has a message to give his fellow men no ecclesiastical rules and regulations should be able to stop him giving it ... (ii) There was obviously a flexibility about the order of service in the early Church which is now totally lacking. There was clearly no settled order at all ... The really notable thing about an early Church service must have been that almost everyone came feeling that he had both the privilege and the obligation of contributing something in it. A man did not come with the sole intention of being a passive listener. He did not come only to receive, he came also to give. Obviously this had its dangers for it is clear that in Corinth there were those who were too fond of the sound of their own voices; but nonetheless the Church must have been in those days much more the real possession of the ordinary Christian'[57].

Professor Arthur Rendle Short wrote, 'When Paul heard what painful meetings they were having in Corinth, he might have said: "Do not listen any longer to all these ignorant people, mostly slaves; make Stephanos your minister, and let him do it all". No doubt this would have helped very much in some directions; but the Apostle was not prepared to give up the open meeting; it was far too valuable. He did not want to make churches like comets – with a brilliant head, and a long nebulous tail. He told them however – and it is very important to put the injunction into practice – that the assembly was not called upon to listen to everybody who chose to make a nuisance of himself, or who talked unprofitably. There were some "whose mouths must be stopped" (Tit. 1:11). The listeners were to be the judges (1 Cor. 14:27-29). It was an open meeting; but there were rules to be obeyed. It was a meeting open for the Spirit to speak by whom He would, not open for men to say what they pleased'[58].

---

[57] William Barclay, *The Letters to the Corinthians*, Edinburgh: The Saint Andrew Press, 2nd Ed., 1956, p149-50

[58] Arthur Rendle Short, *The Principles of Christians called 'Open Brethren'*, London: Pickering and Inglis, 1913

CHAPTER 3

1 THESSALONIANS 5:19-21: DO NOT QUENCH THE SPIRIT

Do not quench the Spirit. Do not despise prophecies. Test all things; hold fast what is good. (1 Thessalonians 5:19-21)

Paul's first letter to the Thessalonians was written to new Christians who were facing persecution. Paul's letter was intended to strengthen their faith, to confirm his love for them, and also to encourage their hope by pointing to the coming of the Lord. But as Paul nears the end of the letter, from 5:12-28, he turns his attention to church matters.

Amongst a number of brief general exhortations, we find Paul's instructions in 5:19-21 about the use of spiritual gifts in the church. We see a number of points of correspondence with the verses in 1 Corinthians 14:26-40:

1. The Holy Spirit was operative, speaking through His servants in the church gatherings (cf. 1 Cor. 12:7-11). There was opportunity for participation; 'quenching the Spirit' appears to relate to stifling the voice of God as heard through those using their spiritual gifts in the church.
2. Prophecies were able to be uttered (cf. 1 Cor. 14:1-5, 26-40). In other words, people spoke about what God had laid on their hearts, rather than preaching on a set topic, or at the invitation of a preaching committee.
3. All contributions had to be tested before being accepted (cf. 1 Cor. 14:29).

I. Howard Marshall writes, 'What is set out in detail in 1 Cor. 12-14 is stated here summarily. The Spirit is powerful and active like fire in the congregation (cf. Rom. 12:11, 2 Tim. 1:6 for the metaphor). Gifts for ministry were being exercised, but some people were trying to suppress them (we don't know just how), but it is wrong to do so'[59].

These exhortations appear to depict a church whose gatherings were participatory.

What Does it Mean to 'Quench the Spirit'?

There is a difference of opinion among the commentators as to what the expression 'do not quench the Spirit' means. As we have seen, some commentators like Marshall take quenching the Spirit to refer to the attempt to suppress and limit the opportunity for God's people to use their spiritual gifts in the church gatherings.

However, other commentators argue that we 'quench the Spirit' by sinful habits, which hinder the Spirit's working. Leon Morris argues that 'quenching the Spirit' here refers to the same thing as 'grieving the Holy Spirit of God' in Ephesians 4:30, that is, by sinful habits, unclean living or unloving attitudes. He writes, 'It is possible to 'quench' the Spirit (or to 'grieve' him) by such matters as those mentioned earlier in the epistle – despondency, idleness, immorality and the like – and it is best to take the words in such a general sense. Masson acutely points out that the words refer to the Spirit, not the inspired!'[60] The Macarthur Study Bible similarly says, 'the fire of God's Spirit is not to be doused with sin'[61].

Four facts tend to point to the opposite conclusion – that quenching the Spirit refers to trying to limit opportunity for the use of spiritual gifts in the church, and that quenching the Spirit is something different to grieving the Spirit:

---

[59] I. H. Marshall, *New Bible Commentary*, 4th Ed., Leicester: IVP, 1994, p1284
[60] Leon Morris, *1 and 2 Thessalonians*, TNTC, Nottingham: IVP, 2009 reprint, p105
[61] *The Macarthur Study Bible*, Nashville, TN: Thomas Nelson, 1997, p1850

1. The Context is the Church

John Stott writes, 'One New Testament picture of a gospel church portrays it as the family of God, whose members recognize and treat one another as sisters and brothers. This seems to be the key concept in the second half of 1 Thessalonians 5, since the word *adelphoi*, 'brothers' (which includes the *adelphai*, 'sisters', in the one *adelphotes*, 'brotherhood'), occurs five times (verses 12, 13 (sic, 14), 25, 26 and 27)'[62].

The context of the passage in 1 Thessalonians 5 is the Christian community, the church, rather than the lifestyle of the individual Christian. Here in the second half of chapter 5, we have a series of short injunctions about shepherding the church (verses 12-14), about mutual doing good within the church and without (verse 15), about speaking in ways that fulfill God's will (verses 16-18), and about prophetic ministry and its need to be tested (verses 19-21).

The church is pictured, particularly in verses 12-14, as a brotherly mutual edification society. Paul addresses the believers as 'brethren' in v12, urging them to esteem those who are laboring among them and leading them in the Lord. Then he addresses their leaders with the same word, 'brethren' in v14, urging them to care for the flock by admonishing, comforting, upholding and being patient with others. It is interesting that Paul uses exactly the same term ('brethren') for both groups, making no attempt to distinguish between the leaders and the led, or to somehow dignify with special titles the emerging leaders of the church.

F. F. Bruce writes: 'The Christian community is to be a little welfare state, a society practising mutual aid among its members in spiritual and material respects alike. Within its fellowship those who need help should be given the help they need. A special responsibility in this regard rests on the leaders of the community, but it is a ministry in which all can have some share'[63].

---

[62] John Stott, *The Message of Thessalonians*, BST, Nottingham: IVP, 1991, p117
[63] F. F. Bruce, *1 & 2 Thessalonians*, WBC, Nashville, TN: Thomas Nelson, 1982, p126

2. Verses 16-18 describe Various Expressions of Christian worship.

In 1 Thessalonians 5:16-18, Paul encourages a number of verbal expressions of Christian worship like rejoicing, praying, and giving thanks. These exhortations immediately precede his words about 'not quenching the Spirit' in verse 19 and his instructions about prophesying in verses 20 and 21.

R. P. Martin[64] notes that these instructions take a certain form: they are all very short, the verb stands last in each directive, and there is also 'a preponderance of words beginning with p' (in Greek, 'always', 'pray', 'everything', 'Spirit', 'prophecy' and 'all things' begin with 'p'). Martin suggests that when the passage is set out in lines, it almost looks like the headings for a church service: first rejoicing (in song), then prayer and thanksgiving, then a liberty to prophesy under the influence of the Spirit, and finally (in verse 22), 'the avoidance of anything unseemly' (F. F. Bruce[65]).

John Stott likewise argues that, 'at first reading one might not think that this section relates to the nature and conduct of public worship. But there are clear indications that this is primarily what Paul has in mind. To begin with, all the verbs are plural, so they seem to describe our collective and public, rather than individual and private, Christian duties. The prophesying of verse 20 is obviously public ... It is this context, then, which suggests that the rejoicing, the praying and the thanksgiving of verses 16-18 ... are also meant to be expressed when the congregation assembles'[66].

However, it is obvious that Martin and Stott are reading too much into the passage. The activities of rejoicing, praying and giving thanks in verses 16-18 are to characterize Christians 'always' (v16), 'without ceasing' (v17) and 'in everything' (v18), not just in church. Nevertheless, we are licensed to say this: if Christians are to be rejoicing, praying, and giving thanks all of the time, surely these activities cannot be excluded

---

[64] R. P. Martin, *Worship in the Early Church*, London: Marshall, Morgan and Scott, 1964, p135-6
[65] F. F. Bruce, *1 & 2 Thessalonians*, p122
[66] John Stott, *The Message of Thessalonians*, p124

from, but should be form part of, Christian gatherings for worship. While this is not some primitive 'order of service', yet neither is there anything inappropriate in arguing that these were precisely the sorts of expressions that should be found in Christian worship.

As Stott points out, the expression 'Do not quench the Spirit' (v19) binds together the verses that went before it and the verses that follow it, both in form and content. Thus, the structurally similar short, sharp 'staccato commands'[67] of verses 16-18 continue after verse 19 until verse 22. Similarly, the content of verses 16-22 is concerned with verbal expressions of Christian worship: rejoicing, praying, giving thanks, prophesying, testing. Thus, 'quenching the Spirit' should be taken to refer here to any attempt to silence any of the various 'expressions' of the Spirit described in this passage, whether by rejoicing, praying, giving thanks (vs 16-18) or prophesying (v20).

By contrast, the immediate context of the verse in Ephesians 4:30 which warns against 'grieving the Spirit' is surrounded with injunctions about Christian behavior (e.g. warnings against lying, stealing, corrupt language, bitterness, evil speaking, etc). The two passages are completely different, and to suggest they relate to the same matter seems wide of the mark.

3. The Description of the Spirit Suggests a Different Emphasis

It is interesting to notice the different ways the Spirit is referred to in these two passages. Here in 1 Thessalonians 5:19, the Spirit of God's activity is emphasized using the metaphor of fire, reminiscent of Acts 2 and the tongues of fire that sat upon the Christians. It points to the powerful work of the Spirit in inspiring God's people to be witnesses. F. F. Bruce, having noted that 'the verb quench is related to the figure of fire', lists references which use the picture of fire 'to denote the Holy Spirit or his activity': Matthew 3:11, Luke 3:16, Luke 12:49, Acts 2:3, Romans 12:11. Bruce then points to the way that Jeremiah's desire to speak no more in God's name resulted in God's word becoming 'a

---

[67] I. H. Marshall, *New Bible Commentary*, p1284

burning fire shut up in my bones' (Jeremiah 20:9) 'which could not be quenched or controlled'[68].

By contrast, in Ephesians 4:30, it is the holiness of the Spirit that is emphasized, for we grieve 'the holy Spirit of God' by sinful behaviour.

4. Paul has Already dealt with Ethical Matters in 1 Thessalonians 4

A final reason which suggests that Paul is not writing here about grieving the Holy Spirit in ethical and moral matters is the fact that he has already dealt with these issues in 1 Thessalonians 4:1-12. There Paul wrote about the need for Christians to 'please God' (v1), to 'abstain from sexual immorality' (v3), about 'brotherly love' (v9), and to 'work with your own hands' (v10). Paul even linked such godly living with the Holy Spirit in v8: 'for God did not call us to uncleanness, but in holiness. Therefore he who rejects this does not reject man, but God, who has also given us His Holy Spirit'.

Having already written about such ethical and moral issues in chapter 4, and stressed that we thus sin against the Holy Spirit, it seems more plausible that Paul is moving on in Chapter 5 to speak about a different area of Christian life in which it is possible to hinder the working of the Holy Spirit: in the life of the Christian community and its expressions of worship.

Summary

To 'quench the Spirit' refers to trying to stop the powerful working of the Spirit of God in the life of the church by restricting the freedom of the people of God to use their spiritual gifts. Henry Alford writes: 'Chrysostom (and others) understand this ethically … but there can be no doubt that the supernatural agency of the Spirit is here alluded to, - the speaking in tongues, &c., as in 1 Cor. 12:7ff. It is conceived of as a flame, which may be checked and quenched'[69]. J. A. Frame writes, 'the reference, however, is not to the ethical fruits of the Spirit (cf. 1:5-6, 4:8,

---

[68] F. F. Bruce, *1 and 2 Thesslonians*, p125

[69] Henry Alford, *The Greek New Testament*, London: Rivingtons, 1856, Vol. 3, p266

2 Thess. 2:13) but, as *propheteias* makes certain, to the extraordinary gifts of the Spirit, the charismata'[70].

Do Not Quench the Spirit (verse 19)

James Denney, the Scottish theologian, gives us a very helpful practical application of 'do not quench the Spirit' in his commentary on 1 Thess. 5:19-21. It is worth quoting at length:

'When the Holy Spirit descended on the Church at Pentecost, 'there appeared unto them tongues parting asunder, like as of fire; and it sat upon each one of them'; and their lips were opened to declare the mighty works of God. A man who has received this gift is described as fervent, literally boiling with the Spirit ... In the First Epistle to the Corinthians Paul describes a primitive Christian congregation. There was no one silent among them. When they came together every one had a psalm, a revelation, a prophecy, an interpretation. The manifestation of the Spirit had been given to each one to profit withal; and on all hands the spiritual fire was ready to flame forth. Conversion to the Christian faith, the acceptance of the apostolic Gospel, was not a thing which made little difference to men; it convulsed their whole nature to its depths; they were never the same again; they were new creatures, with a new life in them, all fervor and flame'.

'A state so unlike nature, in the ordinary sense of the term, was sure to have its inconveniences. The Christian, even when he had received the gift of the Holy Ghost, was still a man; and as likely as not a man who had to struggle against vanity, folly, ambition, and selfishness of all kinds. His enthusiasm might even seem, in the first instance, to aggravate, instead of removing, his natural faults. It might drive him to speak – for in a primitive church anybody who pleased might speak – when it would have been better for him to be silent. It might lead him to break out in prayer or praise or exhortation, in a style which made the wise sigh. And for those reasons the wise, and such as thought themselves wise, would be apt to discourage the

---

[70] J. A. Frame, *1 Thessalonians*, ICC, Edinburgh: T & T Clark, 1912, p205

exercise of spiritual gifts altogether. 'Contain yourself', they would say to the man whose heart burned within him, and who was restless till the flame could leap out; 'contain yourself; exercise a little self-control; it is unworthy of a rational being to be carried away in this fashion'.

'No doubt situations like this were common in the church at Thessalonica. They are produced inevitably by difference of age and of temperament. The old and phlegmatic are a natural, and, doubtless, a providential, counterweight to the young and sanguine. But the wisdom which comes of experience and of temperament has its disadvantages as compared with fervour of spirit. It is cold and unenthusiastic; it cannot propagate itself; it cannot set fire to anything and spread. And because it is under this incapacity of kindling the souls of men into enthusiasm, it is forbidden to pour cold water on such enthusiasm when it breaks forth in words of fire. That is the meaning of 'Quench not the Spirit'. The commandment presupposes that the Spirit can be quenched. Cold looks, contemptuous words, silence, studied disregard, go a long way to quench it. So does unsympathetic criticism'.

'Everyone knows that a fire smokes most when it is newly kindled; but the way to get rid of the smoke is not to pour cold water on the fire, but to let it burn itself clear. If you are wise enough you may even help it to burn itself clear; by rearranging the materials, or securing a better draught; but the wisest thing most people can do when the fire has got hold is to let it alone; and that is also the wise course for most when they meet with a disciple whose zeal burns like fire. Very likely the smoke hurts their eyes; but the smoke will soon pass by; and it may well be tolerated in the meantime for the sake of heat. For this apostolic precept takes for granted that fervour of spirit, a Christian enthusiasm for what is good, is the best thing in the world. It may be untaught and inexperienced; it may have all its mistakes to make; …

but it is of God; it is expansive; it is contagious; it is worth more as a spiritual force than all the wisdom in the world'[71].

Denney is surely correct: we need the power of the Holy Spirit, as much as ever. The solution to the problems we face in the modern church is not better musicians or multimedia presentations, electronic gadgets, glossy advertising brochures or more attractive facilities. We need the fire of God's Spirit. Why would we ever want to quench it?

A Contrast with 1 Corinthians 14

We have already noted three points of correspondence between 1 Thessalonians 5:19-21 and the passage in 1 Cor. 14:26-40. However, a contrast with 1 Corinthians 12-14 is also evident. This passage introduces another force at work in the church in addition to that of the Spirit of God. There seems to be a desire to restrict the freedom of God's Spirit, a desire to limit the opportunity for the exercise of certain gifts, particularly the gift of prophecy. This desire is not based, as in Corinth, on a preference for more spectacular gifts like speaking in tongues. Rather, there seems to be a human desire to control, for something more orderly and predictable than the fire of God's Spirit's utterances.

It is a sad truth that the history of the church shows that the Spirit-directed freedom we read about in 1 Corinthians and 1 Thessalonians soon gave way to a controlled environment where ceremony and liturgy took the place of Spirit-led opportunity.

The church historian A. N. Renwick tells the story as follows: 'The very essence of church organization and Christian life and worship in the first two centuries was simplicity. There was an absence of that formalism and pomp which took possession of the field in later times when spiritual life declined ... Their worship was free and spontaneous under the guidance of the Holy Spirit, and had not yet become inflexible through the use of manuals of devotion. The Church was vigorously

---

[71] James Denney, "The Epistles to the Thessalonians", in *The Expositor's Bible*, ed. W. Robertson Nicoll, London: Hodder and Stoughton, 1902, Baker Books 1982 reprint of 1903 US edition, p354-5

active. Not only the pastor but also many of those present took part in the services, for to them the priesthood of all believers was a tremendous reality'[72].

James Denney describes the spiritual decline of the church in these terms: 'I have hinted at ways in which the Spirit is quenched; it is sad to reflect from one point of view the history of the church is a long series of rebellions of the Spirit. 'Where the Spirit of the Lord is', the Apostle tells us elsewhere, 'there is liberty'. But liberty in a society has its dangers; it is, to a certain extent, at war with order; and the guardians of order are not apt to be too considerate of it. Hence it came to pass that at a very early period, and in the interests of good order, the freedom of the Spirit was summarily suppressed in the church. 'The gift of ruling', it has been said, 'like Aaron's rod, seemed to swallow up the other gifts'. The rulers of the church became a class entirely apart from its ordinary members, and all exercise of spiritual gifts for the building up of the church was confined to them. Nay, the monstrous idea was originated, and taught as a dogma, that they alone were the depositaries, or, as it is sometimes said, the custodians, of the grace and truth of the gospel; only through them could men come in contact with the Holy Ghost. In plain English, the Spirit was quenched when Christians met for worship. One great extinguisher was placed over the flame that burned in the hearts of the brethren; it was not allowed to show itself; it must not disturb, by its eruption in praise or prayer or fiery exhortation, the decency and order of divine service . . . I say that was the condition to which Christian worship was reduced at a very early period; and it is unhappily the condition in which, for the most part, it subsists at this moment. Do you think we are gainers by it? I do not believe it. It has always come from time to time to be intolerable. The Montanists of the second century, the heretical sects of the middle ages, the Independents and Quakers of the English Commonwealth, the lay preachers of Wesleyanism, the Salvationists, the Plymouthists, and the Evangelistic associations of our own day, – all these are in various degrees the protest of the Spirit, and

---

[72] A. N. Renwick, *The Story of the Church*, Leicester: IVP, 2nd Ed. 1985, pp22-23

its right and necessary protest, against the authority which would quench it, and by quenching it impoverish the church'[73].

Do Not Despise Prophecies (verse 20)

Stott writes, 'Here is a clear command to the church to listen to whatever messages purport to come from God, and not to 'despise' (RSV, REB) or reject them unheard and untested. In the post-Pentecost era all God's people receive the Holy Spirit and all may therefore 'prophesy' [Stott footnotes Acts 2:17ff], that is, know and speak God's mind and will. Nevertheless, in the early church a number of people were called in a more specific way 'prophets' or 'prophetesses', e.g. Agabus, Judas and Silas, Philip's four daughters, and others (Acts 11:27-28; 21:10-11; 15:32; 21:8-9; e.g. 1 Cor. 14:1ff) . . . Because we affirm the supremacy and sufficiency of Scripture, we naturally recognize a major difference between Paul's time and our own, namely that we have the completed canon of Scripture, the written Word of God. Certainly, therefore, there are today no apostles . . . and no prophets comparable to the biblical prophets, whether the Old Testament authors or John who called his book (the Revelation) a 'prophecy'. . . Nevertheless, once the uniqueness of the biblical prophets (and apostles) has been conceded, we should be ready to add that there are today secondary and subsidiary kinds of prophetic gift and ministry. For God undoubtedly gives to some a remarkable degree of insight either into Scripture itself and its meaning, or into its application to the contemporary world, or into his particular will for particular people in particular situations'[74].

William MacDonald defines prophecy as follows: 'In its primary New Testament sense, to prophesy meant to speak the word of God. The inspired utterances of the prophets are preserved for us in the Bible. In a secondary sense, to prophesy means to declare the mind of God as it has

---

[73] James Denney, "The Epistles to the Thessalonians", p355
[74] John Stott, *The Message of Thessalonians*, p127-8

been revealed in the Bible'[75]. F. F. Bruce defines prophecy here as 'the declaration of the mind of God in the power of the Spirit'[76].

Test all Things; Hold Fast what is Good (verse 21)

W. E. Vine argues that the expression in verse 21, 'test all things', applies to more than simply prophecies, but extended to all contributions made in the church gathering. He writes: 'the adjective ('all') which is plural … = all spiritual gifts, 1 Corinthians 12:1, including prophecy … From the scope of this injunction not even the utterances of an apostle were exempt, Acts 17:11; 2 Timothy 2:7, cf. Isaiah 8:20, for the duty and the right, the responsibility and the privilege, of the individual believer to judge for himself, 1 Corinthians 10:15; Galatians 1:8, 9, and to act upon his judgement, Romans 14:4, 5, are an essential feature of Christianity'[77].

Thus, this passage is dealing with more than simply the gift of prophecy. The fact that prophecies were in danger of being despised in the church suggests that other spiritual gifts were being preferred in their place. Paul urges that all spiritual gifts and messages contributed in the church gatherings were to be tested.

The two following expressions 'hold fast what is good' and 'abstain from every form of evil' (verse 22) describe the result of the testing. After testing, we are to 'hold fast what is good', while on the other hand, we are to 'abstain from every form of evil'. We are to hold fast to the truths brought before us in the church gatherings, and such truths should have a practical effect upon our behaviour ('abstain from every form of evil').

Vine puts it like this: 'hold fast that which is good' … i.e. that "prophesying" or "tongue" which is being tested commends itself to the spiritual mind as having its origin in God, or that teaching which accords with His revealed will' (p93). Then commenting upon 'abstain from', he writes, 'if, on being tested, the tongue, prophesying or teaching, was not approved, the saints were to turn away therefrom … To give heed to that

---

[75] William MacDonald, *Believers Bible Commentary*, p2043
[76] F. F. Bruce, *1 & 2 Thessalonians*, p127
[77] W. E. Vine with C. F. Hogg, "1 Thessalonians", *The Collected Writings of W. E. Vine*, Vol. 3, Nashville, TN: Thomas Nelson, 1996, p92

which cannot be approved when tested by the Scriptures ... is to submit to influences that must ultimately lower the tone of spiritual life and affect for evil the conduct of the believer' (pp93-94).

Conclusion

Here, then, we have a passage which shows that the participatory, Spirit-led, picture of church gatherings we find in 1 Corinthians 14:26-40 was not unique to the Corinthian church. It was also found in the church at Thessalonica and, as we shall see, everywhere else too.

Denney concludes: 'An open meeting, a liberty of prophesying, a gathering in which any one could speak as the Spirit gave him utterance is one of the crying needs of the modern Church'[78].

---

[78] Denney, p357

CHAPTER 4

PARTICIPATORY CHURCH GATHERINGS IN THE PASTORAL EPISTLES

The Pastoral Epistles (1 and 2 Timothy and Titus) present us with another fascinating picture of New Testament church life. Our interest lies in what Paul says about how the church should be organised, and how Timothy and Titus are to encourage its growth.

Timothy's Mission (1 Tim. 1:3-7)

As I urged you when I went into Macedonia - remain in Ephesus that you may charge some that they teach no other doctrine, ⁴ nor give heed to fables and endless genealogies, which cause disputes rather than godly administration which is in faith. ⁵ Now the purpose of the commandment is love from a pure heart, from a good conscience and from sincere faith, ⁶ from which some, having strayed, have turned aside to idle talk, ⁷ desiring to be teachers of the law, understanding neither what they say nor the things which they affirm. (1 Timothy 1:3-7)

A large part of the Pastoral Epistles deals with promoting healthy teaching in the church. These letters repeatedly stress the importance of 'sound (i.e. healthy, Gk. *hygiaino*, from which our English word 'hygienic' is derived) teaching' – that is, teaching that produces healthy Christian living. Paul deals with this matter in the very first paragraph of 1 Timothy, showing the tremendous importance of good teaching in the church.

Good biblical teaching is Paul's prescription in the Pastoral Epistles for the health of the churches in Ephesus and Crete. Paul lists the following benefits of good teaching in the church and in the lives of believers in 1 Timothy 1 verses 4-5:

1. godly administration[79] (v4) – godly order, as opposed to a church full of disputes.
2. love (v5) – again, as opposed to Christians fighting among each other
3. pure hearts (v5) – clean hearts, because good Bible teaching has a corrective and cleansing effect upon believers lives.
4. good consciences (v5) – not 'clean consciences', but rather consciences in good working order, showing discernment both morally and doctrinally.
5. sincere faith (v5) – vibrant, unhypocritical Christian lives.

Paul also lists some of the sorts of unhelpful teaching that were producing poor spiritual health among the believers:

- false-teaching (v3)
- fables (v4) – myths and superstitious stories
- endless genealogies (v4; probably OT historical speculations, but whatever these refer to, they seem to have been tiresome and long-winded)
- idle talk (empty jabber-jaw, v6)
- Jewish legalism (v7)

Some churches today do not place much of a premium on good Bible teaching. They instead use their services for light entertainment or motivational talks. Other churches use their main services for evangelism or worshipping (worthy causes, it is true), but their flock becomes spiritually malnourished because Bible teaching is relegated to a mid-week evening (if at all) when few people are impacted by it.

---

[79] The KJV reads 'edification' instead of 'administration', Gk. *oikodomian* instead of *oikonomian*, however this reading is found in hardly any manuscripts and has little claim to being original.

Timothy was not asked to remain in Ephesus to help with evangelism, to focus upon worship or even to deal with division or a serious case of discipline. His mission was to deal with teaching in the church. This shows the great importance of Bible teaching.

Participatory Church Teaching

Our interest in 1 Timothy 1 focuses chiefly upon what it says about how New Testament churches organized their teaching. Notice three points from the mandate that Timothy is given in this passage:

1. Timothy was not told to take over the teaching in Ephesus.
We learn from 1 Tim. 1:3 that Timothy was to charge *some* not to teach false-doctrine, which shows firstly that there were multiple false-teachers in the church, and secondly, that not all teachers were false-teachers (only some), implying that there were multiple good teachers as well as false-teachers. Harry Ironside writes, 'It is interesting to trace that little word *some* through this Epistle. You will find it frequently' (he lists references in 1:6, 19, 4:1, 5:15, 'and so on'). Ironside continues: 'There were those who were teaching things contrary to the truth of God; so Paul says to Timothy, "Stay there if you will and help the saints, and warn those teachers of false things, and charge them that they teach no other doctrine than that which has been delivered unto the saints"'[80].

What sort of situation is this? There obviously was no Minister, or Senior/Teaching Pastor who did all the teaching, for we read of multiple teachers. Nor does Paul tell Timothy to fill the position of Senior Pastor, or take responsibility for all the Bible teaching.

There were many other teachers in Ephesus besides Timothy, as is evidenced by the multiple varieties of poor-quality teaching that Timothy had to deal with, as well as no doubt many other good teachers. Some might suggest that only the elders had the right to teach in church, but this is nowhere stated in 1 Timothy, and it is rendered unlikely by the fact that some teachers were peddling serious false-doctrine. Further, in

---

[80] H. A. Ironside, *Timothy, Titus and Philemon*, Neptune, NJ: Loizeaux Brothers, 1947, p17-18

Titus 1:10-11, one reason for the appointment of elders was to refute false-teachers, which again implies that the elders were not the only ones teaching. Stephen Short writes, 'Amongst the implications of that passage is that although teaching in a church was the duty of that church's elders, liberty for teaching was afforded also in church services for those who were not elders, though those in this category who abused their liberty in this needed to be restrained'[81].

2. Timothy was not told to appoint suitable preachers or to organize a preaching roster.

Was there a stable of approved teachers who took it in turns? Obviously not, for Paul never tells Timothy to remove those from the roster who were less gifted or to make sure only the best preachers were on it. Timothy is given no powers to 'hire and fire' preachers, or to restrict teaching to an approved list, nor given the job of inviting speakers. False teachers needed to be silenced (Titus 1:10-11), and other abuses needed to be publicly corrected, but Timothy was not even instructed to tell certain long-winded and unprofitable speakers to cease preaching. Instead, Timothy's mandate involved charging preachers to handle the Word of God rightly and profitably.

Paul nowhere says that Timothy should consider organizing the subjects for consideration or the passages for exposition, nor was he told to set out some plan for consecutive teaching. Nor is he told to get the elders working on such a plan. This would be our immediate response to such a situation: get rid of those teaching false-doctrine or long-winded bores, and substitute some consecutive teaching program or lectionary system. But Timothy's instructions do not say anything like what we have in our modern churches.

3. Timothy was told to correct poor teaching and model good teaching.

Timothy was told to take a two-pronged approach to the problem of teaching in the church. Firstly, he was urged to take a stand against false-doctrine and unprofitable preaching by means of public correction (1

---

[81] Stephen Short, "The Ministry of the Word", *The Witness*, February 1965, p45

Tim. 1:3) and warnings about the sorts of teaching that did not encourage and build up God's people. Secondly, Paul's method of encouraging 'healthy teaching' involved urging Timothy (and Titus) to get heavily involved in teaching the Bible themselves so that (a) the Christians would be fed and taught, and (b) the other preachers would have good examples and models to imitate.

Paul gives Timothy another reminder of this mandate in his second letter: 'Remind them of these things, charging them before the Lord not to strive about words to no profit, to the ruin of the hearers. Be diligent to present yourself approved to God, a worker who does not need to be ashamed, rightly dividing the word of truth' (2 Tim. 2:14-15).

Stephen Short, commenting on the opening verses of the first letter, writes: 'Timothy's task in Ephesus therefore, was not to take over the task of teaching from those who were already attending to it, but to instruct these teachers – in private, doubtless, for the most part – to deliver to the church that which was true and profitable, rather than that which was false, or that which was unprofitable. This having been done, after quite a short stay, he departed from Ephesus for Rome (so we infer from 2 Tim. 4:9). A reference to the teaching by the Ephesian elders of their own church during the actual residence of Timothy among them is contained in 1 Tim. 5:17, which reads: 'Let the elders that rule well be counted worthy of double honour, especially they who labour in the Word and doctrine'[82].

Bearing in mind that it was Paul who founded the church in Ephesus himself only a few years earlier, it would seem that the following characteristics of the church in Ephesus had been established by Paul himself:

- **Multiple preachers in the church.** As we have noticed, Timothy is told to 'charge *some* to teach no other doctrine', which implies multiple preachers, some good and profitable, while others were poor and needed guidance or correction.

---

[82] Stephen Short, "The Ministry of the Word", *The Witness*, February 1965, p44

- **With freedom to preach upon subjects of their own choosing**. Some of these preachers were preaching upon subjects that Paul considered to be either wrong ('other-doctrine', verse 3) or unprofitable ('idle talk', verse 6). It is obvious that some of these preachers had chosen poor subjects to speak upon of their own will ('desiring to be teachers of the law', verse 7), not at the invitation of a committee.
- **Even allowing Opportunity for Some who were poor quality Preachers**. The variable quality of the preachers (some good, some less so), suggests that such preachers were neither authorised or approved to preach by some accrediting board that enforced some selection or quality control policy.
- **Being held to account for their messages**. One of the main tasks that Timothy was charged with by Paul was to evaluate and respond to teaching in the church, refuting false-teaching, and alerting believers to the varieties of preaching that were unprofitable. The critical evaluation thus related both to the suitability of the content and quality of the preaching style.

It might be objected that we are just piling up inferences here. We are saying that Paul did not mention anything about Timothy (a) doing all the teaching, (b) picking the speakers, or (c) organising the teaching program. However, (some will argue), this does not prove that there was *not* some preaching roster that Timothy re-organized or a consecutive teaching program that was already in place. Maybe some sort of preaching system already existed, or was simply a standard practice in New Testament churches, and Paul did not need to mention it.

This is an argument from silence. It would carry some force if there were other examples in the New Testament of some such organized, consecutive, clerical, or liturgical model of church life. But the New Testament nowhere mentions any such system of church gatherings that objectors would try to substitute for the biblical picture. We have already seen positive evidence from various places in the New Testament that explicitly describes how church gatherings were conducted. The picture we find here in the Pastoral Epistles again matches the participatory, open, free, interactive gatherings we find described elsewhere. The

Pastoral Epistles add to and corroborate the form of participatory church gatherings we find described elsewhere in the New Testament.

In addition, the point of 1 Timothy is precisely to set in order the way that things should be done in the church: 'so that you may know how you ought to conduct yourself in the house of God, which is the church of the Living God, the pillar and ground of the truth' (1 Tim. 3:15). Paul does not leave things to the imagination. Instead, he spells out things that Timothy (surely) knew full well. Paul's letter to Timothy was not primarily written to educate Timothy, but to provide written authority for Timothy's mission in such a way that no one could contradict Timothy's mandate. Nor was 1 Timothy written for Timothy's time alone, but to provide instructions for the governance of the church in Ephesus after Timothy left. Therefore, the fact that Paul neither instituted nor referred to a roster of preachers or some consecutive teaching program suggests that Paul did not intend Timothy to organize such a system to operate in the church.

In summary, we can draw a number of very simple lessons from this passage about the way New Testament churches carried out this most important task of Bible teaching. Many (if not all) of the brothers were free to speak, upon whatever subject they wished, but abuses that this system allowed were not left uncorrected, and high standards of teaching were encouraged and expected.

The sort of Christian ministry that Paul pictures here involved letting people use their gifts and share the message that God had laid upon their hearts, not a control-freak mentality that required pulpit professionalism. Paul gave Timothy guidelines here; he did not call for graduates of some theological seminary. Paul told Timothy to correct unhealthy ministry; not to set up a closed-shop. Paul urged high-standards in Bible teaching, but not an ordained or organized ministry.

In the New Testament, God gave His servants freedom to teach the Scriptures upon whatever subject they felt burdened to speak about. If this yielded less than perfect results, the system was not abandoned. Instead, God's people learned through the public correction of false-teaching, through repeated warnings against unedifying talk and through the blessing received through faith-building teaching coming from men like Timothy and Titus.

There are numerous benefits to this participatory style of church gathering: it allows people to develop their gifts, it means that God's people get different kinds of ministry from God's Word, it allows the Holy Spirit to prompt people so the meeting is Spirit-led and we can be open to hearing God speak through His Word. In the early church, it meant that their meetings were a spiritual feast, a conference of different contributions, every Sunday. No wonder these early New Testament churches grew so spectacularly.

Yet, there were not only numerous benefits from participatory church gatherings; there were also many potential pitfalls and real problems. This is precisely why Timothy was asked to stay in Ephesus.

Why are most modern Church services so different to the New Testament? Maybe it is simply because many Christians are unaware of what the New Testament says about the way the early churches ran their gatherings. We have become used to following the traditions of men rather than the Word of God. But, knowing the way the churches of the New Testament ran their gatherings, are we actually prepared to be 'apostolic' (one of the four traditional marks of a true church)? Or are we afraid to try to do things in a scriptural way because it might get a bit messy? Is our problem a lack of faith in God to do things the way His Word describes?

Were Timothy and Titus Bishops or Pastors?

Timothy and Titus were asked by Paul to remain in Ephesus and Crete to deal with certain matters in the churches there. One of the important issues that both 1 Timothy and Titus dealt with concerned the appointing of elders (1 Tim. 3) or bishops (i.e. overseers, Titus 1). What was Timothy's and Titus' relationship to these elders and overseers? What was Timothy's and Titus' position and role in these churches?

The KJV footnotes at the end of 2 Timothy and Titus say that Timothy and Titus were the first bishops in these respective churches. Other modern commentators suggest that Timothy and Titus served as the Pastors of these churches (e.g. see the Macarthur Study-Bible introductory notes on 1 Timothy). To understand Timothy's and Titus' position in these churches, and which of these positions is correct, we need to first survey what the New Testament teaches about church leadership.

The terms 'Elder', 'Bishop' (or, Overseer) and 'Pastor' (or, Shepherd) are Synonymous

In New Testament times, an elder (Greek: *presbyteros*) was the same thing as a 'bishop' (or 'overseer', Greek: *episkopos*) and a 'shepherd' (i.e. 'pastor', Greek: *poimen*). The three titles elder, overseer, and shepherd are applied interchangeably to the same people in the New Testament. This can be seen in the following passages:

- In Acts 20, Paul called for the *elders* of the Church in Ephesus (v17). Then in verse 28, Paul says to them: 'Therefore take heed to yourselves and to all the flock, among which the Holy Spirit has made you *overseers*, to *shepherd* the Church of God which He purchased with His own blood'.
- In 1 Peter 5, Peter uses all three of these same expressions again when writing to the *elders* (v1), urging them to *shepherd* the flock of God (v2), serving as *overseers* (v2).
- In Titus 1, Paul tells Titus to appoint *elders* (1:5). In verse 7, listing their qualifications, he then says, 'For an *overseer* must be blameless …'.

The three terms 'elder', 'overseer' (i.e. bishop) and shepherd (i.e. pastor) are synonymous; they are three ways of describing the work of the same people. Further proof that elders and overseers are exactly the same people is seen in the fact that the qualifications of both are, for all practical purposes, identical in 1 Tim. 3 and Titus 1. William Barclay points out that while the apostles appointed elders in all the churches (Acts 14:23), in Philippians 1:1, Paul greets 'all the saints in Christ Jesus who are in Philippi, with the bishops (overseers) and deacons'. Barclay writes: it seems 'quite impossible that Paul would have sent no greetings to the elders, who, as we have already seen, were in every Church; and therefore the bishops and the elders, must have been one and the same body of people'[83]. He concludes: 'modern scholarship is practically unanimous in holding that in the early Church the *presbuteros* and the *episkopos*, the elder and the bishop or overseer, were one and the same person'[84].

In the New Testament, the bishop (i.e. overseer) was not a distinct office to that of the elder. Neither was the pastor (i.e. shepherd) a different office to that of the elder. All three words, elder, overseer and shepherd, referred to the same one person. Or better still, as we are about to see, the three words refer to the same *group* of people.

Church Leadership was Plural and Shared, not Singular
In the New Testament there was more than one elder or overseer or pastor per church. There is no such thing in the New Testament as one man who is the leader of the church. Notice the plural forms of the words 'elders' and 'overseers' in the following verses:

1. In Acts 11:30; 15:2, 4, 6, 22, 23; 16:4 and 21:18, we learn that the church in Jerusalem had a body of elders who functioned as official representatives of the church there.
2. In Acts 14:23, after Paul's first missionary journey, we read: 'So when they had appointed ***elders*** in ***every church***, and prayed with fasting, they commended them to the Lord in whom they had believed'.
3. In Acts 20:17, Paul called for the ***elders*** of the Church in Ephesus to meet him in Miletus.
4. Paul, when writing to Timothy says: 'Let the ***elders*** who lead well be counted worthy of double honour' (1 Tim. 5:17).
5. In writing to Titus, Paul directs him to 'appoint ***elders*** in every city' (Titus 1:5).
6. In Peter's First Letter, he writes: 'The ***elders*** who are among you I exhort, who am also an elder' (1 Peter 5:1). Then again, in verse 5 of

---

[83] William Barclay, *The Letters to Timothy, Titus, Philemon*, The Saint Andrew Press, Edinburgh, 1960, p82
[84] Ibid, p82

the same passage, he writes: 'Likewise you younger people, be subject to the *elders*'.
7. James writes: 'Is anyone sick among you? Let him call for the *elders* of the church and let them pray over him, anointing him with oil in the name of the Lord' (James 5:14).
8. In 1 Timothy 4:14, Paul uses the term 'presbytery' or 'eldership' - meaning the collective body of elders: 'Do not neglect the gift that is in you, which was given to you by prophecy with the laying on of the hands of the *eldership*'.
9. In Acts 20:28, Paul speaking to the Ephesian elders said: 'Take heed to yourselves and to all the flock, among which the Holy Spirit has made you *overseers* (ie. bishops) ...'
10. In Philippians 1:1, Paul addresses his letter 'to all the saints in Christ Jesus who are in Philippi, with the *overseers* and deacons'

Stephen Short, writing about Paul's greeting in the opening verse of Philippians, notices that there is 'no mention of the church's 'minister', where such mention, surely, would have been expected. Indeed, in the introduction of none of the New Testament Epistles is the 'minister' addressed; nor, at the conclusion of any of the New Testament Epistles are greetings sent to him – even (as in the epistles to the Romans and the Colossians) where greetings are sent to many people. One might even go so far as to submit that in no New Testament letter to a local Christian church is there any allusion made anywhere to what the author might have termed the 'minister' of that church, or the 'pastor' of that church; and it is difficult to suggest any other reason for this than that 'ministers' and 'pastors' as we know them today did not then exist. What did then exist, and what fulfilled the function which is fulfilled now by 'ministers' and 'pastors', was a body of 'elders', or 'overseers', or 'bishops', so that Paul could here write: 'Paul and Timotheus, the servants of Jesus Christ, to all the saints in Christ Jesus which are at Philippi, with the *bishops*'[85].

---

[85] Stephen S. Short, "The Ministry of the Word", *The Witness*, February 1965, p43. This printed thesis was originally read to about two hundred ministers of

Elders, Overseers and Shepherds were the Leaders of the churches

Elders/overseers/shepherds in the New Testament were the actual leaders of churches. They were not some subservient class or advisory board to a minister, bishop or pastor. They were the church leaders:

- 1 Tim. 5:17 reads, 'let the *elders* who *lead* well be counted worthy of double honour'.
- Notice the way that shepherding and leading are connected in Hebrews 13:7, 17, 20 and 24. Christ is the Great **Shepherd** (i.e. 'pastor', verse 20) who never leaves us (verse 5), whereas human '*leaders*', 'those watching out for your souls' (i.e. '*overseers*', verse 17) will come and go ('remember those *leading* you, who spoke the word of God to you, whose faith follow', verse 7).
- Notice that in 1 Thess. 5:12, when referring to the leaders in the Church at Thessalonica, Paul again refers to them in the plural: 'we urge you, brethren, to recognise those who labour among you and are over you' (literally, govern you, *lead* you) in the Lord and admonish you, and to esteem them very highly in love for their work's sake'. These leaders in the Church were involved in teaching ('admonish you', verse 12) and are encouraged to 'warn the unruly, comfort the fainthearted, uphold the weak, be patient with all' (verse 13). In other words, they were shepherding God's people.

So, we may say that the four following terms are synonymous: elders ('presbyters'), overseers ('bishops'), shepherds ('pastors') and leaders. Furthermore, the New Testament requires us to understand a plurality of such men in leadership of each local church.

Summary

In the New Testament, the bishop was not a separate office to that of an elder. The idea of the monarchical bishop, ruling over the elders, only arose in the second century. Nor was the pastor a separate office to that

---

evangelical churches at a meeting at Welwyn, Hertfordshire, England, on the 17th of June, 1964.

of the elder (as in many modern churches). Nor is it right to think of the pastor as someone with different responsibilities to the other elders, or someone on staff who is paid for his work whereas an elder is a volunteer. In the New Testament, as both Acts 20 and 1 Peter 5 make perfectly clear, all of the elders were told to pastor (i.e. shepherd) the flock. The modern evangelical distinction between a pastor (or pastors) and elders is unbiblical, as is the modern evangelical title of Senior Pastor, for the only references in the New Testament to a Senior Pastor are found in 1 Peter 5:4 where the title is ascribed to Christ as the 'chief shepherd' (Greek: *archipoimen*) and Hebrews 13:20 which calls Christ 'the Great Shepherd'.

Many people attempt to read modern denominational structures and ecclesiastical traditions back into the New Testament by calling Timothy or Titus 'the bishop' of the church, or 'the pastor' of the church. However common or convenient these titles may be in our day, they are neither part of the biblical picture nor do they accord with its shared (as opposed to hierarchical) leadership structure. The modern evangelical concepts of 'bishops' and 'pastors' cannot rightly be projected backwards onto the roles that Timothy and Titus played.

What shall we make of Timothy's and Titus' roles in the New Testament? Neither Timothy nor Titus are given honorific titles anywhere in the New Testament, unless we count the terms 'brother', 'servant', 'partner' or 'co-worker'[86]. Some would attempt to give them the title of 'apostolic-delegate' but such a term is nowhere found in the New Testament (and has no more biblical authority than the modern Roman Catholic equivalent, 'papal nuncio'). They were simply Paul's ministry-partners and fellow-workers, sent by him to work in growing churches alongside the existing elders (for the church in Ephesus had elders long

---

[86] Descriptions of Timothy elsewhere in the NT include 'fellow worker' (Romans 16:21), 'my beloved and faithful son in the Lord' (1 Cor. 4:17), 'Timothy the brother' (2 Cor. 1:1, Col. 1:1, Philem. 1:1), 'bondservant of Jesus Christ' (Phil. 1:1), 'servant of God and fellow-labourer' (1 Thess. 3:2), 'a true son in the faith' (1 Tim. 1:2), '[my] child' (1 Tim. 1:18), 'beloved child' (2 Tim. 1:2), and 'our brother' (Heb. 13:23). Titus is called 'my brother' (2 Cor. 2:13), 'my partner and fellow-worker' (2 Cor. 8:23) and 'a true son' (Tit. 1:4).

before Timothy's arrival, Acts 20:17), or in the case of Titus, to appoint the new elders.

What were their roles within the churches at Ephesus and Crete? Nowhere are we told that either men officially became part of the eldership (or presbytery, 1 Tim. 4:14) in these churches, nor did they occupy some clearly-defined position that ruled over the elders. Even Paul refused to talk of himself as ruling over the churches ('Not that we have dominion over your faith, but are fellow workers for your joy', 2 Cor. 1:24).

We may conclude that Timothy and Titus were neither bishops nor pastors in the modern usage of those terms. While they were actively involved in teaching, correcting, encouraging and working among the flock (i.e. they were doing a similar work to the elders/overseers/shepherds), they were not officially part of the elderships of these churches, nor did they hold any official titles in such a capacity. They were simply the Lord's servants working in the churches.

False Teaching in the Church

We read numerous references to false-teaching in the Pastoral Epistles: law-keeping (1 Tim. 1:7 and Titus 1:10, 'the circumcision'), asceticism ('forbidding to marry and commanding to abstain from foods', 4:3), and those denying the future resurrection ('saying the resurrection is already past', 2 Tim. 2:18). There also seem to have been some whose teachings did not encourage godly living (e.g. 2 Tim. 3:1-10, Titus 1:12-16), for Paul regularly speaks about the need for godliness. The question all this false-teaching raises is, How was it possible for such errors to be taught publicly in the church?

Stephen Short raises the question in the analogous situation we read about in Colosse. He says, 'The Epistle to the Colossians was written to counteract a heresy which was being propounded in the church at Colossae. . . . Paul pleaded as follows (ch. 2 v.8): 'Beware lest any man spoil you through philosophy and vain deceit, after the tradition of men, after the rudiments of the world, and not after Christ' (v. 16): 'Let no man therefore judge you in meat, or in drink, or in respect of an holyday, or of the new moon, or of the Sabbath days' (v. 18): 'Let no man beguile you of your reward in a voluntary humility, and worshipping of angels, intruding into those things which he hath not seen, vainly puffed up by his fleshy mind'.

Short continues: 'What situation, in writing this, is Paul envisaging? Is he hinting to the Colossians that the minister of their church is a heretic, and is preaching to them false doctrine? Obviously he is not; for had that been the case, he would surely have instructed the church to dismiss their minister, and appoint in his place someone who was sound in the faith. Why did not Paul issue these instructions? Because it was not the case of a false teacher who was the church's minister (there being in fact no minister in the church). Rather was it the case of a man in the church who, in the middle of the church's meetings, would rise to his feet not infrequently to give an address – as did many other men in the church – but propounded false ideas in his addresses. Paul's resort therefore, was knowing that the church might have to continue to listen to such misleading addresses, to fortify its members against the particular errors to which they were apt to be exposed. But the very fact that heretics could propound such notions in the churches of Apostolic times shows that the teaching such churches received came, in each case, through more than a single pair of lips'[87].

Short also raises the case of the Judaizing false-teachers in Galatia: 'It was thus, one intuits, with the Judaizers. It would have been useless for Paul to have told the Galatians, 'Don't invite these men to preach to you'. The Judaizers did not wait for such an invitation. Knowing the liberty for ministry which there was in the churches of Christians, they rose to their feet and expounded to those present their misguided opinions whenever an opportunity for this occurred. They could not have done that had only one person authority to preach in each Christian church'[88].

There seems to be a clear parallel in the Galatian and Colossian churches to the situation we find here in the Pastoral Epistles, not only

---

[87] Stephen Short, "The Ministry of the Word", *The Witness*, February 1965, pp43-4
[88] Ibid., p 44

in the sorts of falsehoods being taught in the church, but also in the way in which they were introduced. Just as Short argues that the liberties of the open, participatory church gatherings in Galatian and Colossae allowed an opportunity for false-teaching, so we may assume that the many references to false-teaching in the Pastoral Epistles flow on from an open, participatory style of church gathering.

Debate and Discussion in the Church

Church gatherings in the New Testament, at least as seen through the window of the Pastoral Epistles, were more like a modern parliament with its multiplicity of speakers contributing to informed debate, rather than the monologue of a medieval cardinal.

References that describe the to-and-fro of vigorous and spirited debate taking place in the church gatherings are commonly found throughout the Pastoral epistles, indicative of the fact that there were different viewpoints expressed on some issues.

Notice the references to 'disputes', 'arguments', 'fights', 'quarrels', 'opposition':

- 'disputes' (1 Tim. 1:4)
- 'disputes and arguments over words' (1 Tim. 6:4),
- 'fights over words' (2 Tim. 2:14),
- 'disputes' (2 Tim. 2:23),
- 'quarrels' (2 Tim. 2:24),
- 'opposition' (2 Tim. 2:25),
- people 'resisting the truth' (2 Tim. 3:8),
- 'resisting our words' (2 Tim. 4:15),
- 'foolish disputes' (Titus 3:9),
- 'contentions' (Titus 3:9)

All of these references are to debate of a troublesome nature and it is obvious that Paul is not encouraging a model of church that is characterised by arguments and disputes. On the contrary, Paul argues that the *'servant of the Lord must not quarrel but be gentle to all, able to teach, patient'* (2 Timothy 2:24). The reason Paul sent Timothy and Titus to the churches in Ephesus and Crete was to see to it that the churches there became more orderly (1 Tim. 3:15: 'I write so that you may know how you may behave yourself in the house of God').

However, Paul did not sacrifice free discussion for the sake of order. Paul did not curtail freedom just because there are ways in which freedom can be abused. There is no hint of any banning of any preachers (except heretics) or limiting the preaching to a select list of approved men. Paul's consistent method is to encourage mature and profitable debate rather than to ban free debate because it has the potential for unhelpful contributions.

The New Testament pictures a state in which there was freedom of speech in the church. Sadly, many Christians today have about as much participation in church as children sitting in after-school detention. New Testament churches, on the other hand, allowed opportunity for free participation.

How Did Paul Know so Much about Poor Quality Preaching?

Paul's criticisms of poor-quality preaching are an important part of the Pastoral Epistles and they suggest something significant about the meetings in the churches of the apostolic era.

Paul deals with the subject of poor quality preaching on numerous occasions in the Pastoral Epistles:

- 1 Tim. 1:3-4: 'charge some that they *teach no other doctrine*, nor give heed to *fables and endless genealogies*'
- 1 Tim. 1:6-7: 'from which some, having strayed, have turned aside to *idle talk*, desiring to be *teachers of the law*'
- 1 Tim. 4:2-3: '*speaking lies in hypocrisy ... forbidding to marry and commanding to abstain from foods*'
- 1 Tim. 4:7: 'reject *profane and old wives fables*'
- 1 Tim. 6:3: 'if anyone *teaches otherwise* and does not consent to wholesome words, even the words of our Lord Jesus Christ, and to the doctrine which accords with godliness, he is proud, knowing nothing, but is *obsessed with disputes and arguments over words*, from which come envy, strife, reviling, evil suspicions, *useless wranglings* of

men of corrupt minds and destitute of the truth, who suppose that godliness is a means of gain.
- 1 Tim. 6:20: 'avoiding the *profane and idle babblings* and *contradictions of what is false called knowledge*'
- 2 Tim. 2:14: 'charging them before the Lord not to *strive about words to no profit*, to the ruin of the hearers'
- 2 Tim. 2:16-18: 'shun *profane and idle babblings*, for they will increase to more ungodliness and their message will spread like cancer. Hymenaeus and Philetus are of this sort, who have strayed concerning the truth, *saying that the resurrection is already past*, and they overthrow the faith of some'
- 2 Tim. 4:3-4: 'the time will come when they will not endure sound doctrine, but according to their own desires, because they have itching ears, they will heap up for themselves teachers; and they will turn their ears away from the truth, and be *turned aside to fables*'
- Titus 1:10: 'there are many insubordinate, both *idle talkers and deceivers, especially those of the circumcision*, whose mouths must be stopped, who subvert whole households, teaching things which they ought not, for the sake of dishonest gain'
- Titus 3:9: 'avoid *foolish disputes, genealogies and strivings about the law*, for they are unprofitable and useless'

We can learn a few lessons from these references. Firstly, of course, we must learn the obvious lesson: the quality of preaching in the church is of great importance. Paul repeatedly contrasts the varieties of poor quality preaching with 'sound teaching' (that is, teaching that is spiritually health-promoting). That is because good teaching is what makes for well-fed, healthy, growing Christians. Paul obviously believes in preaching – he is not interested in the 'everybody sharing a short thought' format that most home bible studies resemble. He wants to see good preaching that builds healthy Christians in the church.

Secondly, however, we are forced to ask the question: How did Paul know so much about poor quality preaching? He mentions not only false-teaching (law-keeping, resurrection-deniers, legalists teaching commandments of men, fable-tellers and other 'deceivers'), but also people who were obviously true Christians but whose preaching was not particularly edifying. He mentions idle babblers, those telling 'genealogies' - which could mean that they either read out genealogies, or maybe told long boring 'histories'. He talks about argumentative souls engaging in word-fights, those whose messages were profane - that is, lacking anything godly or sacred, their preaching instead consisted of worldly talk – and finally those whose preaching merely tickled 'itching ears' – that is, those who preached comfortable falsehoods that their audiences wanted to hear.

Perhaps the reason that Paul knew so much about poor-quality preaching was that he heard reports about it from others. No doubt this was true, for people will talk. However, the most obvious possible reason that Paul was so familiar with and so animated in his criticism of the great variety of poor quality preaching was that he himself had more than second-hand experience of it. And if Paul had to listen to poor quality preaching in church, it means that Paul did not monopolise the preaching when he was establishing and visiting churches in the apostolic world. He himself was a listener as well as a preacher. This does not fit well with our modern model of church, in which we almost worship our modern celebrity preachers, who are expected to preach every Sunday to the exclusion of all others.

It appears that Paul in his own day did not monopolise all the preaching. From what we know of Paul, it is likely that he *did* preach every Sunday in a church (if there was one to attend), but from the evidence of poor quality preaching that he writes about, it does not appear that he was the only preacher every Sunday. Instead, there seems to have been a multiplicity of preachers, some of them of dubious quality, in the apostolic churches.

Thirdly, the reason why Paul did not monopolise the preaching in the church is important. We see from other places in the New Testament that the church meeting was a participatory church gathering in which those prompted by God's Spirit were freely able to contribute. There was no Pastor who did all the preaching, no 'stable' of preachers who took their turns, no secretary booking up speakers, nobody drawing up a list of contributors to the meeting in advance. Nor is there anybody setting out a program of consecutive bible studies or a series of topics to be addressed. All of this is completely foreign to the gatherings of the New Testament church. There was nobody – not even the elders – 'running the show'.

Fourthly, it needs to be acknowledged that such participatory church gatherings can often lead to poor quality preaching. We see the problem in Corinth, where some of the contributors were more interested in showing off their spirituality than trying to encourage and build up the other believers. We see it here in Ephesus where some of the preaching was long-winded, disputatious, legalistic, even heretical. And we see it in our modern day, too – when some preachers who are not very gifted can be tiresome and unedifying. This is the downside of having participatory church gatherings.

Fifthly, however, we need to consider what Paul did about this problem of poor quality preaching. Whilst Paul is scathing in his criticism of the sorts of poor quality preaching in church, he does not seem to have taken matters into his own hands and organised matters so as to eliminate the problem. Even though he is an apostle, he does not exercise his authority to change the participatory model of church gatherings. Nor does he issue Timothy or Titus with any such authority. He does not make some sort of rule (like we would) that meant that only approved or accredited people could preach. Instead, while certain heretical teachers' mouths must be stopped, for the remainder all Paul says is that Timothy and Titus are to set a good example of 'healthy teaching' and publicly warn about the dangers of unedifying contributions. There is not a word – despite all the problems – of Paul legislating some solution to the problem of poor quality preaching.

Paul prefers spiritual solutions to political fixes. He is not prepared to fall back on the 'arm of flesh' instead of relying upon God. Instead, he will let Christ be Lord in the Church. He avoids the quick fix, and instead waits in faith upon God's help, in His time and way, to sort out the problems. He is prepared to tolerate less than perfect preaching and instead allow God to work producing growth and spiritual maturity, rather than restrict the liberty of the Holy Spirit to work through the different gifts of the different believers. He is prepared to let the Holy

Spirit direct affairs in the church rather than allow any man – even an apostle – to lead the church according to his own lights, taking the place of head of the church that rightly belongs only to Christ.

Elders and Teaching in the Pastoral Epistles

There are a number of verses about elders and teaching in the Pastoral Epistles. These verses are important for an understanding of what the role of elders was in relation to teaching in the church.

- 1 Tim. 3:2: 'An overseer then must be blameless, the husband of one wife, self-controlled, sober-minded, respectable, hospitable, *able to teach*'
- 1 Tim. 5:17: 'Let the elders who lead well be counted worthy of double honour, *especially those labouring in the word and teaching*'
- Titus 1:9: '[for an overseer must be one] *holding to the faithful word as he has been taught, that he may be able, both to encourage by sound teaching and convict those who contradict*'

We learn some important lessons from these verses:

1. Elders Taught in the Church

1 Tim. 3:2 says that the overseer must be 'apt to teach' (KJV). The Greek word behind the expression 'apt to teach' here is difficult to translate simply into English. The idea is that the man must be able *and* active in teaching the Scriptures. Perhaps the best all-encompassing translation is that an overseer must be a 'capable teacher'. So, teaching is one of the qualifications or characteristics of an elder. Notice carefully the often-overlooked verse in Titus 1:9 where this is stated forthrightly: the overseer must be 'able, *by sound teaching*, both to encourage and convict those who contradict'.

    1 Tim. 5:17 says, 'Let the elders who lead well be counted worthy of double honour, especially those *labouring in the word and teaching*'. The fact that some elders are noted for 'labouring in the word and teaching' does not mean that the other elders do not teach at all. This would be like arguing that because some elders 'lead well', then the other elders cannot be leading at all. In both of these areas (leading and teaching),

there would be some elders who were not as outstanding as others, yet who nevertheless did both of these jobs.

Some would argue against what is being taught in these verses by saying that while an elder must be able to teach, the requirement is not necessarily that the elder should be able to *publicly* teach. Instead, it is enough that he be able to privately counsel and advise. However, this argument is poor and flawed. Titus 1:9 is referring to the church gatherings when it speaks about an elder being able to 'encourage by sound teaching and convict those who contradict'. The 'public/church' context is undeniable here, for how would an elder be able to 'convict those who contradict' what is being taught in the church if he was 'not a public-speaker'? Further, how would such an elder really be able to function as a 'leader' of the church if he was unable or unfitted to open his mouth in public to deal with false-teaching?

Such a man would appear to be excluded from eldership. A spiritual man who is not a leader (that is, a man who is deeply pious, but also private and shy, who is not able to give a public lead to the people of God) would appear to be unable to fulfil one of the crucial functions of an elder. Of course, he would be better than an unspiritual leader (one who is quite prepared to voice his opinions in public but without the requisite spirituality and knowledge of the truth to be able to give scriptural guidance).

Exceptional circumstances would be required for such a person to be appointed as an elder. Sadly, many churches today have appointed men who are not actively teaching publicly in the church, and therefore (according to 1 Tim. 3:2 and Titus 1:9) unqualified to be elders of the church. The usual reason for such appointments is that the church is in such desperate need for elders that they accept people who are not really qualified. Alternatively, 'political appointments' of like-minded (and often passive) 'yes-men' are made for the smoother government of the church, rather than following the guidelines given in the New Testament.

The result in many churches today is that the elders are neither able nor given opportunity to teach at all. They are allowed to open the doors, straighten the seats, and sometimes even (if given sufficient notice) to publicly pray in the church. But the preaching has been taken over by a professional 'pastor', or visiting speakers, or a ministry team, whose participation excludes anyone else.

2. Men had to be capable teachers *before* being appointed elders

It has often been pointed out that in 1 Timothy 3 and Titus 1 we are not really given a job description of an elder, so much as a character description. That does not mean that we lack information about what the work of an elder/overseer/shepherd/ leader involved, for this can easily be discerned from a consideration of the passages of the NT associated with the work they perform, and indeed, from the names used to describe their position.

However, the important point to notice here is that the character descriptions we find in 1 Timothy 3 and Titus 1 are not a list of functions a man must perform *after* he becomes an elder or overseer. These are instead the pre-requisites for someone who is being considered for the position.

Therefore, it follows that elders are not the only ones who teach in the church – there must be others besides the elders who are showing signs of ability in teaching. Someone who is being considered for appointment to the presbytery must already be a capable teacher in the church, and this would logically infer that this man must already be doing a good deal of it.

Why is this significant? For the simple reason that the Pastoral Epistles obviously envisage a multiplicity of teachers in the church in New Testament times. There was no solitary 'teaching elder' or 'senior pastor' who did all the teaching in the church, nor was teaching restricted to the elders as a body. There were many other men involved in teaching the church. In fact, we see from 1 Corinthians 14 that there was opportunity for any of the men to teach in the church gatherings. To see that the Pastoral Epistles imply as much, we may consider one last point.

3. Elders were not the Only Ones who Taught in the Church

Not only did the teaching ministry in the churches in the New Testament involve and include the elders, but the Pastoral epistles show us that the teaching ministry extended far beyond them. Philip Towner writes, 'There is no indication that participation in ministry was necessarily limited to those named overseers, elders, and deacons, or that the charismatic gifts [i.e. the freedom to use a wide array of spiritual gifts] had been absorbed into the roles designated by those titles ... [Allusions] to Spirit-filled ministry going beyond the official leadership structure are few but nonetheless telling (1 Tim. 4:14, 2 Tim. 2:2)'[89].

Thus, in Titus 1: 9-11, (directly after Paul's instructions for the appointment of overseers), we read about the sort of false-teaching that the elders needed to be able to correct: '[an overseer must] *be able, by sound doctrine, both to exhort and convict those who contradict, for there are many insubordinate, both idle talkers and deceivers, especially those of the circumcision, whose mouths must be stopped, who subvert whole households, teaching things which they ought not, for the sake of dishonest gain*'.

Such false-teachers were hardly men who were considered 'eldership material' or being given trial sermons. They were not 'trainee elders', but rather troublemakers teaching things that were false. The reason that they were allowed opportunity to teach things that were false was because the churches afforded opportunity for people to participate; it was because New Testament churches practised a participatory form of church gathering.

It might be argued that these false-teachers were not preaching in the church but in private, however, this is shown to be false by two facts. Firstly, the fact that the false-teachers were said to 'contradict' would appear to indicate that their arguments were made publicly, and secondly, the fact that the overseers were told to see to it that the false-teachers 'mouths must be stopped' would appear to most naturally refer to the church gatherings, for how could an overseer muzzle a false-teacher in a private home or in the market-place?

Elders (and also deacons, 1 Tim. 3:9) thus had to be men who knew the truth and stood up for it in the church because there was free

---

[89] Philip H. Towner, *The Letters to Timothy and Titus*, NICNT, Grand Rapids, MI: Eerdmans, 2006, p244

opportunity for others to speak in the church, sometimes teaching things contrary to sound doctrine.

The Timothy Training Program

2 Timothy 2:2 reads as follows: *'And the things which you heard from me among many witnesses, the same commit to faithful men, who will be able (competent) to also teach others'*.

This verse mandates for ministry training, primarily in the local church and possibly beyond. Training for ministry was an important part of our Lord's three years spent with his disciples and it also characterised the way Paul nurtured other younger men like Timothy and Titus. Here Timothy was told to invest in the lives of others so that they would, in turn, transmit the truth of God to the generation to follow them. We live in an age that requires training for everyone from street-sweepers to surgeons, so we should not find this biblical injunction hard to accept.

Why is there a need for such training? Timothy was told to commit the truth to 'faithful men' to counteract the influence of false-teachers and because of other people who contribute in church in unprofitable ways. 'Idle talkers' who rise to speak but only weary God's people come in a number of different varieties. There are some who are gifted as well as spiritual, but not very well taught. Timothy was told to teach these the great doctrines of the faith, so that the breadth and depth of their ministry might increase. Others are very spiritual but not very gifted; they are passionate but have little of real substance to say. These not only need knowledge, but also training so they may study Scripture more profitably and preach in more orderly and helpful ways. There are also some who are neither gifted, spiritual nor knowledgeable. G. Campbell Morgan said that good preaching involves three elements: truth, clarity and passion. These people fail on all three counts. They put on a deep, pious voice, and drone on with empty words. Others rise to speak because they want to be heard; they have a desire for power and position. Not all benefit from training; it is hard to teach old dogs new tricks.

There is a need to 'invest in the best', for 'talent identification', particularly when people are young. A church cannot thrive on mediocrity. Those who show spiritual keenness, who are teachable and humble, who are sincere and faithful, irrespective of their knowledge or giftedness, these are the ones to be sought out, encouraged and helped. This verse shows that there is a need to develop discipleship and train for service in more personal and small group settings outside the church gatherings.

This verse is the nearest Paul comes to authorising a certain class of people to perform the teaching in the church; except, of course, that Paul does not actually go as far as that. Notice the crucial omission. This verse does not state that the faithful men that Timothy trains are the *only* people who may teach in the church. Nor is there any mention of guarding the teaching office against untrained or unsuitable people outside the group that Timothy trains.

In fact, this verse implies the very reverse. Timothy was to train 'faithful men who will be competent to teach' because of the need for better quality teaching in the church and to counter-balance the sometimes poor-quality contributions of 'empty-talkers', as well as to combat the false ideas of those promoting doctrines contrary to the truth. Training was necessary because of the abuses that a participatory form of church gathering opens up.

As we have noticed elsewhere in the Pastoral Epistles, nowhere does Paul license Timothy to 'hire or fire' preachers or teachers, nor does he tell Timothy to coordinate or organize the teaching program in the church. Nor is there any idea of Timothy being the sole preacher, the Senior Pastor or the bishop.

Yes, Paul repeatedly stresses the need for teaching to be profitable and health-promoting. He repeatedly points out the sorts of teaching which are spiritually helpful and harmful to the life of the Christian and the Church. But Paul does not specify that organising the teaching personnel or program is part of the prerogative of either Timothy or the elders. The only restrictions Paul places upon teaching are to silence heretics and women (1 Tim. 2:9-15), for different reasons.

Thus, Paul's three-pronged strategy in the Pastoral epistles is (a) negatively – to repeatedly speak out against the unhelpful types of teaching that may be given in the church gathering, (b) positively – to send Timothy and Titus to teach in these churches and thus set a good example of sound, helpful teaching, and (c) to encourage Timothy to invest his time in training the more promising spiritual men in the sorts of teaching that builds the church and the doctrines that need to be defended. It would have been far easier to simply appoint certain trusted people to teaching positions (as most churches today do), but Paul does not take this soft option. He believes in the open, participatory, sharing sort of church gathering that we notice in 1 Corinthians 14 and elsewhere.

To summarize, then, this verse mandates training, and nothing more. No clerical office is created by this verse. Nor does this verse legislate for some qualification or licence or standard (academic or otherwise) to be met before a man may teach in the church. The reason is simple: Paul had no right to restrict the exercise of the gifts of God's Spirit. Paul knew that all Christians are priests and prophets, indwelt by God's Spirit and able to speak for and from God. Of course, Paul knew that not everything stated by someone in church comes from God – that is why discernment and judgment of what had been taught was required. But equally, Paul was not prepared to quench the Spirit by resorting to the human expedient of assuming he could do better than the Holy Spirit. He nowhere licenses Timothy to appoint those who should speak or to dictate what they should say.

CHAPTER 5

IF ANY MAN SPEAKS - 1 PETER 4:10-11 AND JAMES 3:1

As each one has received a gift, minister it to yourselves, as good stewards of the manifold grace of God. If any man speaks, let him speak as the oracles of God, if anyone serves, as from the strength which God supplies, that in all things God may be glorified through Jesus Christ, to whom be the glory and the might for ever and ever, amen. (1 Peter 4:10-11)

Peter here writes about Christians using their spiritual gifts. In his comments about Christians using speaking gifts, we see again a number of parallels with the passages in 1 Corinthians 14:26-40 and 1 Thessalonians 5:19-21:

1. Each one has received a spiritual gift
2. Any man is able to speak ('if any man speaks', not, 'if the Bishop/Pastor/Teacher speaks'),
3. Such speaking gifts are prophetic ('as the oracles of God'); a man should speak because he has a message from God.

Edwin Blum summarizes: 'Every Christian has a gift (Rom 12:6-8; 1 Cor. 12:12-31) that he has received from God ... Since every Christian has a gift, his being equipped with it apparently takes place with the indwelling of the Holy Spirit at regeneration ... One of the longstanding misconceptions in church practice is the idea that only one person is to "minister" in the local church. The biblical principle is that all can and should minister in one way or another ... Peter puts these manifestations of grace in two broad categories: "speaking" and "serving" (v.11). Speaking (*lalein*) covers all forms of oral service – teaching, preaching, prophecy, perhaps even tongues. "The very words of God" translates *logia* or "oracles", which are utterances from God's mouth. So what one says is to be as God says it'[90].

William Kelly remarks upon this passage that it 'suppose[s] an open door for ministry among Christians in the Christian assembly'[91].

We thus learn that the participatory style of church gatherings we read about in 1 Corinthians were not some odd, unique or abnormal practice confined to Corinth. Nor were they only found in churches planted in the sphere of Paul's missionary activities. Here we find participatory church gatherings in Peter's writings.

Stephen Short writes, '1 Peter 4:10 has significance for our study, for it reads: 'As every man has received a gift, even so minister the same to one another'. This verse [1 Peter. 4:10] is one of several which emphasizes that there was a pronounced element of mutuality in the preaching within the New Testament churches; in other words, that there was no 'one way traffic' here (as with a 'pastor' addressing his congregation), but a 'two way traffic'. What the Bible shows is that in the churches of the Apostolic period, the Christians admonished one another, taught one another, edified one another, exhorted one another, and ministered to one another… And how beneficial it proves itself for preachers not to be on the 'giving end' always, but from time to time to be on the 'receiving end' – receiving from the very people to whom one is normally giving. 'Iron sharpeneth iron; so a man sharpeneth the countenance of his friend''[92].

---

[90] Edwin Blum, "1 and 2 Peter", *The Expositors Bible Commentary*, Vol. 12, Grand Rapids, MI: Zondervan, 1982, p256-7

[91] William Kelly, *Lectures Introductory to the Bible*, Vol. 6, 1 Peter 4

[92] Stephen S. Short, "The Ministry of the Word", *The Witness*, February 1965, p45-6

As Each one has Received a Gift ... (verse 10)

These two verses occur at the end of two paragraphs that contrast the Christian's former relationship among the ungodly with life in the new Christian community. In the first paragraph (verses 1-6), before conversion the Christian once lived in idolatry, drunkenness, lusts and loose-living (verse 3), but now he should 'no longer live the rest of his time in the flesh for the lusts of men, but for the will of God' (verse 2). In fact, his former non-Christian associates think it strange that the Christian does not run with them in the same excess of debauchery, speaking evil of him (verse 4).

In the second paragraph (verses 7-11), having left the world behind, the Christian enjoys fellowship in a new spiritual family, the Christian community. In these verses we have repeated reference to 'one another' and 'yourselves':

- 'have fervent love for one another' (verse 8)
- 'be hospitable to one another' (verse 9)
- 'as each one has received a gift, minister it to yourselves' (verse 10)

It is in this context that we find Peter's teaching on the subject of spiritual gifts. Peter confirms virtually every main idea that we find in Paul's writings on the same subject in Romans 12, 1 Corinthians 12-14 and Ephesians 4:

- Peter uses the same language as Paul to describe the phenomena (*charisma*, gift, cf. 1 Cor. 12:4, etc.),
- Peter reinforces the fact that God is the one who gave the spiritual abilities (cf. Romans 12:3),
- Peter confirms Paul's teaching that each and every Christian has received a spiritual gift (1 Corinthians 12:7, Ephesians 4:7),
- Peter also repeats the truth that these gifts are all different ('the manifold grace of God', 1 Peter 4:10, cf. Rom. 12:4, 1 Cor. 12:7-11).
- Finally, the harmony of Peter's and Paul's teaching on the subject of spiritual gifts extends even to their use in the church gatherings, as

Peter here endorses the idea of spiritual gifts being used in church gatherings.

Minister it to Yourselves (verse 10)

Peter's exhortation for the Christians to minister their gifts 'to one another' (literally, 'to yourselves') follows on from the main thought of the paragraph: the mutual love and care the Christians should show to one another. Thus, in verse 8, they are told to have fervent love for one another, and in verse 9, they are to show hospitality to one another. Here in verse 10, their gifts are to be used by each one (for each one has a gift) and for the benefit of each other.

The type of Christian community that Peter encourages is one in which spiritual gifts are exercised in the same way that love and hospitality are to be shown. It should not be just a few folk who are expected to have fervent love for other Christians, but all of the believers, nor just one or two families that are to show hospitality, but all. Peter's mind perhaps goes back to the early church in Acts 2:44-46, where we read that the believers 'were together, and had all things in common', selling their possessions to meet the needs of those who were poor among them, 'breaking bread from house to house, they ate their food with gladness and simplicity of heart'. This picture of the ideal church, where every member no longer thinks of themselves but genuinely cares for others, is what Peter is urging upon his readers.

It is in this same spirit of every member actively showing mutual love that Peter urges the Christians to use their gifts. It is not just the most prominent, gifted, educated or able Christians who are to use their gifts, but all of the Christians. It is not that some are 'givers', while others receive. Instead, all of the Christians are to use their gifts for the benefit of everyone else. Peter encourages mutual edification through the use of spiritual gifts. As we are about to see, this applies even to the speaking gifts in church.

If Anyone Speaks (verse 11)

J. Ramsay Michaels writes that '"Speaking" ... refers not to ordinary conversation (which would not have to be "a word from God") but to authoritative speech in worship assemblies'. He argues that while some commentators limit the speaking to "routine functions like teaching and preaching" (in distinction from "ecstatic utterances"), 'there is no proof of this in the text. The term could embrace all that Paul includes under "prophecy" (Rom. 12:6), "teaching" (Rom. 12:7), and "exhortation" (Rom. 12:8), as well as "wisdom" and "knowledge" (1 Cor. 12:8)'. He concludes by saying that, 'It is clear ... that his focus is not on missionary proclamation ... but on the speech of Christian believers "to each other" (v10) in a setting of worship'[93].

Several commentators, however, take a different view. Calvin in his commentary upon this verse writes, 'He who speaks, then, that is, who is rightly appointed by public authority, let him speak as the oracles of God'. However, Peter says nothing in this verse of someone being 'rightly appointed by public authority' before he is allowed to speak in church. Instead, Peter simply says, 'if *any* man speaks, let him speak as the oracles of God', and there is nothing in the immediate context which further specifies who 'any man' refers to.

Matthew Henry comments on this verse, 'If any man, whether a minister in public or a Christian in private conference, speak or teach, he must do it as the oracles of God, which direct us as to the matter of our speech. What Christians in private, or ministers in public, teach and speak must be the pure word and oracles of God'. However, again, Peter makes no reference to 'ministers' (or laypersons) in this verse. There is no distinction between ministers who (alone) may speak in church and laypersons who are permitted to speak outside of church.

Edmund Clowney writes, 'Peter may already have the elders and deacons of the church particularly in view. His reference to speaking the very words of God surely has special reference to the 'shepherds of God's flock' (5:2)'[94]. Clowney later suggests that 'serving' (verse 10) may be a reference to the ministry of deacons in the church, 'here set beside the

---

[93] J. Ramsay Michaels, *1 Peter*, WBC, Waco, TX: Word, 1988, p250
[94] Edmund Clowney, *The Message of 1 Peter*, BST, Leicester: IVP, 1988, p183

teaching ministry'[95]. Clowney argues that Peter is hinting at two orders of ministry in these verses: the elders speaking and the deacons serving.

Who is Peter referring to when he says, 'if anyone speaks'? Are these 'ministers rightly appointed'? The elders? Is this the Pastor? Or is Peter speaking about the prophets within the church? Is he perhaps referring to those who have a special gift?

If we may borrow the words of Paul Barnett already quoted earlier in relation to 1 Corinthians 14:26, we are struck by the absence of any reference to a presbyter or pastor. The idea that Peter has in mind 'ministers rightly appointed', a pastor, or elders goes beyond what the verse states. Peter instead says the exact opposite: 'if *anyone* speaks'. This is hardly the term we would expect Peter to use if he was trying to restrict the speaking ministry to a select few.

Peter has just assured the Christians in the previous verse that 'each one has received a gift', and it seems that he envisages that anyone could use such a gift in church. If 'each one' has received a gift, then we would assume that the word 'anyone' that immediately follows is also without restriction.

One of the problems we face when reading the Bible is that we sometimes unwittingly read it through the lens of our own cherished church tradition. The suggestions of Calvin, Henry and Clowney represent different attempts to read back into the apostolic time-period the ecclesiastical situations of contemporary times. However, if we place Peter's language in its proper context – the context of 1st Century Christianity – and if we set his words alongside other NT documents like 1 Corinthians, 1 Thessalonians and the Pastoral Epistles, we see that when Peter writes that 'anyone' may speak, he is encouraging the freedom and right enjoyed by all first-century Christians to publicly speak in church gatherings.

Peter does lay down one restriction: that those speaking need to speak 'as the oracles of God'. It is thus not a case of *who* may speak so much as the sort of things that are said that concerns Peter here. He does not attempt to pre-judge someone's contribution before they have

---

[95] Ibid., p185

opened their mouth. Forbidding people to speak unless they met some qualification seems quite foreign to Peter's way of thinking. After all, who would have thought that a fisherman like Peter would have become the chief spokesman for Christ?

Some might argue that the context here does not exactly specify that the church gatherings are in view. However, the primary arena in which spoken gifts are to be used for the benefit of 'one another' is in the church gatherings. When we add to this the further fact that Peter envisages people speaking 'the oracles of God', it would seem unlikely that Peter is thinking in terms of domestic small-talk or commercial transactions in this verse. The context of mutual love and spiritual encouragement among members of the Christian community in this paragraph points to the fellowship of believers, and the primary setting in which the speaking gifts of verses 10-11 are used for mutual edification would be in the church gatherings.

Let Him Speak as the Oracles of God

Whereas the opening words of this verse ('if any man speaks') teach the freedom that each brother had to participate in the early church's gatherings, the words 'let him speak as the oracles of God' balance them by warning that with such freedom comes great responsibility. Tom Carson writes, 'And so ministering the word of God is a very solemn thing; it is not a thing to be taken lightly, and the person who stands up to minister the Word of God should be a man who has spent much time in private, studying the Word. There must be prayerful, careful study of the Word, so that when he stands up he will indeed be able to speak as the oracles of God'[96].

The word 'oracles' carries with it a sense of immediacy: God's words confront and address the hearers; there is a sense of direct communication from God[97]. J. Ramsay Michaels writes, 'In effect, Peter

---

[96] Tom Carson, *Studies in Peter's First Epistle*, Sydney: Christian Outreach Book Service, 1983, p88

[97] The word 'oracles' (Gk. *logia*) is a diminutive form of the usual word 'word' (Gk. *logos*) and originally meant a short word or saying, used mostly in Greek

is broadening traditional understandings of prophecy so as to include all the teaching and exhortation that goes on in connection with Christian worship. "Whoever speaks" (and therefore not just Christian prophets in a technical sense) should speak as if delivering the very oracles of God"[98].

'Speaking as the oracles of God' would still appear to apply today for, as one Christian organization involved in training preachers puts it, 'when the Bible is taught, God himself speaks and His voice is heard clearly today'[99]. Thus, this verse includes within its scope the preacher who waits upon God, studying His word, and then expounds and declares the message of God to His people.

In the context of 1 Peter 4:11, 'the oracles of God' refers to any message given by a man who speaks on behalf of God. However, the word 'oracles' itself does not necessarily require that the utterance is the spontaneous result of an immediate revelation. From its broader usage elsewhere the term includes within it what God has said beforehand, and also what God has written in the Scriptures (see Psalm 12:6, 18:30, Rom. 3:2, Heb. 5:12). The emphasis here lies upon the proclamation of God's mind to others, not so much the way in which the message was received.

William MacDonald writes, 'Even if a man is gifted to preach or teach, he must be sure that the words he speaks are the very words God would have him say on that particular occasion. This is what is meant by the oracles of God. It is not enough for a man simply to preach from the

---

culture for sayings that were claimed to originate from a deity. However, in the OT, its LXX usage includes God's spoken words and promises as well as God's written words in Scripture. It is found elsewhere in the NT in Acts 7:38, Romans 3:2 and Hebrews 5:12 to refer to God's spoken laws for the Israelites given to Moses, and to Scripture generally. BAGD (the standard Greek lexicon) defines the reference here as 'the utterances of those Christians gifted with the charisma of the word'. W. E. Vine, in his *Expository Dictionary*, defines 'oracles' here as 'the utterances of God through Christian teachers'.

[98] Michaels, *1 Peter*, 250
[99] Proclamation Trust, see www.proctrust.org.uk/about

Bible. He should also have the assurance that he is presenting the particular message intended by God for that audience at that time'[100].

'Speaking as the oracles of God' involves four things. A man must speak in a *manner* that is worthy of a spokesman for God. He must declare, without apology, equivocation, or levity, but instead with appropriate urgency, the message of God. Secondly, the speaker's subject *matter* must be faithful to what God's Word actually says. He must declare 'this is the Word of the Lord'. If the preacher has the right subject matter but is not authoritative in his presentation, this is not as great a fault as authoritatively presenting something which is not based on God's Word at all. Thirdly, he must preach the *message* from God that meets the need of the moment in the lives of the hearers. It is not enough to 'deliver a sermon' (however interesting or informative) or to present an exposition (however doctrinally orthodox) that is irrelevant to the lives of those listening. It is true that all scripture is profitable, but the 'oracles of God' implies that it must be the needed message for the moment. Therefore, this verse is not simply talking about orthodox matter and godly manner, but also the right message. But all this requires something more in the preaching: the supernatural *movement* of the Spirit. Earlier generations called this the 'unction' of the Spirit – His guidance and illumination in preparation, His power and clarity in presentation, and His conviction of the hearers in response. This spiritual power (1 Cor. 2:1-4, 1 Thess. 1:5) is the vital ingredient in preaching, and the preacher needs to wait upon God for it in earnest prayer.

All true preaching presents the message of God based upon the Word of God in the power of the Spirit which meets the needs of the moment. It involves a prophetic element, in which God's voice is heard. Thus, the chief aim of the preacher must be to spend time alone in the presence of God with his Bible, waiting upon the Lord for what the Lord would have him to preach upon, waiting for the Lord to give insight into His Word. This assumes, too, that it is also necessary for the preacher to look within and see 'if there is any wicked way in me' (Psalm 139:24), to confess sin and seek to be a 'vessel for honour, sanctified and

---

[100] William MacDonald, *Believers Bible Commentary*, p2278

useful for the Master' (2 Timothy 2:21). Then, finally, there is a need to look to the Lord for the right words to put the message into (Ecclesiastes 12:10).

How often is it true today that a person comes away from Bible teaching and is able to say that the Lord spoke to them from the preaching of His Word? Sadly, this is becoming a less frequent occurrence, and more commonly people today are forced to sit and listen to dry, academic expositions of passages of Scripture devoid of the Spirit of God's presence, or even worse, preaching which is really nothing more than religious entertainment for the amusement of the listeners.

If anyone serves (verse 11)

Peter divides the gifts into two broad groups: speaking gifts and serving gifts. Some people are better at doing things for God than saying things for Him. Peter says that such people should serve with the ability (or strength) which God supplies.

This raises a question: does not Peter's 'division of labour' suggest that not everybody is fitted for teaching in church? Should not such people stick to what they are good at, while letting those more gifted in the teaching department get on with it? Should we not also restrict people to what they are gifted at doing?

It is true that not everybody has the gift of teaching, and such people themselves usually (and thankfully) steer clear of trying to exercise a gift they do not possess, but there seems no reason why the lack of this one speaking gift should prevent them from ever opening their mouth in church. It is a fact that 'practical' people, used to serving God in down-to-earth ways, are precisely the sorts of people who can give the occasional 'word of wisdom' (1 Corinthians 12: 8).

Notice that Peter does not say anything about 'teaching' here, but 'speaking'. Admittedly, because teaching is the virtually the only gift which is exercised in the modern evangelical church culture, this is what we instinctively think of when we read the word 'speak', but this is not what Peter actually wrote. There are, in fact, other speaking gifts that edify the church in the New Testament, like exhortation. There was also opportunity in the NT for people to interact with a speaker after someone had taught, so that what had been taught was evaluated and sometimes corrected (1 Cor. 14:29, 1 Thess. 5:21) and it was possible to ask questions (1 Cor. 14:35). Such opportunities in church gatherings for interaction doubtless had the effect of gently encouraging some people to speak up more frequently in public.

There is, no doubt, much wisdom in the suggestion that people should concentrate on what they are gifted in. However, Peter does not try to discourage, restrict or forbid people from using certain gifts. (Neither does Paul, who encourages the Corinthians to 'earnestly desire the best gifts', 1 Cor. 12:31, by which he means prophesying). Peter does not use the two broad divisions of gift as a reason for disqualifying people from speaking (if their gift is serving), any more than we today would think of prohibiting people from serving if their gift is speaking. Christian life and testimony involves both 'life and lip'. Just as the preacher who never practices what he teaches is a hypocrite, so there is something out of place about a Christian whose relationship with God never amounts to opening his mouth to praise or pray to God publicly or speak for God to others.

The issue of spiritual gifts is a difficult one for some people. No one is told at conversion which spiritual gift they possess, nor are spiritual gifts appointed or accredited by men. Instead, spiritual gifts may be developed and may atrophy (1 Tim. 4:14, 2 Tim. 1:6), new spiritual gifts may be desired (1 Cor. 12: 31) and may possibly even be given at some point after conversion (1 Tim. 4:14). The New Testament teaches that we should graciously and patiently encourage people to use spiritual gifts in ways which are most profitable for the building up of the church, rather than trying to forbid people to use gifts for which we think they are unsuited. Christ did not come to quench smoking flax or break bruised reeds, and there is little of the mind or heart of Christ in the attitude to the use of spiritual gifts that such an objection expresses. Neither is there any of the pastoral wisdom of Paul's prescription for the growth of individual Christians and the collective edification of the church in the suggestion that we should be continually silencing people who aspire to use their gifts but do not come up to our standards of eloquence or spiritual insight.

Under the New Covenant, all of God's people are endued with a prophetic gift in some measure (Acts 2:17-18). All of God's people also know Him (Hebrews 8:11), and are presumably able to express something of this knowledge to others.

Summary

1 Peter 4:10-11 presents a very similar picture to what Paul writes about in 1 Corinthians chapters 12 to 14. Notice the parallels:

1. Each Christian has received a gift (verse 10, compare with 1 Cor. 12:4-11),
2. These gifts are different, hence the 'manifold grace of God' (verse 10) and the two main areas of gifting outlined in verse 11, speaking and serving (compare with 1 Cor. 12:8-11 and also Romans 12:6-7a)
3. Each Christian has a responsibility to use this gift for the benefit of others (verse 10, cf. 1 Cor. 12:7, 12-31)
4. The speaking gifts are prophetic, that is, the oracles of God are communicated thereby (verse 11, cf. 1 Cor. 14:1-25)
5. Any man is able to speak (verse 11, cf. 1 Cor. 14:26ff.)

Thus, we can see here again evidence of the participatory nature of church gatherings in the early church, just as in 1 Corinthians 12-14.

We may conclude with William Kelly's words on this passage. Having argued that this passage 'suppose[s] an open door for ministry among Christians in the Christian assembly', Kelly continues by cautioning, 'No Christian should think or talk about a right of ministry; for although liberty of ministry may be legitimate enough in itself, still I think it is a phrase apt to be misunderstood. It might easily be interpreted as if it meant a right for any one to speak. This I deny altogether. God has a right to use whom He pleases, according to His own sovereign will and wisdom; but the truth is, that if you have received a gift, you are not only at liberty but rather bound to use it in Christ's name. It is not a question of merely having license ...

Kelly continues: 'According to this none ought ever to speak unless he has a thorough conviction that he is giving out God's mind and message, as suited for that time and those souls. Were this felt adequately, would it not hinder a great many from speaking? Nor is there any reason to fear that silence in such a case would inflict a real loss on the church of God... The great matter is, that what is spoken should be from God. Persons ought not to speak unless they have a certainty that what they wish to say is not only true (this is not what is said) but the actual will of God for the occasion. The speaker should be God's mouthpiece for making His mind known there and then. This is to speak "as oracles of God." It is not merely speaking according to His oracles, which is the usual way in which men interpret the passage, and thence derive their license for speaking as they judge fitting without thinking of God's will. They think they have an understanding of scripture, and that they may therefore speak to profit; but it is a totally different thing if one desire only to speak as God's mouthpiece, though it is granted that one may here as elsewhere mistake and fail'[101].

James 3:1

My brethren, let not many of you become teachers, knowing that we shall receive a stricter judgment.

James here cautions against the desire to teach God's people. He was not, of course, forbidding people to teach God's Word, for then there would be no feeding of the flock at all. Instead, he warns that those who teach will be held accountable by God for practicing what they preach. Accordingly, James advises against people being over-eager to teach and urges us to consider the seriousness of the responsibility.

Nevertheless, even James' caution is evidence of the fact that it was theoretically possible for anyone to teach God's people in New Testament times. There is no mention here of any special qualification required for teaching, or ordination to the office. Teaching in the New Testament was not a position occupied only after several years of study at Bible college. Nor do we anywhere find that someone could only teach at the invitation of the elders (James 5:14). On the contrary, in the New

---

[101] William Kelly, *Lectures Introductory to the Bible*, Vol. 6, 1 Peter 4

Testament there was opportunity for 'any man' to 'speak' (1 Peter 4:11). James does not even warn against people attempting to teach who lack knowledge or gifting. His warning, in line with the rest of his epistle, is moral in tone: James warns against people not practicing Christianity.

James uses two expressions here that suggest he is including all of God's people in this warning, not just a select group of teachers. Firstly, he uses the expression 'my brethren' which is elsewhere found seven times in the letter to refer to all his readers (1:2, 2:1, 14, 3:10, 12, 5:10, 12). Secondly, he uses the word 'we' which again is always used in the letter to refer to all believers (1:18, 5:1, etc.).

The setting seems to be the church, for otherwise the warning against the danger of hypocrisy would have far less force or application: it is in the public place that we are most liable to the danger of preaching without practising. The word 'teachers' also suggests that the passage is primarily referring to what happens in the church.

Stephen Short writes, 'That Christians generally had liberty to teach in the churches in question seems to be implied by James' counsel in Jas. 3:1, RV: 'My brethren, be not many teachers, knowing that we shall receive the greater condemnation'. What caused James to write that may well have been his having heard that several people were trying to teach in church who had not been divinely gifted for the task; so James advised them to desist; but his doing so does at least infer that Christians generally were *free* to teach in the churches'[102].

Tom Carson comments, 'In NT churches teaching was not confined to a single channel (cf. Acts 13:1, 1 Cor. 14, 1 Pet. 4:10-11). James links himself with those he warns (cf. 1 Jn 2:1). The greater the light the greater the responsibility'[103].

---

[102] Stephen Short, "The Ministry of the Word", *The Witness*, Feb 1965, p45
[103] Tom Carson, "James", *Zondervan Bible Commentary*, ed. F. F. Bruce, Grand Rapids, MI: Zondervan, 2008, p1579 (formerly *New International Bible Commentary*, London: Pickering and Inglis, 1979)

CHAPTER 6

EPHESIANS 4:7-16 – MUTUAL EDIFICATION

> *⁷ But to each one of us grace was given according to the measure of Christ's gift. ⁸ Therefore He says: "When He ascended on high, He led captivity captive, And gave gifts to men." ⁹ (Now this, "He ascended"—what does it mean but that He also first descended into the lower parts of the earth? ¹⁰ He who descended is also the One who ascended far above all the heavens, that He might fill all things.) ¹¹ And He Himself gave some to be apostles, some prophets, some evangelists, and some pastors and teachers, ¹² for the equipping of the saints for the work of ministry, for the edifying of the body of Christ, ¹³ till we all come to the unity of the faith and of the knowledge of the Son of God, to a perfect man, to the measure of the stature of the fullness of Christ; ¹⁴ that we should no longer be children, tossed to and fro and carried about with every wind of doctrine, by the trickery of men, in the cunning craftiness of deceitful plotting, ¹⁵ but, speaking the truth in love, may grow up in all things into Him who is the head—Christ— ¹⁶ from whom the whole body, joined and knit together by what every joint supplies, according to the effective working by which every part does its share, causes growth of the body for the edifying of itself in love.*

John Piper, commenting on Ephesians 4:16, says: 'So even though growth and upbuilding are from Christ, the head, it is the whole body that builds the body. And the word 'whole' is important. The whole body builds the body. That point is emphasized in the words, 'according to the working of each individual part'. The whole body – that is, each individual part in the body properly functioning – causes the growth of the body. Now I ask you, where and how does that happen in your corporate church life? Can we ever create enough programs that every person would be involved using some particular gift? That's probably not even the right question to ask. Isn't it more likely that Paul envisions a kind of regular gathering of the body in groups small enough so that every member of the body can minister to others with his own unique spiritual gift? ... So what verse 16 means when it says that "the whole body causes the growth of the body" when "each individual part is working properly", it means that all the members have gifts, and all of those gifts are to be used in building up the body "in love". And this is how Christ, the all-supplying, supernatural Head of the body, builds and cares for his Church'[104].

Piper asks, 'where and how does [Eph. 4:16] happen in your corporate church life?' In New Testament times, the answer would have been, 'every Sunday in our church gatherings, of course!' Most Christians today would respond with confused silence.

Gary Inrig writes about Eph. 4:16, 'This is a verse which ought to be clearly underlined in the Bible, and in the thinking, of every Christian. There is certainly no concept of "one-man" ministry or a clergy-laity distinction in such a view of congregational life. Every single Christian is "in the ministry" and it is a ministry dependent on the "proper working of each individual part." In other terms, it is a ministry of spiritual gifts, as each believer functions according to the will of God for him or her as an individual. To allow one man to be known as "the minister" of a church is a serious error, not only of terminology but of understanding of the nature of local church life. To permit only one individual to teach or preach the Word while other gifted believers are not encouraged to discover, develop and exercise their gifts is, in fact, to quench the Spirit (1 Thess. 5:19)'[105].

---

[104] http://www.desiringgod.org/resource-library/sermons/how-christ-enables-the-church-to-upbuild-itself-in-love

[105] Gary Inrig, *Life in His Body*, Wheaton, IL: Harold Shaw Publishers, 1975, p45-46

In an earlier chapter, we observed evidence of participatory church gatherings in the Pastoral Epistles, 1 and 2 Timothy and Titus. Timothy had been sent by Paul to the city of Ephesus on a mission that largely focused on improving the teaching in the church there. It is not surprising, then, that we find further evidence of participatory church gatherings in Paul's letter to the Ephesians. This chapter therefore confirms and strengthens the evidence we have already seen from 1 and 2 Timothy.

Here in Ephesians 4:7-16 we have another key passage in the New Testament teaching that church life is meant to be participatory: each member of the body is gifted and intended to be involved in edifying the other members of the body. As we shall see, this includes participation in the church gatherings.

The Four Main Ideas of this Passage

To introduce this passage, let us notice four of its main themes:

1. Spiritual Gifts

Ephesians 4 is one of the key passages in the NT on the subject of spiritual gifts. Paul teaches that each believer has a spiritual gift ('to each one of us grace was given', verse 7), and that these gifts are different: he enumerates a few of them – apostles, prophets, evangelists, pastors and teachers (verse 11).

2. Church Unity

Paul's letter to the Ephesians majors on the subject of the church and its unity. This is seen in the opening verses of chapter 4, where Paul writes that we should be 'endeavouring to keep the unity of the Spirit in the bond of peace' (verse 3), and then lists six grounds for Christian unity: 'there is one body and one Spirit, just as you are called in one hope of your calling; one Lord, one faith, one baptism, one God and Father of all, who is above all, and through all, and in you all' (verses 4-6).

Paul continues to point out the importance of church unity as he discusses spiritual gifts in verses 7-16. Indeed, he says that the very purpose of spiritual gifts is that we may '*all come to the unity of the faith,* and of the knowledge of the Son of God, to a perfect man' (verse 13). In verse 16, Paul says that the effect of the use of spiritual gifts is that we may be *'joined and knit together by what every joint supplies*, according to the effective working by which every part does its share' (verse 16).

The participatory use of spiritual gifts promotes church unity in two important ways, doctrinally and practically. Firstly, as different spiritual gifts are exercised by different believers, the believers are built up in the faith as they hear from different perspectives, and thus become more doctrinally rounded, balanced, and spiritually mature (verse 13). Secondly, by each believer using his or her gifts in the life of the church, we become more involved practically in the work of the church, and so drawn closer together to one another (verse 16).

3. Spiritual Growth

Another point of Paul's in this passage is that spiritual gifts result in spiritual growth. Paul focuses particularly in verses 12-15 on the aim and goal of Christian development and growth. He thus speaks about:

- 'the perfecting of the saints' (verse 12)
- 'till we all come to ... a perfect (i.e. complete, mature) man' (verse 13)
- 'that we should no longer be children' (verse 14)
- 'but ... may grow up in all things into Him' (verse 15)
- 'caus[ing] growth of the body' (verse 16)

4. Participatory Edification

A fourth prominent idea in the passage is the participatory nature of the edification envisaged. Paul encourages the mutual use of gifts by all for the benefit of all:

- 'to *each one* of us grace was given' (verse 7)
- 'till we *all* come' (verse 13)
- 'the *whole* body' (verse 16)
- 'what *every* joint supplies' (verse 16)
- '*every* part does its share' (verse 16)
- 'for the edifying *of itself* in love' (verse 16)

Here we have a picture of church life that is participatory: 'the whole body' is equipped by Christ, so that every member of the body 'supplies', 'works', and 'every part does its share', with the result that the body edifies 'itself'. The aim of the gifts is not only that all of the believers grow to spiritual maturity, but additionally, that development occurs through all the individuals using their gifts, the whole church playing a part and contributing to the well-being of all of the members.

Alternative Interpretations of this Passage

There are two main alternative interpretations of this passage that we need to consider before proceeding any further. The first of these is the traditional Protestant (and Roman Catholic) interpretation that held sway up until nearly one hundred years ago, and the second is the now-standard evangelical view that sprung up in response to the obvious faults in the traditional interpretation. We shall argue here that both views have flaws and that a third alternative interpretation is required.

1. The Clergy Model

The traditional Protestant view of this passage is that Ephesians 4 is talking about the work of the clergy. Thus, Calvin in his commentary writes about the passage, 'The meaning may be thus summed up. "The external ministry of the word is also commended, on account of the advantages which it yields. Certain men appointed to that office are employed in preaching the gospel. This is the arrangement by which the Lord is pleased to govern his church, to maintain its existence, and ultimately to secure its highest perfection."'

Similarly, Charles Hodge summarizes verses 12-16 as follows: 'The gifts which Christ bestows on his church are the various classes of ministers, apostles, prophets, evangelists, and pastors who are teachers. v. 11. The design of the ministry is the edification of the church, and to bring all its members to unity of faith and knowledge, and to the full stature of Christ; that they should no longer have the instability of children, but be a firm, compact, and growing body in living union with Christ its head'[106].

By the word 'ministry', these commentators mean an ordained clergy. T. K. Abbott says about the word 'ministry' (or 'service') in verse 12 that it 'can only mean official service, and this does not belong to the saints in general'[107].

Arguments for this clerical interpretation of the passage include the following:

1. Paul lists five gifts in verse 11, starting with the foremost gift, the apostles, then other important gifts, prophets and evangelists, and finishes with pastors and teachers. These are all official, public leaders using their preaching gifts, not minor or mundane ministries. These are the ministries in view in verses 12-16 when Paul writes about the work of the ministry and the edification of the church.
2. The public preaching gifts of verse 11 are precisely the sorts of gifts that bring about the Christian maturity we read about in verses 13 and 15. In 1 Corinthians 14, for example, Paul urges the importance of prophecy for the edification of the church. Thus, Paul is writing about the teaching office here.
3. One of Paul's main concerns in this passage (in verse 14) was that the believers would not be carried off by wrong doctrine: 'that we should no longer be children, tossed to and fro and carried about with every wind of doctrine, by the trickery of men, in the cunning craftiness of deceitful plotting'. The gifts of verse 11 and the 'work of the ministry' of verse 12 were given to prevent doctrinal departure from the faith; by 'ministry', Paul is not concerned here with minor acts of service, but with the major work of teaching the truth.
4. The word 'ministry' is used in Ephesians to describe Paul's work as an apostle (3:7) and to describe the work of Tychicus (6:21), Paul's messenger to the Ephesians. These were official rather than everyday ministries.

---

[106] Charles Hodge, *A Commentary on the Epistle to the Ephesians*, New York: Robert Carter and Bros., 1860

[107] T. K. Abbott, *Ephesians*, ICC, Edinburgh: T. & T. Clark, 1909, p119

Despite these arguments, the main problem with the 'Clergy Model' is the fact that a number of times throughout the passage we read about all of God's people being involved and important for the growth of the church. Thus, we read about 'each' of God's people being given a gift (v7), 'till we all come ... to a perfect man' (v13), 'by what every joint supplies', 'every part does its share' and 'the body ... edifying ... itself in love' (v16). This passage clearly emphasizes the importance of the work of all the members of the church, not just a clerical elite.

Further, this passage is not teaching about church government or office, even in verse 11 where it mentions apostles. This passage is about gifts and growth, not government. It is not about the office of a clergyman, but about the use of spiritual gifts by all.

Worst of all, the idea that there are two classes of Christians, the clergy and the laity, is a denial of the main point of Ephesians 4:1-16 – the unity of the body of Christ. The idea that Christians can be divided into two groups is not found here in Ephesians 4, and it is foreign to the NT.

Ray Stedman writes, 'When the ministry was left to the "professionals", there was nothing left for the people to do other than come to church and listen. They were told that it was their responsibility to bring the world into the church building to hear the pastor preach the gospel. Soon Christianity became little more than a Sunday-morning spectator sport, much like the definition of football: twenty-two men down on the field, desperately in need of rest, and twenty thousand in the grandstands, desperately in need of exercise. . . The work of ministry belongs to the entire body of believers, who should be equipped, guided, and encouraged by those who are gifted by God to expound and apply His Word with wisdom and power. The entire body has received gifts from the Spirit, and it is the task of those in the pastoral ministry to encourage the entire body to discover and exercise those gifts. When we rediscover the pattern and strategy of Ephesians 4, when we have given all Christians in the body their God-given role as ministers of God's eternal plan, then the entire body comes alive with resurrection power.

Lives are changed. Ministries explode. Communities are touched and healed. The church becomes healthy and exciting again'[108].

2. The Clergy-Laity Model

Against this first 'Clergy Model' stands a second view that is far better and much closer to the biblical picture, yet it also has problems. This second view has come to virtually dominate, not only the interpretation of Ephesians 4, but also the modern evangelical church scene. Here is how this model works:

1. The pastor/teacher(s) equip the saints (through Bible teaching)
2. The saints do the work of serving (they run the ministries of the church)
3. The body is built up (the church expands and grows)

In other words, there is a division of labour within the church: the clergy are responsible for the teaching of the Word of God, which equips the saints. They act as a coach might in a sporting team: providing strategic leadership, sound teaching, wise counsel, and helpful correction. The Pastor-Coach cheers from the sideline as the saints do the service (they run the crèche, the cleaning rosters, the soup kitchen, etc). The clergy cannot do all the work of ministry themselves – instead, they are the Pastor-Teacher-Coaches who equip everyone else to play their part and perform their various ministries.

Ray Stedman describes this view as follows: 'Note that neither the apostles and prophets nor the evangelists and pastor-teachers are expected to do the work of the ministry! They are not even expected to do the work of building up the body of Christ! Those tasks are to be done only by the people – the ordinary, plain-vanilla Christians we often call "the laity". The four offices of apostle, prophet, evangelist, and pastor-teacher exist for one function and one function only: to equip

---

[108] Ray C. Stedman, *Body Life*, Grand Rapids, MI: Discovery House, 1972, 1995, p116-8

everyday Christians to do the work God has given them – and gifted them! – to do'[109].

This view is partly correct, and presents a huge improvement over the previous view, in that it states that all the people of God are involved in ministry. But it is also clearly wrong in stating that evangelists, pastors and teachers are *not* involved in ministry nor in building up the body of Christ.

This interpretation depends on a particular reading of Eph. 4:12. In contrast to the KJV which translated this verse in three phrases ('For the perfecting of the saints, for the work of the ministry, for the edifying of the body of Christ'), virtually every modern version translates the verse as two phrases: 'to equip the saints for the work of ministry, for building up the body of Christ' (ESV), 'to equip his people for works of service, so that the body of Christ may be built up' (1984 NIV).

As John Stott explains of the earlier three-phrase translation: 'It will be noted that according to this translation, Christ had three distinct purposes in mind. I think Armitage Robinson was the first commentator to insist that this was a mistake. 'The second of these clauses', he wrote, 'must be taken as dependent on the first, and not ... as coordinate with it'. In other words, the first comma ('the fatal comma') – which is 'without linguistic authority but with undoubted ecclesiological bias' – must be erased. If it is allowed to stand, we are faced with 'a saddening result', for 'the verse then means that only the special ministers, not all the saints, are called to do 'the work of ministry' and to cooperate in the 'building of the body'. This interpretation 'has an aristocratic, that is, a clerical and ecclesiastical flavour, it distinguishes the (mass of the) 'saints' from the (superior class of the) officers of the church'. If the comma is erased, however, we are left with two purposes – one immediate and the other ultimate – for which Christ gave gifts to his church. His immediate purpose was ... 'to equip God's people for work in his service' (NEB), and his ultimate purpose 'for building up the body of Christ'[110].

---

[109] Ray Stedman, *Body Life*, p120

[110] John Stott, *Ephesians*, BST, Nottingham: IVP, 1979, 1989, p166

Thus, whereas in the 'Clergy Model', the clergy do all three of the things in verse 12 (perfecting the saints, the work of ministry and edifying the body), in the second 'Clergy-Laity Model', the clergy do the first (equip the saints) enabling the saints do the second and third (works of service and building up the body).

Vance Havner puts it like this: 'Every Christian is commissioned, for every Christian is a missionary. It has been said that the Gospel is not merely something to come to church to hear but something to go from church to tell – and we are all appointed to tell it. It has also been said, 'Christianity began as a company of lay witnesses; it has become a professional pulpitism, financed by lay spectators!' Nowadays we hire a church staff to do 'full-time Christian work', and we sit in church on Sundays to watch them do it. Every Christian is meant to be in full-time Christian service … There is indeed a special ministry of pastor, teachers and evangelists – but for what? … For the perfecting of the saints for their ministry'[111].

The majority of modern commentators follow this 'Clergy-Laity' line of interpretation, and the promotion of 'every-member ministry' that this view encourages is commendable. However, there are some problems with this interpretation that see it falling short of being a convincing explanation.

Here is how Max Turner, rejecting the Clergy-Laity Model (as well as the Clergy Model) expresses it: '(The) leaders are said to have been given for three co-ordinate purposes. Christ gave them to equip or complete the saints; to serve the church's needs, and to build up the body of Christ. Traditional Protestant interpretation (now reflected in all modern translations including the NJB) has limited the function of the leaders to the first of these, arguing it is the equipped saints who then minister to the church and build it up, not the leaders. To propose that the latter are the subject of all three phrases is taken to be 'Catholic' and 'clericalist' interpretation. But while any 'clericalist' interpretation is clearly excluded by vs 7 and 16 (where the saints definitely have a part in

---

[111] Vance Havner, *Why Not Just be Christians?* New York: Fleming H. Revell, 1964, p63

the building up of the church), it is more probably the leaders' functions which are still in view throughout v12"[112].

Here are four problems of a textual, biblical, grammatical and practical nature with the Clergy-Laity model:

i. **Textually**: the text of the verse does not clearly say what this model suggests. For example, a relative pronoun could have been added to make it clear that it is the saints who do the ministry: 'for the equipping of the saints, *who* do the work of the ministry …'. But Paul did not use such a relative pronoun to make his meaning clear. Again, Paul could have made this point a little clearer by adding an infinitive verb: 'for the equipping of the saints, *to do* the work of the ministry …'. This is how the New Living Translation paraphrases the verse, however there is no infinitive verb in the original text. Or, Paul could have used a conjunction: 'for the equipping of the saints, *so that* they do the work of the ministry …'. This is the way the NIV paraphrases the latter part of the verse, however, the NIV conjunction is without any warrant, for it is not present in the original Greek. There are perhaps other ways that Paul could have made clear that it was not 'the clergy' but rather 'the laity' who do the second of the three tasks, the work of the ministry, but Paul used none of these simple textual devices. If Paul had used any of these simple flags to show that a different group was doing the work of the ministry, we could be more certain that this is what he meant. But he did not, so this interpretation remains unclear.

ii. **Biblically**: While the Clergy Interpretation insisted that it is the Clergy who do the ministry, the Clergy-Laity Interpretation insists that (a) the laity do the ministry and (2) the pastors and teachers do *not* do the ministry (nor do they even edify the body of Christ). But this is false: pastors and teachers are involved in doing 'the work of ministry'. Numerous verses show that all Christians – the leaders as well as ordinary Christians – are involved in 'the work of ministry'.

---

[112] Max Turner, "Ephesians", *New Bible Commentary*, Leicester: IVP, 1994, p1238

Thus, we have already seen references to Paul's and Tychicus' ministry in Ephesians 3:7 and 6:21. The twelve apostles' ministry is referred to in Acts 1:17, and Paul's ministry in Acts 20:24 and Romans 11:13. But on the other hand, ordinary Christians are also involved in 'ministry'. We have seen that 1 Peter 4:10-11 says, 'as each one has received a gift, *minister* it to one another', and Peter goes on to broadly define the two main areas of gifting – speaking 'as the oracles of God', and serving. These verses are saying that preaching and teaching form part of 'ministry' (or service). Thus, ministry or service is something that all Christians are to be involved in.

iii. **Grammatically**[113]: The Clergy-Laity interpretation depends heavily upon the fact that Paul uses different Greek prepositions before the three phrases in v12: *pros* before the first and *eis* before the second and third. However, both of these prepositions mean virtually the same thing; they both express purpose and both are translated by 'to' or 'for'. Frederick Rendall, writing about this verse, says, 'The nice distinctions of the classical period were not maintained in later Greek'[114]. Chrysostom the famous 4th-century Greek expositor argued that the prepositions mean the same thing as each other here, and that there are three parallel clauses (as in the KJV). As we have seen, the Clergy-Laity model argues that the first phrase gives us the immediate purpose of the gifts, while the second and third phrases are parallel to each other and give us the ultimate purpose of the gifts. However many older commentators (like Alford and Ellicott) argue that the first phrase is the ultimate purpose, and the second and third phrases are the immediate purpose (they point to the use of the same prepositions in Rom. 15:2 where *pros* expresses ultimate purpose). Still other commentators argue that the phrases are

---

[113] Strictly speaking this argument is really lexical or syntactical, but seeing ordinary readers are unfamiliar with these terms, we are using the term here to refer to 'Greek grammar' in the broadest sense.

[114] F. Rendall, "Ephesians", *Expositors Greek New Testament*, London: Hodder and Stoughton, 1903, p330

successive, the first immediate, the second intermediate, and the third ultimate. What this all means is that the Greek experts are far from united, and the meaning of the Greek prepositions does not settle the argument. Daniel Wallace writes about the preposition *eis* in Eph. 4:12-13: 'the problem here is not so much meaning as it is the question of subordination and coordination'[115]. The fact that Paul uses two slightly different Greek prepositions is not a decisive argument in favour of the Clergy-Laity interpretation.

iv. **Practically**: The Clergy-Laity Interpretation encourages the laity to get involved in the work of ministry, which is good. However, in practice, the laity are encouraged to be involved in every ministry except one: the pastor-teacher's role of using his spiritual gifts in the church gathering to teach, encourage and equip the saints. The laity are shut off from doing anything that encroaches upon the preserve of the clergy, and advised to get involved in the ordinary duties of keeping the church's weekly machinery running. Thus, in practical terms, there is virtually no difference between this model and the Clerical Model – both perpetuate a clergy-laity distinction that is foreign to the New Testament, and both direct the laity to do menial, semi-administrative tasks that the clergyman is either too busy, or finds it beneath his dignity, to do. Not only are the clergy excused from doing mundane 'works of service', but worse, the laity has no role to play in the first task: equipping other saints. The work of the laity is to pay and to pray, to bring others to hear the clergy preach or to interact with needy souls out in the world – but crucially (just like in the Clergy Model), the laity are not to use their spiritual gifts in the church gathering. For all the talk of 'every-member ministry' that the Clergy-Laity model generates, the reality is that this model protects the clerical privilege of participating in church almost as jealously as the first model, and promotes the same end result: spectator Churchianity.

---

[115] Daniel Wallace, *Greek Grammar beyond the Basics, An Exegetical Syntax of the New Testament*, Grand Rapids, MI: Zondervan, 1996, p371

The Clergy-Laity model thus results in untenable conclusions (bible teachers are not doing the work of ministry or edifying the church?) and in practical terms makes little difference to the way the Clergy Model works. The older translation of verse 12 (as three clauses) is not some 'mistake'; it is a legitimate option and provides a more sensible way to understand the passage. The modern fashion for translating verse 12 as two clauses is simply bandwagon exposition – everyone suddenly started interpreting the verse this way in the mid-20th Century for reasons that are not particularly convincing.

3. The 'Collaborative' Model

While the Clergy Model denies that the ordinary saints can do the work of ministry (only the Clergy can), and the Clergy-Laity Model denies that specially gifted Christians can do the work of ministry (only the 'laity' can), the Collaborative Model says that all of God's people – leaders and ordinary Christians – should use their gifts to equip the saints, do the work of ministry and build up the body of Christ. The gifts listed in verse 11 are not exhaustive, but only the most important gifts. Nevertheless, all Christians have gifts (verse 7) which exist for the same purpose – to help other Christians, to serve God, and to build the church. Both of the first two models are deficient, the Clerical model because it ignores the emphasis in the passage upon the giftedness of all of God's people in the church, and the Clergy-Laity model because of its attempt to demarcate a dubious division of labour between the clergy and laity within verse 12. Instead, Paul seems to be balancing the two following truths about spiritual gifts:

a. spiritual gifts have been given to all God's people (verse 7), and all of God's people are to be actively involved in using these gifts so that there is growth in the body (verse 16);
b. nevertheless, certain spiritual gifts (like those listed in verse 11) are more important for the up-building of the church (verses 12-15); not all people have the same gifts.

Or we might put it this way: while the Clergy Model teaches that the specially-gifted do all the work of ministry, and the Clergy-Laity Model says that the saints do all the work of ministry (with the pastor-coaches cheering on from the sidelines), the Collaborative Model argues that *both* those who are specially-gifted as well as all of the ordinary saints are involved in (a) equipping the saints, (b) doing the work of the ministry, and (c) building up the church by using their gifts. To continue the sporting analogy, we might say that the church's most gifted leaders are on the field as 'player-coaches', the most involved of all, alongside all the other believers in the work of the ministry.

G. C. D. Howley links Ephesians 4 with 1 Corinthians and the participatory use of gifts there: 'the bestowal of the prominent gifts by the risen Lord was not to give a monopoly to a comparatively small number of persons, but that the exercise of these gifts might, in turn, train and develop (perfect) the members of Christ so that all would be fulfilling their individual ministry. The final words in the passage (vv. 15, 16) reveal the consequences of the functioning of all the members in the binding together, nourishment, and growth of the Body. And this is what we find at Corinth, the result of the work of such gifts, a church 'enriched in Him' and 'coming behind in no gift' but showing many expressions of the endowment of the Spirit'[116].

This model mirrors what we are told in 1 Cor. 12-14: that each of us has a spiritual gift (which we can use to contribute in the church gatherings), but that we should concentrate upon using the gifts that are more profitable for edifying the church (prophesying in 1 Cor. 14). All of us are gifted and necessary (1 Cor. 12), but some gifts are more profitable than others (1 Cor. 14).

Thus, we need to balance the egalitarian emphasis of verses 7 and 16 (everyone is gifted, every part of the body works to cause growth in the body) with the functional emphasis in verse 11 (some gifts are more useful than others). All the gifts do not reside in one single person (the

---

[116] G. C. D. Howley, "The Christian Ministry", in *The Church: a Symposium of Principles and Practices*, ed. J. B. Watson, Kilmarnock: John Ritche Ltd, 1999, p111

Clergy model), but neither should we swing to the opposite extreme and ignore the importance of those who are specially gifted by God. While there is no room for the sort of elitism seen in both the Clergy model and the Clergy-Laity model, neither should we take the route of radical uniformity (of the sort that expects all believers to take turns doing the Bible teaching in church). The idea that all Christians are expository teachers is false. But to forbid on this account a man from opening his mouth and using other gifts in church is equally misguided. It is important to stress the priority of the preaching and teaching gifts found in verse 11 for the building up of the body of Christ, while not downplaying the importance of the contribution of the gifts of all the members.

Speaking the Truth in Love

The expression 'speaking the truth in love' at the beginning of verse 15 is important. Many commentators argue that this should really be translated *'living out the truth* in love', based on the usage of the word *aletheuo* in Classical Greek. However, certain pieces of evidence point strongly towards the traditional translation of '*speaking the truth* in love':

- the LXX (Greek translation of the OT) consistently uses this word with the meaning of 'speaking the truth'
- the only other place the word is used in the NT (Gal. 4:16) carries the meaning of 'speaking the truth'
- this meaning makes better sense in the context of Eph. 4 where Paul is writing about spiritually-gifted preachers and speakers (v11). Paul contrasts this with the work of false-teachers: being 'tossed to and fro and carried about with every wind of doctrine, by the trickery of men' (v14).
- Paul is not writing about ethical honesty or living uprightly in the immediate context (that comes later in verses 25ff.)

Who is it that is 'speaking the truth in love'? If we track backwards, we see that it is the 'we all' of verse 13. The work of 'speaking the truth in love' is not the function of the 'pastors and teachers' of verse 11 alone, but of *all* the believers ministering to each other: teaching, encouraging, discipling, comforting, correcting and supporting. This is the reason that verse 16 goes on to emphasize the participatory nature of body-growth: 'the *whole* body, being knit together by what *every* joint supplies, according to the effective working by which *every* part does its share, causes growth of the body for the edifying of itself in love'.

Verse 16 is particularly important for understanding the Collaborative model of mutual edification that this passage teaches:

a. the church is a body made up of different parts
b. every part supplies an essential element to the functioning of the whole
c. every part works and does its share
d. every part causes growth of the body
e. the body edifies itself

The body is a self-edifying structure in which every part works together to cause growth, not only of all the individual parts, but of the whole.

It is also very important to notice the way that growth comes from Christ, the head of the body in verses 15 and 16. We have already seen that Christ is the One from whom each believer receives their gifts (verse 7). But even more significantly here, Christ as the head of the body is the One from whom *all the body* (verse16) receives guidance and direction for service. It is not the role of a clerical caste, a 'senior pastor' or even the elders to take the role of the 'head', dictating the ministry of individuals within the church (although wise guidance is helpful). Just as Christ directed the service of his apostles, so too with all of the gifts: the body is dependent upon its heavenly Head for direction.

In the Church Gatherings
It could be objected that this passage does not talk specifically about the church gatherings, and therefore the idea that it gives encouragement to the idea of participatory church gatherings is unwarranted. It is true that the scope of this passage goes beyond the church; the evangelist, for example, is active in the world bringing people into the church.

However, as we will see, the scope of this passage includes the church and its gatherings.

Paul's great subject in Ephesians is the church (mentioned nine times). The church is the main focus of this particular passage in Ephesians 4:1-16. While it does not use the word 'church', it mentions the 'body of Christ, which we know is a picture of the church with Christ as its 'Head'. It also uses the word 'edify' twice, which is again associated with the word-picture of the church as a temple being built.

The passage is teaching about spiritual gifts, and it is focussed on the twin objectives of unity (which implies corporate rather than individual Christianity) and truth (which involves people speaking). In the New Testament, truth, unity and spiritual gifts intersect in the public setting of the church gatherings. In addition, the gifts that Paul mentions in verses 7 and 11 are gifts that are primarily used in founding, establishing and building up the church. Here we have a passage that teaches us about the use of gifts, and in particular, speaking gifts. There is no division of gifts here into those that may be used in the church (by the clergy) and gifts that may be used elsewhere (by the laity). Indeed, some of the gifts listed by Paul are primarily used in the church gatherings (particularly, the gifts of pastor and teacher).

The sorts of expressions that Paul uses in this passage again primarily apply to activities which occur when the church meets:

- Edifying the body of Christ (verse 12, cf. 1 Cor. 14),
- growing in the unity of the faith (verse 13)
- and of the knowledge of the Son of God (verse 13),
- being protected against wrong doctrine (verse 14), and
- 'speaking the truth in love' (verse 15)

Thus, the church gatherings are the principal venue where the contribution of the gifts of all the different believers, as directed by the Head, should be realised. While this passage does not specifically mention the church gatherings, nor describe the functioning of a church meeting, we learn that all the Christians are to be involved in using their gifts to build each other up, and we know (from elsewhere in the NT) that the principal venue where this edification happens is the meetings of the church. While we cannot limit this passage to the church gatherings, what it teaches should nevertheless characterize the church gatherings.

Conclusion

Paul is writing about the growth and building up of the church in Ephesians 4:7-16, and in doing so he uses the words 'all', 'each' and 'every' five times in the passage as well as saying that the body edifies 'itself'. Each and every Christian is to be involved in the work of building up the body of Christ. This is not the role of a select few leaders with gifts that set them apart from the rest, but the responsibility of every Christian. Christ is the Head of the body, and He is the one who not only has given the gifts but should be directing their operation in the church by His Spirit.

CHAPTER 7

PARTICIPATORY CHURCH GATHERINGS IN ACTS

A Participatory Prayer Meeting: Acts Chapters One and Two
B. B. Warfield, commenting on 1 Cor. 14, wrote: 'This, it is to be observed, was the ordinary church worship at Corinth in the Apostles' day. It is analogous in form to the freedom of our modern prayer-meeting services ... There is no reason to believe that the infant congregation in Corinth was singular in this. The Apostle does not write as if he were describing a marvellous state of affairs peculiar to that church. He even makes the transition to the next item of his advice in the significant words, 'as in all the churches of the saints'. And the hints of the rest of his letters and in the Book of Acts require us, accordingly, to look upon this beautiful picture of Christian worship as one which would have been true to life for any of the numerous congregations planted by the Apostles in the length and breadth of the world visited and preached to by them'[117].

The point to notice here is that Warfield likened the church gathering described in 1 Cor. 14 to the freedom of a modern-day prayer meeting. This is an interesting observation, which becomes even more significant when we remember that this is actually how the church started out in the book of Acts: as a simple Prayer and Bible Study gathering.

---

[117] B. B. Warfield, *Miracles Yesterday and Today, True and False*, Grand Rapids, MI: Eerdmans, 1954, pp4-5

> *'These all continued with one accord in prayer and supplication, with the women and Mary the mother of Jesus and with his brothers. And in those days Peter stood up in the midst of the disciples (altogether the number of names was about a hundred and twenty), and said, "Men and brethren, this Scripture had to be fulfilled, which the Holy Spirit spoke before by the mouth of David concerning Judas, who became a guide to those who arrested Jesus"* (Acts 1:14-15).

The church was born on the Day of Pentecost in Acts chapter two. But the Day of Pentecost was the tenth day that the disciples had continued in prayer since the Ascension[118]. In these ten days, the disciples gathered in Jerusalem to pray and discuss the Scriptures (see Acts 1:16ff.) while waiting for the coming of the Holy Spirit.

Thus we can trace a line of descent from the freedom of the participatory nature of the churches in Corinth and Thessalonica (among others) back to the freedom of the prayer meeting out of which the church in Jerusalem grew in Acts 1 and 2. The participatory nature of church life that we find in the New Testament letters was an outgrowth of the situation in Acts 1 from which the Church was born.

Now, it might be argued that the picture of the embryonic and infant Church seen in Acts 1 and 2 provides no proof that the church continued to proceed in the same way, or should still proceed in the same way today. We can ignore these issues for now. At the moment, all that is being argued is that here we have another example of simple, interactive church gatherings in the New Testament. It is therefore unsatisfactory to argue that participatory church gatherings are found in a few sporadic places in the New Testament, like the church in Corinth, or the churches in Ephesus and Crete (as we see in the Pastoral Epistles). Instead, we find a definite pattern of participatory church gatherings as we look through the New Testament, going right back to the beginning of the church in Acts 1.

---

[118] If we calculate from the Ascension, forty days after Christ's Resurrection, until Pentecost, fifty days after the Resurrection, there were ten days in between the Ascension and Pentecost.

What we find in Corinth or Ephesus is not some eccentric aberration, therefore, but in keeping with the apostolic origins of the Church as pictured in the book of Acts. That might not convince some people that we should practise what the apostolic church practised, but the accumulating evidence for participatory church gatherings throughout the New Testament shows up the hollowness of the boast of some who argue that their church is genuinely Apostolic (one of the four traditional marks of a true Church), all the while continuing to be unapostolic in the way its primary activity, the church gathering, is carried on.

Peter Stood Up

There are not many church gatherings described in the book of Acts, but among those that are, there is an interesting incidental description that we find repeated in relation to them:

- '*in those days* Peter stood up *in the midst of the disciples ... and said*, "Men and brethren, this Scripture had to be fulfilled ..."' (Acts 1:15).
- 'Peter standing up with the eleven, *raised his voice and said to them*, "Men of Judea and all who dwell in Jerusalem, let this be known to you ..."' (Acts 2:14)
- '*then one of them, named* Agabus, stood up *and showed by the Spirit that there was going to be a great famine*' Acts 11:28
- '*but some of the sect of the* Pharisees who believed rose up, *saying, "It is necessary to circumcise them, and to command them to keep the law of Moses"*' (Acts 15:5)
- '*and when there had been much dispute,* Peter rose up *and said to them,* "Men and brethren, you know that a good while ago God chose among us, that by my mouth the Gentiles should hear the word of the gospel and believe"' (Acts 15:7)

The interesting point in each case is the way the Scripture records these people either standing up or rising up to speak in the early church. These descriptions remind us of what we read about in 1 Cor. 14:30-31. A. C. Thiselton comments upon the words there about something being 'revealed to another who sits by': 'In this case, the one who is sitting down nearby may well have stood to indicate his readiness to communicate what was disclosed to him for the congregation'[119]. Gordon Fee makes the same point: 'The clear implication is that the one prophesying stands while doing so; probably this would be true of the other manifestations as well'[120].

'Rising up' could, of course, be taken in a metaphorical sense to mean people opposing or protesting what was being taught. We find people 'rising up' metaphorically a few times in Acts (e.g. the opponents of the gospel, 5:17, 6:9). But this does not appear to be the meaning in the case of Peter 'rising up' to speak in Acts 15, nor would 'standing up' be naturally taken in a metaphorical sense, as when Agabus stood up in Acts 11. The two expressions seem to be simply describing, in physical terms, what was happening.

Further, it is clear that the people 'standing up' did so to publicly address either their fellow Christians, or in the case in Acts 2 the people generally, for we have their summarised speeches after the note about them standing up. It is clear also from these references that we are reading about a gathering of disciples or a gathering of the church. The passages either mention the fact that, for example, Peter stood up in the midst of the disciples, or they record his words addressing the congregation, "Men and brethren".

So, while these references to people who 'stood up' are nothing more than incidental touches, yet they are illustrative glimpses into how participation took place in the early church gatherings in the book of Acts. Further, the repetition of this incidental detail is indicative of the fact that this matter of standing up to address the congregation was characteristic of how participation occurred in the church gatherings in the book of Acts.

---

[119] A. C. Thiselton, *The First Epistle to the Corinthians: A Commentary on the Greek Text*, NIGTC, Grand Rapids, MI: Eerdmans, 2000, p1143

[120] Gordon Fee, *The First Epistle to the Corinthians*, NICNT, Grand Rapids, MI: Eerdmans, 1987, p695 footnote 35

We must not place too much weight upon this expression, nor argue that it constitutes proof of participatory church gatherings in Acts. However, we may explore the implications that this expression suggests.

Firstly, we are not told that the person was first invited to address the congregation before they 'stood up'. This was certainly not the case in Acts 2 where, amid the confusion, Peter and the eleven 'stood up' to explain what was happening to the crowds who had gathered.

Nor are we told that the person asked permission from others before they 'stood up'. There is no evidence of some chairman who approved their right to speak or forbad certain other people from speaking. In Acts 1, the disciples were gathered praying and there would not have been any need of a chairman. Nor does James who some argue (without any textual evidence) was the chairman in Acts 15 approve or invite Peter to speak in that chapter.

Nor can it be argued that this freedom to stand up and address the congregation was limited to certain people who perhaps enjoyed 'presidential status', like Peter, for not only does Agabus stand up to speak in Acts 11, but also certain of the sect of the Pharisees who believed also stand up, as we see from Acts 15.

Nor, from the context of events, and particularly the nature of the debate in Acts 15, does it seem reasonable to assume that the order of the discussion had been pre-planned and that the person had stood up at the time appointed to them.

Instead, the book of Acts simply states that they 'stood up' and then spoke. What was happening? It would appear that the person stood up to gain the attention of the congregation so that there would be an opportunity to speak. This is what happened in Acts 2 amid the commotion of the tongues. It would also appear to be the reason why Peter stood up in Acts 1, amid the 120 disciples crowded into the upper room, engaged in prayer.

The fact that the person stood up seems to indicate that they themselves were taking the initiative in addressing the congregation. This seems most apparent in the case of Agabus in Acts 11 who, as a prophet, was not appointed by some other person to deliver an exposition or encouragement, but felt the need to pass on a message from God.

This again best explains Peter's desire to speak in Acts 15, on the basis that he felt compelled to share his personal experience of having been given the responsibility of first preaching the gospel to Gentiles.

In summary, the expression is suggestive of the fact that there was no pre-arranged program nor was official permission required for people to speak. Rather, the person standing up was doing so to indicate that they themselves personally wished to say something. This was the easiest way to draw peoples' attention in their direction so that the audience would listen to what was going to be said.

This appears to be the most natural explanation of what was happening, and it thus appears consistent with the picture we find in 1 Cor. 14 and other passages in the New Testament where prophets and other gifted people spoke in the church, not because they were invited to speak, or because they had been arranged to speak, but because they had a right to address the congregation, because of the freedom that was permitted to people to use their spiritual gift, and because of the inner prompting of the Holy Spirit who had not only originally given the gift but also was being manifested through its use.

The Church in Antioch

The church in Antioch is one of the most important churches in the New Testament. It was here that the disciples of the Lord were first called Christians. It was here that the first racially-integrated Christian church was planted. It was from this base that the mission to the Gentiles was launched in Acts 13.

References to the church at Antioch in operation are found in Acts 11:19ff., Acts 13:1-3, 14:26 - 15:2, 15:30-35. We shall notice three particular features of the church at Antioch, characteristic of a participatory type of church life:

1. Multiple teachers and preachers
2. The Holy Spirit speaking through people
3. Different ways of speaking

Multiple teachers and preachers

The book of Acts tells us about the following preachers and teachers speaking in Antioch:

- Barnabus and Saul teaching the new Christians (Acts 11:26),
- Agabus and other prophets who came down from Jerusalem (Acts 11:27),
- Barnabus, Simeon called Niger, Lucius of Cyrene, Manaen who had been brought up with Herod the tetrarch and Saul (13:1),
- 'certain men who came down from Judea (teaching that) unless you are circumcised according to the custom of Moses you cannot be saved' (15:1),
- Judas and Silas, 'being prophets also, exhorted and strengthened the brethren with many words' (15:32), and
- 'Paul and Barnabus also remained in Antioch, teaching and preaching the word of the Lord, with many others also' (15:35).

Some would argue that the five teachers and prophets mentioned in Acts 13:1 was a complete list of all those who were permitted to speak in the church. S. P. Tregelles argued for a 'stated ministry' ('that is, that in every assembly those who are gifted of God to speak to edification will be both limited in number and known to the rest') on the basis of this verse. He quoted G. V. Wigram approvingly: 'I see that at Antioch there were but five whom the Holy Ghost recognized as teachers - Barnabus, Simeon, Lucius, Manaen and Saul. Doubtless, at all the meetings it was only these five, one or more of them, as it pleased the Holy Ghost, who were expected by the saints to speak. This was a *stated* ministry'[121].

However, this argument runs aground on the fact that we read that many others spoke in the church at Antioch, including the prophets who came with Agabus in Acts 11 and the 'many others' who taught with Barnabus and Paul in Acts 15:35. Even more tellingly, we read that certain men came teaching a doctrine which was not accepted, namely the Judaizing doctrine (Acts 15:1). These were not 'approved' teachers! Luke does not even say that they were 'brethren' - indeed, Paul's letter to

---

[121] quoted by G. H. Lang, *The Churches of God*, pp83-84

the Galatians refers to some of these people as false-brethren (Gal. 2:4). Everywhere that Paul later preached the gospel, these Judaizers seemed to follow and were granted opportunity to teach their false-doctrines, at least for a while. The idea, then, that there was some 'official list' of ordained or approved preachers or teachers seems difficult to maintain from the text. There was opportunity for many, not for the few. There was opportunity for those who spoke, motivated by the Spirit of God, and even for those whose message was tried and found wanting.

Further, the fact that prophets spoke in the church at Antioch conclusively settles the issue all by itself: prophets speak as prompted by the Holy Spirit, not at the invitation or permission of mere men, whether elders or not.

It should be obvious, then, that the opening verses of Acts 13 are not so much intended to teach that there was an official list of accepted speakers in the church at Antioch (or even that these were the only ones who ministered in the church), but rather simply the fact that certain notable prophets and teachers in the church were spoken to by the Holy Spirit about the need to send forth Barnabus and Saul for the work elsewhere. To conclude from these verses that there needs to be a list of approved names drawn up for preaching in the church is beside the point of the passage and goes beyond what the verses themselves state.

To try to limit the preachers and teachers in a church on the basis of this verse is unwarranted: whether we like it or not, the early church conducted their gatherings in such a way that any men prompted by the Spirit were able to speak.

Of course, in any church, those who are most gifted in teaching or preaching will be easily identified by the members of the church. But the ever-expanding pool of teachers in the church at Antioch (from Barnabus and Saul in Acts 11, to the five listed in Acts 13, to the 'many others' of Acts 15) argues against the idea of a 'stated ministry'. Indeed, the 'stated ministry' concept would kill off, or at least severely stunt, any possibility of any others developing their gifts and using them for the benefit of the body.

The Holy Spirit Spoke

A second noteworthy feature of the church of Antioch is the way that the Holy Spirit spoke through the preachers. This feature is important because of the way it is repeated in the book of Acts. Thus, we read, in Acts 11:28 that 'then one of them, named Agabus, stood up and showed by the Spirit that there was going to be a great famine throughout all the world, which also happened in the days of Claudius Caesar'. Likewise, in Acts 13:2, as the five prophets and teachers 'ministered to the Lord and fasted, the Holy Spirit said, "Now separate to Me Barnabus and Saul for the work to which I have called them"'. Alongside these two references we may place the record of the Jerusalem conference in Acts 15, where the apostles and elders claimed that it was the voice of the Holy Spirit Himself speaking through their deliberations: 'it seemed good to the Holy Spirit, and to us, to lay upon you no greater burden than these necessary things ...' (Acts 15:28).

Here in the church at Antioch we have the clearest illustration of what Paul writes about in 1 Corinthians 12:7, 'the manifestation of the Spirit is given to each one for profit'. Paul is making the claim that the Holy Spirit is manifested through different people speaking (and serving, too), by the gifts that He has given them. The church is meant to be the place where the Holy Spirit is manifested, and where His voice is heard.

We see further evidence of the way this happens in 1 Corinthians 14:24-25 where an unbeliever comes in and is convicted of God's presence through the message of the prophets, who speaks of things that only the unbeliever is aware of: 'the secrets of his heart are revealed'. There is another veiled allusion to the way the Holy Spirit works in 1 Cor. 14:30 where we read that truths are 'revealed' to people during the messages of others in the meeting.

This was the record of the church at Antioch: the Holy Spirit spoke through His servants the prophets and teachers in the church.

Different Ways of Speaking

Finally, in the church at Antioch we also see the impact of different gifts in the life of the church. The Holy Spirit was able to speak through a prophet like Agabus who predicted a famine (11:28). However, other prophets like Judas and Silas delivered messages that 'exhorted and strengthened the brethren with many words' (Acts 15:32). Obviously, here they were not foretelling the future so much as fortifying the believers in their faith. Again, we have others who were noted for being teachers, particularly Barnabus and Saul in 11:26, and some (or all) of the five listed in Acts 13:1 were prophets, although which ones were prophets and which were teachers is not stated. The reason might indeed be the fact that there is a substantial overlap between these two gifts, just as there appears to be an overlap between prophecy and exhortation in the case of Judas and Silas in Acts 15:32. Then, again, in 14:27, we have the word of testimony: 'Now when they (Paul and Barnabus) had come and gathered the church together, they reported all that God had done with them, and that He had opened the door of faith to the Gentiles'.

That there are different ways that the Holy Spirit may speak in the church is the plainest conclusion that could be drawn from passages like Romans 12 or 1 Corinthians 12. However, in our modern day, virtually the only way that the Holy Spirit is permitted to speak is through the three-point sermon. This is not to downplay the benefits of good preaching, nor is it meant to ridicule preaching which is well-structured and easily digested. Rather, it is simply to state that the Holy Spirit would probably get our attention more easily if we did not force His every message into the same mould. Sometimes, all that needs to be said could be stated in one sentence. Just like the Lord in the synagogue in Nazareth, it might even be the case that simply reading half of a sentence of Scripture would have more impact than half an hour of preaching.

The church at Antioch bears clear witness to the fact that diversity and variety are the trademarks of the Holy Spirit's work and witness. Why are these things not characteristic of our churches? Is it because the Holy Spirit is not allowed His proper place among us – a place the Bible records Him being given among the churches of the New Testament?

Summary

These glimpses into the church at Antioch thus offer further evidence of the fact that the church gatherings in Acts were participatory. This is not to say that these occasional glimpses of the operation of the church at

Antioch amount to proof of participatory church gatherings, but simply that the picture that Acts presents is remarkably consistent with the picture we see in Corinth, Ephesus or Thessalonica. Thus, to the list of places where we see participatory church gatherings in operation, it would seem we have to add Antioch.

The Jerusalem Council

The Jerusalem council, convened to deal with the question of whether Gentile believers were required to keep the law of Moses, was one of the most important events in the book of Acts. Participatory church gatherings, by contrast, are not a high priority in the book of Acts. Nevertheless, certain incidental features of the council described in Acts 15 are indicative of a participatory style of church gatherings.

Our argument here is not that procedural features of the Jerusalem council are proof that New Testament church gatherings were conducted in a participatory way, but rather that because New Testament church gatherings were conducted in a participatory way (as seen in various passages in the epistles), it is not surprising that we see further evidence of this in Acts 15. We will notice particularly three features seen from Acts 15:

1. the participants
2. the 'order of service'
3. the activity of the Holy Spirit

The Participants

When we look at Acts 15 and consider who participated, we read: *'And when [***Paul and Barnabus***] had come to Jerusalem, they were received by the church and the apostles and the elders; and they reported all things that God had done with them. But* **some of the sect of the Pharisees who believed** *rose up, saying, "It is necessary to circumcise them, and to command them to keep the law of Moses." Now the apostles and elders came together to consider this matter. And when there had been much dispute,* **Peter** *rose up and said to them: "Men and brethren"' (Acts 15:4-7) ...* Then **all the multitude** *kept silent and listened to* **Barnabas and Paul** *declaring how many miracles and* *wonders God had worked through them among the Gentiles. And after they had become silent,* **James** *answered, saying, "Men* and *brethren, listen to me' (12-13) ... Then it pleased* **the apostles and elders, with the whole church**, *to send chosen men of their own company to Antioch with Paul and Barnabas,* namely**,** *Judas who was also named Barsabas, and Silas, leading men among the brethren. They wrote this* letter *by them:* **The apostles, the elders, and the brethren**, *To the brethren who are of the Gentiles in Antioch, Syria, and Cilicia: Greetings . . .'* (22-23).

The first question to be considered in relation to the council is who attended. Verse 6, with its reference to the apostles and elders being gathered together, might at first appear to indicate that only the apostles and elders were present. However, as we shall see, there were plenty of other people too: Paul and Barnabus, no small number of believing Pharisees, 'all the multitude' who kept silent after Peter's speech, and finally, in verse 22, we read about 'the whole church' who along with the apostles and elders sent chosen men to Antioch with Paul and Barnabus.

Another interesting point to notice is that the apostles spoke last, not first. The main speakers (Peter, Barnabus, Paul and James) did not rush in and try to organize the meeting, or to steer its direction, play politics, try to force some conclusion or even clamp down on disruptive or disputatious people. The most spiritually mature and sensitive participants were prepared to sit back and wait and see what would happen. Their decisive speeches occur after there had been much dispute among others. The patience they showed, the humility (not trying to dominate, as others did), and the faith in the Holy Spirit's orchestration of events, are a model for our participation in the church.

It would therefore appear that the Jerusalem council was no 'closed-door' committee meeting restricted just to the apostles and elders at Jerusalem, but a very large gathering of Christians. Maybe the term 'council' gives the wrong impression altogether. There appears to have been freedom for anyone who was interested to attend, to sit and observe, listen to and (as we shall see) even participate in the discussion.

The Order of Service

As to the way proceedings developed, Acts 15:7 tells us that after there had been 'much dispute', Peter, Barnabus and Paul, then finally James all spoke. The fact that there were multiple speakers is not particularly noteworthy here. Even though multiple speakers is a feature of participatory church gatherings, any conference worthy of the name will have multiple speakers. Even a church business meeting will have multiple speakers.

Instead, the significant thing is that the whole affair was more like a church business meeting than a modern-day church service. Thus, we read that there was spirited debate and discussion. There were also two silences that the inspired record deems worthy of mention. These silences indicate three things. Firstly, they indicate that a passionate crowd was following the debate and discussion closely, even to the point of making background noise and then falling quiet. Second, these silences indicate points of significant break-through in the course of discussion, firstly after Peter's speech (verse 12), and then after Paul and Barnabus' account of the way God had worked to the salvation of the Gentiles on their first missionary journey (verse 13). Thirdly, the silences indicate that there was nobody scripted to take the 'pulpit' next and give their thoughts on the matter. Silence fell because opposition was crumbling and a consensus was in the process of being achieved. The silences were not scripted any more than the speeches were.

The debate was conducted in a natural and free-flowing manner, not according to some pre-arranged plan. The noise of debate resulted from the fact that there was freedom for people to argue their point of view. Silences happened as a result of the impact of what certain speakers had said.

There were no pre-arranged speakers, nor was there any president who directed affairs, or who allowed certain people to speak at certain points – there was no order of service at all. There was freedom for anybody who wished to contribute to do so, and enough mutual respect among the participants for the discussion to be conducted in such a way as to achieve a real breakthrough.

The type of Christianity we see on display at the Jerusalem council was that of mature, Spirit-filled Christians. In contrast to the control-freak Christianity of modern churches trying to put on a TV-quality performance scripted down to the last minute, the atmosphere at the Jerusalem council was one of freedom and respectful attention paid to the views of all interested parties.

The Activity of the Holy Spirit
Finally, at the end of the meeting, the apostles, elders and the whole church at Jerusalem could write in their letter to the church at Antioch that 'it seemed good to the Holy Spirit and to us …' (Acts 15:28). Significantly, even though only men had spoken in the meeting, the participants believed that the Holy Spirit had spoken. A few necessary points should be noted here.

Whilst individual members of churches using their gifts are said to be manifesting the Spirit (1 Cor. 12:7), yet 1 Cor. 14 cautions against accepting everything that is spoken in a church gathering as being from the Spirit of God. Instead, prophecies must be judged and spirits must be tested. The fact that the Spirit indwells every Christian means, not that everything that every Christian says is from God, but rather that the entire body of Christians can come to a Spirit-filled conclusion through the combined insights of different believers. The Holy Spirit's voice was thus heard in the cumulative words of different speakers and in the way the Holy Spirit orchestrated a satisfactory conclusion to the matter.

The individual contributions were an important part of the process by which the Holy Spirit spoke. For example, what Peter said was not wrong – it was from God's Spirit. But it was not sufficient to settle the debate. Nor was Paul and Barnabas' report of the ways that God had worked through them to the conversion of Gentiles the end of the matter. A satisfactory conclusion was not reached until James' speech had taken into account the needs of Jewish believers and their concern for law-observant Jews in Gentile lands (verse 21). Even the Pharisaical party, though their theological argument was wrong, had a legitimate concern: if Gentile Christians in Gentile cities claimed to be 'right with God' but continued in certain practices that were highly offensive to sensitive Jews, these Jews would never accept the gospel. Certain accommodations were needed to ensure that Jews would not be stumbled by a gospel that embraced all people regardless of race. James' speech sorted out this problem.

Further, perhaps the most important thing to note about the way the Holy Spirit spoke is the sensitivity the Christians had to the Holy Spirit. Why is it that they sensed that the Holy Spirit was pleased with the outcome? Surely because there was first of all an openness to listen to the voice of God, a familiarity with the presence of the Holy Spirit in the normal gatherings of the church, and an awareness of the need to wait upon God. The Christians here did not seem to feel that the manifestation of the Spirit in this meeting was some extraordinary or unusual thing. The reason they felt confident to claim that the decision was from the Holy Spirit was because this was their normal experience.

Most modern Christians would consider it presumptuous to claim that a decision 'seemed good' to the Holy Spirit. The reason why most modern Christians would be reluctant to claim that the Holy Spirit had spoken in such a situation (apart from the fact that we do not have apostles with us today) is simply because we rarely have church meetings that are anywhere like this one where there is opportunity for God's people to freely participate, where everyone is listening carefully to the Spirit's voice, scrutinizing what different people say to test whether it comes from God or not. It rarely enters our head to think of God directing the outcome of a church meeting for the simple reason that *we* run our church meetings, not the Holy Spirit. We run our meetings according to our tried and trusted traditions and pre-arranged programs. Of course, sometimes we do hear from God, individually or collectively – He is a gracious God. But usually we simply proceed with our pre-arranged church programs, asking God to add His blessing. The result is that God is not really the One in charge, and only rarely do we really hear His voice, or sense His presence.

For these early Christians, however, it was all different. They were open to God's leadership and direction. That is why they patiently waited for and listened to God's Spirit as they are met together. That is why they sensed the Spirit's voice when it came.

Conclusion

In summary then, the Jerusalem council was a gathering at which multiple people spoke, a meeting that was not humanly-scripted, but through which the Holy Spirit directed His servants to a satisfactory conclusion. We, too, need to leave room and opportunity for the Spirit to speak in the church through whom He wills, and using the gifts that He chooses to manifest Himself through.

The Origins of Participatory Church Gatherings in the Gospels

Not only have we seen evidence of participatory church gatherings in the book of Acts; we can go even further back than this. If we look back into the Gospels, we see none of the pomp, pageantry, performance or programming of modern Christianity, but instead simplicity and informality. The Lord Jesus gathered his disciples around himself in a similar manner to a modern prayer, Bible study or discipleship group. In this setting there was no starched churchiness nor any liturgical order of service, but instead the freedom of perfect fellowship. There was no lecture-hall learning-style, but rather the interchange of questions and answers, the Lord gently instructing and correcting them.

The Archetypal Church Gathering

In fact, it is in the Gospels that we have the original and archetypal church gathering. That is, on the night in which He was betrayed, the Lord gathered his disciples around him and spent precious hours with them, sharing a meal and speaking to them about things they needed to know in view of His departure.

Here is how G. H. Lang describes this event: 'The simple and informal nature of the Supper is marked by the conversational feature of the occasion. That was naturally seen in the Passover feast, it being a family and social event. There was converse between Jesus and the disciples, and among themselves as to who would betray Him. They disputed with one another as to priority, which led the Lord to rebuke and warn them, and prompted Peter to protest that he was ready to die with Christ, causing the Lord to foretell his coming denial of the Master. There was further interchange of thought as to the matter of now taking purses and swords. A brief colloquy arose as to whether Peter's feet should be washed, and another between the Lord and Judas. While Christ was imparting the instruction recorded in John 14, Thomas interposed a remark and Philip added another, to which the other Judas shortly added a question. A little later (John 16:17ff.) the disciples are heard chatting over a difficulty they feel, and the Lord talks to them about it'[122].

If we place the three brief synoptic Gospel accounts of that evening alongside John's account, we observe that alongside the institution of what we call the Lord's Supper there was also an extended period of time given to teaching his disciples (John chapters 13-17). This teaching was not one long sermon, but was instead an interchange of thought as questions interrupted proceedings on a number of occasions, which the Lord proceeded to answer. Nor was this teaching restricted to 'devotional' topics (as some argue that the only sort of Bible teaching appropriate to the Lord's Supper is concerning the Person or Work of Christ). On the contrary, the teaching given on that night was very practical.

- The Lord spoke of the need for his followers to have their feet cleansed, that is, through the teaching of His Word (cf. John 13 and John 15:1-3).
- The Lord spoke of the need for his disciples to love one another (John 13:34).
- The Lord taught about the coming and work of the Holy Spirit (John 14)
- The Lord taught the secret of Christian fruitfulness: abiding in Him (John 15)
- The Lord taught about the Christian's witness in the world and the world's persecution of God's people (John 15:18 - 16:4)

The whole occasion was characterised by the sweetness of true fellowship and the joy of Christ's presence. How strange our church services would

---

[122] G. H. Lang, *The Churches of God: Their Constitution, Government, Discipline and Ministry*, London: Paternoster, 1959, pp75-6

seem to these disciples if they were to time-travel and stumble one Sunday morning into one of our modern carefully-crafted spiritual variety shows. How shocked they would be to see the sterile and cold ritualism of modern Christendom with people who hardly know each other sitting half-asleep in their pews, only ever looking at the backs of each other's heads. What a contrast with the warm and spontaneous fellowship that existed between Jesus and His disciples.

The biblical record of that archetypal church gathering presents us with a picture of the Lord Jesus among His disciples that is intended to be the basis for the church's gathering in every age. Few would argue that the Lord's Supper ceased (at some point of church history) to be of any further validity or importance. Nor would there be many who would claim that Bible teaching has no place in a church gathering. Nor would there be many who would forbid the singing of hymns (Matthew 26:30), nor intercessory prayer (John 17).

Nobody would dare argue against any of these elements of the church gathering. Why then should we feel that we might be able to improve on the atmosphere in which the original church gathering was held? This was a participatory, communal, fellowship where the perfect freedom of love bound them all together and linked them all with Christ their leader.

CHAPTER 8

PRINCIPLES UPON WHICH PARTICIPATORY CHURCH GATHERINGS ARE BASED

This chapter will look at seven general principles upon which participatory church gatherings are based.

1. The Work of the Holy Spirit

A clergyman and a Christian were talking on a train. The clergyman said, 'I tell my parishioners that they should do about spiritual things as they do about their groceries: go where they are best served. If the Methodist parson does them more good, let them go to him'.

The Christian disagreed and said that we ought to go to a church which does what the Lord has commanded. The clergyman replied, 'I don't think God has given instructions as to these matters. I believe He leaves us at liberty to do what we consider most suitable, and that we are justified in choosing accordingly'.

'On the contrary', said the Christian. 'I find the Word of God just as explicit about these things as it is about the way of salvation'.

'I should very much like you to show me where', said the clergyman.

So they opened their Bibles together in the train and turned to one passage after another. They saw how those who gladly received the Gospel were baptized and continued steadfastly in the apostles' doctrine, in fellowship with one another, in the breaking of bread and prayers (Acts 2:41-42); how disciples used to come together on the first day of the week to break bread (Acts 20:7); how that when gathered together all might contribute, one by one, to their mutual edification (1 Cor. 14:31,

32); how elders in each assembly were to feed the flock, looking for their reward when the Chief Shepherd shall appear (1 Peter 5:1-4).

Much more was considered. At last, as the journey was nearing its end, the clergyman said: 'I have been deeply interested in all you have said. It is very beautiful; indeed as a theory it seems perfect. But it appears to me that in practice it would need some supernatural power to make it work'.

'Undoubtedly', replied the Christian, 'that is just what it does need. What do you suppose that the Holy Spirit was given for?'[123]

Professor Arthur Rendle Short wrote about participatory church gatherings: 'Someone will say, "But will not things get into dreadful confusion if you seek to follow out these practices? In those days they had the Holy Spirit to guide them, and shall not we go wildly astray, and have dull, confused, unprofitable, perhaps even unseemly meetings, unless we get someone to take charge?"

'Is that not practically a denial of the Holy Spirit? Do we dare deny that the Holy Spirit is still being given? The Holy Spirit is at work today as much as He was at work in those days, and we may all join in that creed of all the churches: "I believe in the Holy Ghost".

'Please do not think that what is sometimes called the 'open-meeting' means that the saints are at the mercy of any unprofitable talker who thinks he has something to say, and would like to inflict himself upon them. The open meeting is not a meeting that is open to man. It is a meeting that is open to the Holy Spirit. There are some whose mouths must be stopped. Sometimes they have to be stopped by the godly admonition of those whom God has set over the assembly. But because there is failure in carrying out the principle, do not let us give up the principles of God'[124].

The work of the Holy Spirit in the book of Acts demonstrates not only the power of the Holy Spirit but the way that God works. Someone called Jeremy Taylor once said, 'Since the days of Pentecost, has the

---

[123] Harold P. Barker, *Christ's Vicar*, Easton: C. W. Beales, n.d., p221-2

[124] Arthur Rendle Short, *Young Believers and Assembly Life*, London: Pickering and Inglis, pp13-14, quoted in G. H. Lang, *The Churches of God*, London: Paternoster, 1959, p86

whole church ever put aside every other work and waited upon Him for ten days, that the Spirit's power might be manifested? We give too much attention to method and machinery and resources and too little to the source of the power'.

E. M. Bounds, the great man of prayer, wrote, 'What the church needs today is not more machinery or better, not new organizations or more and novel methods, but men whom the Holy Ghost can use – men of prayer, men mighty in prayer. The Holy Ghost does not flow through methods, but through men. He does not come on machinery, but on men. He does not anoint plans, but men – men of prayer'[125].

While we all say we believe in the Holy Spirit, it is possible for us to push the Holy Spirit to one side, while we try to build the church with our intelligence, our money, or our organisational skills. C. T. Studd said, 'How little chance the Holy Spirit has nowadays. The churches and missionary societies have so bound Him in red tape that they practically ask Him to sit in a corner while they do the work themselves'.

Sadly, the history of church life down through the centuries has been the story of attempts to substitute human organisation for the Spirit's fire. Arthur Wallis writes, 'In those early days, the manner of life of the believers, their church order and fellowship were marked by divine simplicity and spiritual power. As faith and spirituality waned the power of the Spirit was gradually withdrawn. Soon it became necessary to substitute human arrangements, which could be worked without the Spirit's power, for the divine arrangements, which were dependent upon that power. Thus by degrees the simple apostolic pattern ordained by the Spirit was abandoned in favour of the complex ways of man, and those concerned with the building up of the churches forgot the exhortation of God to Moses concerning His house, "See that thou make all things according to the pattern." Some asserted that God had revealed no pattern; others that the pattern did not matter, that every man could do that which was right in his own eyes. Since revivals bring a renewal of

---

[125] E. M. Bounds, *Power through Prayer*, Ch. 1, www.biblebelievers.com/em_bounds/index.html

the power of the Spirit, they are commonly accompanied by a return to the simple apostolic pattern'[126].

Instead of relying on the Holy Spirit's power and direction, it is possible for us to restrict and quench God's Spirit's activity within the church. This is what was happening in Micah's day: "'Do not prattle,' you say to those who prophesy. So they shall not prophesy to you; they shall not return insult for insult. You who are named the house of Jacob: "Is the Spirit of the LORD restricted? Are these His doings? Do not My words do good to him who walks uprightly?"' (Micah 2:6-7). God's servants the prophets had a message that they had to deliver. But they were told to be quiet and to cease their warnings. Similarly today, by programming affairs in God's House according to our own wisdom, we can limit opportunities for the Spirit of God to speak through His servants.

God's Spirit is compared in the Bible to the wind, for 'the wind blows where it wishes' (John 3:8). At Pentecost, one of the signs accompanying the coming of the Holy Spirit was 'the sound of a rushing, mighty wind' (Acts 2:2). There was no containing, controlling, restricting or stopping His activity. God's Spirit worked in people's lives to bring them to salvation, and He worked sovereignly amongst His people to build up the church.

A Church in which God's people are indwelt by the Spirit of the Lord should be characterised by freedom. Notice what 2 Cor. 3:17 says: 'Now the Lord is the Spirit, and where the Spirit of the Lord is, there is freedom'. There should be freedom – in the church of all places! – for the Holy Spirit to work. This includes freedom for those with spiritual gifts to freely use them, and thus to 'manifest the Spirit' (1 Cor. 12:7). Indeed, Hans Küng, the radical Roman Catholic liberal theologian, has turned this verse around and said, 'The Spirit of the Lord is absent where there is no liberty'[127].

---

[126] Arthur Wallis, *In the Day of Thy Power*, Alresford: Christian Literature Crusade, 1956, pp 91-92

[127] Hans Küng, *Why Priests?* London: William Collins Sons & Co, 1972, p21

By curtailing the spiritual freedom that rightly belongs to God's people we restrict the working of the Holy Spirit. All of God's people are indwelt by God's Spirit and, as such, have the ability and right to speak on God's behalf, as His messengers and spokesmen (i.e. prophets, Acts 2:17-18), for 'we have the mind of Christ' (1 Cor. 2:16).

W. E. Vine traces the rise of human organisation in the churches of the second century, particularly the offices of monarchical bishops, and puts it down to:

> a 'gross failure to recognize the prerogatives of the Spirit of God! According to the apostolic teaching "there are diversities of gifts but the same Spirit": "to each one is given the manifestation of the Spirit to profit withal. For to one is given through the Spirit the word of wisdom; and to another the word of knowledge, according to the same Spirit." All gifts are wrought by "the one and the same Spirit, dividing to each one severally even as the Spirit will" (1 Cor. 12:4-11). Further, oral ministry in the church, instead of being confined on any given occasion to one individual, was open for the leading of the Spirit of God, so that it might be exercised by one and another of those to whom He had imparted spiritual gifts for the edification of the church (1 Cor. 14:29-33). So in the epistle to the Ephesians, "unto each one of us was the grace given, according to the measure of the gift of Christ," who gave "some to be apostles; and some prophets; and some evangelists; and some, pastors and teachers; for the perfecting of the saints, unto the work of ministering, unto the building up of the body of Christ." This exercise of the variety of gifts in the church, instead of being a temporary arrangement for apostolic times, was to continue "till we all [that is, the whole Church, the body of Christ] attain unto the unity of the faith, and of the knowledge of the Son of God, unto a full-grown man, unto the measure of the stature of Christ" (Eph. 4:7-13)'[128].

---

[128] W. E. Vine, "The Origin and Rise of Ecclesiasticism and the Papal System", *The Collected Writings of W. E. Vine*, Vol. 4., Nashville, TN: Thomas Nelson, 1996, p359-60

A 19th-century missionary to India, George Bowen, wrote, 'On successive Sabbaths ... we visit various churches. We ... hear the sermon that is preached and observe the worship that is rendered to God. Again we worship with those of another denomination ... At length we come to a worshipping body whose customs are so fundamentally different from those of the churches previously visited that the differences among the latter appear to be quite trifling. In the church we have stumbled upon (the church at Corinth) instead of one man officiating for all, while all sit silent save when they sing or make common responses, and where everything is arranged to exclude as much as possible anything like spontaneousness, we find that when the members come together, "everyone has a psalm .. a doctrine .. a tongue .. a revelation" ... May we not learn from this that the Holy Spirit loves a larger liberty than is accorded by our arrangements? ... Is it not possible that the apostle Paul, coming into one of our staid and orderly churches, would look upon the whole of the decorous and tasteful service as one unmitigated abuse? He would, perhaps, say, Is the Holy Ghost dead, that you make no provision for his manifestation? Is there no communion of the saints in the assemblies of the saints?'[129].

Does the 'freedom of the Spirit' characterise your church? Is your church characterised by the fire of God's Spirit or the machinery of men? Is there room for the Holy Spirit in your church, or would it be more true to say that your church is characterised by the cleverness, organisation, ability and energy of human beings?

2. Spiritual Gifts

There are four main passages in the New Testament dealing with spiritual gifts: Romans 12:6-8, 1 Cor. 12-14, Eph. 4:7-16 and 1 Pet. 4:10-11. These passages teach three general lessons.

Firstly, spiritual gifts are not the possession of the clergyman, or of a few select saints, but of all believers. Romans 12:6 says, 'Having then gifts differing according to the grace that is given to us'. 1 Cor. 12:7 says,

---

[129] George Bowen, 'Daily Meditations', quoted in G. H. Lang, *The Churches of God*, p81

'the manifestation of the Spirit is given *to each one* for the profit of all'. Eph. 4:7 says, 'but *to each one* of us grace was given according to the measure of Christ's gift'. 1 Peter 4:10 says, 'As *each one* has received a gift, minister it to one another as good stewards of the manifold grace of God'.

Donald Grey Barnhouse, commenting on Romans 12, writes: 'A great error in our modern way of doing things is to expect one man to possess all the necessary gifts for leadership. Thus, a church may have several hundred members but only one pastor. He is supposed to be able to preach, comfort and so on. In fact, of the eight gifts mentioned in our text (Rom. 12:6-8) seven are usually considered to be the functions of the ordained minister, while the eighth is the function of the congregation. And what one gift is left to the congregation? It is that of paying the bills. Something is out of order here. Someone may ask if I am suggesting that laymen should preach. Without question, when a layman has a grasp of the Scriptures he should exercise his gift and preach at every opportunity. The growth of laymen's movements is significant and is a step in the right direction – back to the New Testament way of doing things'[130].

Secondly, there is a great variety of spiritual gifts. Romans 12 mentions eight gifts, 1 Cor. 12:8-11 mentions nine (and the other gift-list at the end of chapter 12 mentions another four, and in chapters 12-14 there are about twenty different spiritual gifts mentioned), Eph. 4:11 mentions five, and 1 Peter 4:10-11 mentions the two broad categories of speaking and serving gifts.

Alan Cole (commenting on the great variety of gifts and ministries of the Spirit in 1 Cor. 12:4ff) says, 'Perhaps there has been no greater folly in the Church down the ages than the steady attempt to 'standardize' the ministry, leading to repeated refusals to make room for those to whom the Spirit has given gifts that do not fit into our tidy ready-made patterns ... what we have done is to confine the ministry to one or two of the Spirit's channels, instead of enjoying the many-sided

---

[130] Donald Grey Barnhouse, *The Measure of Your Faith*, Bible Study Hour Broadcasts, Book 69, Evangelical Foundation, Inc., 1957, p21

richness of his giving. Our limiting of the idea of 'ministry' to the regular work of ordained office-bearers is indeed calculated to quench the Spirit in our churches'[131].

In modern evangelical churches there is a shrinking gift-pool due to the increasing professionalization of Christian ministry. Large churches will hire staff to do all the jobs that need doing, and the result is that the gifts of large numbers of people are allowed to atrophy and wither. Teaching is virtually the only sort of spiritual gift used in modern evangelical churches. Other gifts are still present and occasionally evident – serving, showing mercy, giving, leading – but people seem to be less and less inclined to use these gifts of their own accord. People have to be dragooned into serving God, and appeals for help with various 'serving' tasks (helping set up, etc.) are becoming more frequent. The modern attitude is that people 'turn up, pay up and shut up'. But even the turning up is becoming less frequent, and the paying up is down. What a contrast with the effervescence of the early Christians as seen, for example, in the spiritual giftedness at Corinth. Handley Moule said he would rather tone down a fanatic than resurrect a corpse, and in many churches today the body of Christ is almost in a coma.

Thirdly, the New Testament exhorts individual Christians to use their spiritual gifts. 1 Peter 4:10 says, 'as each one has received a gift, minister it to one another'. Romans 12:6-8 says, 'Having then gifts differing according to the grace that is given to us, *let us use them*: if prophecy, in proportion to our faith ...'. The words in italics are not present in the underlying Greek, but they are implied, for the instructions that follow set out the way in which the gifts should be used.

The exhortation to use spiritual gifts implies that individual Christians are responsible for using their God-given gifts. This is most obvious in the case of prophecy where a person speaks as prompted – not by a request from the elders or some committee – but by the Holy Spirit. The person prophesying is specifically told to do so 'in proportion to faith' – according as the prophet's faith permits him to speak. But the

---

[131] Alan Cole, *The Body of Christ: A New Testament Image of the Church*, London: Hodder and Stoughton, 1964, pp44-45

principle applies equally to the gifts of exhortation, or giving, or leading, or showing mercy (12:8). These gifts are the individual and instinctive responses of people whose hearts burn with a desire to do something for the Lord and because of their concern for people around about them. Christians using these gifts are self-motivating (or Spirit-motivated); they see a need and cannot help but try to meet that need. They are not usually the sorts of gifts exercised only when someone has been asked by another. Instead, they involve people rising up and willingly taking the initiative.

Nowhere in the New Testament are elders or other Christian leaders said to be responsible for organising people so that they identify and use their gifts. There were no 'spiritual gift seminars' in the early church. Instead, the exhortations for Christians to use their gifts imply that individual Christians are personally responsible. Since some of these gifts mentioned are most prominently used in the church gatherings, we conclude that Christians are expected to participate of their own volition in the church gatherings, not in response to an invitation from the church planning committee, or to fill a slot in a church program. The early church seems to have been characterised by people rising up and prophesying, teaching and exhorting each other without the need (or mention) of others asking them to do so. They did so because their hearts were on fire for the Lord.

Stephen Short, commenting on 1 Cor. 12, summarises the matter (note especially his last line, and by implication, its application to all gifts): '1 Cor. 12:8 states: 'To one is given by the Spirit the word of wisdom; to another the word of knowledge by the same Spirit'. Both of these gifts, manifestly, were gifts of utterance (and we can remind ourselves in this connection how that Paul told these people in 1:5, that, as a church, God had 'enriched' them in gifts of utterance). The 'word' of wisdom, demonstrably, was the ability to communicate wisdom, whereas the 'word of knowledge' was the ability to communicate knowledge; and what, tentatively, one would suggest is that the Christian with the word of 'knowledge' is the one who is gifted at expounding the contents of the Bible, whereas the Christian with the word of 'wisdom' is the one who is gifted at applying the contents of the Bible – (much, indeed, as the 'teacher' and the 'exhorter' of Rom. 12). *And if both gifts have been divinely provided, liberty should be provided, surely, for both to be exercised*[132].

3. Mutual Edification

In the New Testament there are over fifty 'one another' commands and statements like 'love one another' (John 13:34), 'serve one another' (Gal. 5:13), 'bear one another's burdens' (Gal. 6:2), 'be kind to one another ... forgiving one another' (Eph. 4:32), 'encourage one another' (Hebrews 3:13), and 'be hospitable to one another' (1 Pet. 4:9). These 'one another' commands emphasize that church life involved caring fellowship and mutual encouragement; not only receiving but also giving. The numerous 'one another' references are significant in that it is not said to be the responsibility of the Pastor, or the elders, to foster genuine fellowship among the believers. Instead, it is the responsibility of each and every individual Christians one toward another.

In his book *Body Life*, Ray Stedman writes: 'What is terribly missing in all too many churches is the experience of "body life" - that warm fellowship of Christian with Christian which the New Testament calls *koinonia*, and which was an essential part of early Christianity. The New Testament lays heavy emphasis upon the need for Christians to know each other, closely and intimately enough to be able to bear one another's burdens, confess faults one to another, encourage, exhort, and admonish one another; and minister to one another with the Word, song and prayer. As we carry out the various "one another" ministries of New Testament-style body life, we will come to comprehend "with all the saints", as the apostle Paul says, "what is the breadth and length and height and depth, and to know the love of Christ which surpasses knowledge" (Ephesians 3:18-19)'[133].

Included in these 'one another' commands are the following instructions that would normally relate to spoken gifts used in the church gatherings:

---

[132] Stephen S. Short, "The Ministry of the Word", *The Witness*, Jan 1965, p7 (emphasis added)

[133] Ray Stedman, *Body Life*, Discovery House Publishers, 1995, p151

- 'teaching one another' (Col. 3:16)
- 'admonishing (or instructing) one another' (Col. 3:16 and Rom. 15:14)
- 'comforting one another' (1 Thess. 5:11)
- 'edifying one another' (1 Thess. 5:11), and
- 'washing one another's feet' (John 13:14, which we learn from the Lord's own words in John 15:1-3, 'You are already clean because of the word which I have spoken to you', refers not so much to the physical activity of foot-washing, or even to humble service, but to the spiritual ministry of cleansing defilement through 'the washing of water by the word', see Eph. 5:26)
- in Hebrews 10:24-25, we read, 'Let us consider one another to stir up love and good works, not forsaking the assembling of ourselves together, as is the manner of some, but exhorting *one another*, and so much the more as you see the Day approaching'. The second 'one another' is in italics because it is not in the original, but the words are implied by the first reference to 'one another', by the emphasis upon unity and togetherness, and by the words 'assembling of ourselves together'. Virtually every English translation uses 'one another' or 'each other'. Whereas Heb. 3:13 say to 'encourage (or exhort) one another daily', in Heb. 10, exhorting one another is set in contrast with forsaking the assembling of ourselves together, and we may conclude that the exhorting one another privately in day to day life (of Heb. 3) is to be carried over into exhorting one another publicly in the church gatherings in Heb. 10.

These activities involve spiritually sharing together the things concerning the Lord in the church gatherings – the normal setting for teaching, edifying and exhorting.

Elton Trueblood, writing in *The Company of the Committed*, wrote, 'The key words are "one another". There are no mere observers or auditors; all are involved. Each is in the ministry; each needs the advice of the others; and each has something to say to the others. The picture of mutual admonition seems strange to modern man, but the strangeness is only a measure of our essential decline from something of amazing power'[134].

Some might argue that these 'one another' commands do not apply to a church setting. However, once we place these 'one another' commands alongside what the New Testament elsewhere uniformly teaches about participatory church gatherings, it is clear that the church gathering is where this mutual edification and encouragement happened. We are to share the lessons we have learned in our own lives, to comfort others by the comfort we have received from the Lord and to teach each other from the Word of God.

4. The Priesthood of All Believers

In the New Testament, all Christians are priests. Rev. 1:6 and 5:10 speak about us being made a 'kingdom of priests'. Similarly, 1 Peter 2:5 says 'you also, as living stones, are being built up a spiritual house, a holy priesthood, to offer up spiritual sacrifices acceptable to God through Jesus Christ'. A few verses later, in 1 Peter 2:9, we read, 'But you are a chosen generation, a royal priesthood, a holy nation, His own special people, that you may proclaim the praises of Him who called you out of darkness into His marvellous light'.

The most important book in the New Testament about the priesthood of all believers is the Epistle to the Hebrews. There (and only there) are we told that Christ is our Great High (or literally, Chief) Priest (Hebrews 3:1; 4:14,15; 5:10; 6:20; 7:26; 8:1; 9:11; 10:21). This would seem to imply that under Christ there exist other priests, over which He is the chief, but it is not until we come to Hebrews 8 that we find out more about who these other priests are. The writer's argument, particularly in chapters 8 to 10, draws a contrast between the 'service' or 'ministry' carried on under the Old Covenant with that of the New Covenant. The word 'service' or 'ministry' used here is *latreia* (and its verb *latreuo*), and in the context it becomes clear that the service referred to is religious service, and particularly that of priests. Thus, in Heb. 8:4-5

---

[134] Elton Trueblood, *The Company of the Committed*, New York: Harper and Row, 1961, p32

we read that on earth the Old Testament priests, 'serve (*latreuo*) the copy and shadow of the heavenly things' (i.e. in the tabernacle). Heb. 9:1 says, 'Then indeed, even the first covenant had regulations of *service* and the earthly sanctuary' and verse 6 says, 'Now when these things had been thus prepared, the priests always went into the first part of the tabernacle, performing the *services*'. Again, in verse 9, we have yet another reference to the 'service' of the OT priests: 'in which both gifts and sacrifices were offered which cannot make him performed the *service* perfect in regard to the conscience'.

But in Heb. 9:14, we have an astonishing statement setting out the service of the Christian: 'how much more shall the blood of Christ, who through the Eternal Spirit offered Himself without spot to God, cleanse your conscience from dead works to serve (*latreuo*) the Living God'. It is obvious here, from the repeated use of the word 'service' in relation to the Old Testament priestly service in the build-up to this verse, that all those who are cleansed from sin, i.e. all New Testament saints, are called to perform a service which is equated with its Old Testament counterpart, the work of the priests in the earthly tabernacle.

In short, all Christians are to perform priestly service. In Heb. 12:28 we read, 'Therefore, since we are receiving a kingdom which cannot be shaken, let us have grace, by which we may *serve* God acceptably with reverence and godly fear'. Finally, in Heb. 13:10-16, we are presented with a final contrast – between the Old priests who '*serve* the tabernacle' and the Christian who is called to offer priestly sacrifices: 'Therefore by Him let us continually offer the sacrifice of praise to God, that is, the fruit of our lips, giving thanks to His name. But do not forget to do good and to share, for with such sacrifices, God is well pleased'.

W. H. Griffith-Thomas wrote, 'The truth, therefore, is that Christianity *is*, not *has*, a priesthood'[135]. T. C. Hammond writes, 'Scripture asserts that Christians as a whole constitute a priesthood (1 Peter 2:5). Scholars are agreed that sacerdotal [i.e. priestly] terms are not discoverable in Christian writers until the close of the second century. . . .

---

[135] W. H. Griffith-Thomas, *The Principles of Theology*, London: Church Book Room Press, 1956, p316

The idea of a distinction between the ministry and other Christians, leading to the setting up of a clerical 'caste', is unknown to Scripture. The word clergy (derived from *kleros*) indicates Christians as a whole and not an aristocracy in the Church (cf. Acts 26:18)'[136].

Thus, the concept of the priesthood of all believers is affirmed in the New Testament. There is no mediatorial class of Christians who stand in a higher relationship to God than other believers. There is no such thing as a clergy/laity division in the New Testament. The question for us is whether our churches show the practical reality of the doctrine of the priesthood of all believers?

Lawrence Richards writes, 'Luther proclaimed the priesthood of all believers; nearly 500 years later church forms still deny it'[137]. G. D. Fee writes 'Although most Protestants in theory deny apostolic succession to reside in its clergy, *de facto* it is practiced in vigorous and sometimes devastating ways - in the "one-man show" of many denominational churches or in the little dictatorships in other (especially "independent") churches. And how did such a pluralism of papacies emerge? Basically from two sources (not to mention the fallenness of the clergy whose egos often love such power): (a) from the fact that the local pastor is so often seen (and often sees him/herself) as the authoritative interpreter of the "sole authority" - Scripture; (b) from the pastor's functioning in the role of authority, thus assuming the mantle of Paul or of a Timothy or Titus'[138].

Protestant Christianity repudiated the Roman Catholic Church's theology of mediatorial offices, rites and works that gave people access to God (Mary, saints, priests, Mass, penance, payments, good deeds). It retained, however, the Roman Catholic clergy/laity division by which the Protestant clergyman alone was authorised to administer the sacraments

---

[136] T. C. Hammond, *In Understanding Be Men*, London: Inter-Varsity Fellowship,1954, p168

[137] Lawrence O. Richards, *A New Face for the Church*, Grand Rapids, MI: Zondervan, 1970, p38

[138] G. D. Fee, "Reflections on Church Order in the Pastoral Epistles, with Further Reflection on the Hermeneutics of *Ad Hoc* Documents", *JETS* 28/2 (June 1985), p149

and preach the Word. The Church of England's Thirty-nine articles reads, 'It is not lawful for any man to take upon him the office of public preaching, or ministering the Sacraments in the Congregation, before he be lawfully called and sent to execute the same' (Art. 23). Similarly the Westminster Confession of Faith (followed by Presbyterian and Reformed churches) states, 'There be only two sacraments ordained by Christ our Lord in the gospel, that is to say, Baptism, and the Supper of the Lord; neither of which may be dispensed by any but by a minister of the word, lawfully ordained' (27.4). Such sacerdotal ideas find no basis in New Testament scripture.

There is little need to elaborate on the connection between the priesthood of all believers and participatory church gatherings. In the New Testament, the priesthood of all believers was a glorious reality, not a shallow slogan, for one of the rights the believers enjoyed was to use their gifts publicly in the church gatherings for edification.

5. Church Government

It is generally agreed that there are three main forms of Church Government today: episcopalian, presbyterian and congregational. Episcopalian church government involves rule by a bishop (Greek: *episkopos*) over a number of churches. Under the bishop there are priests and deacons. While Episcopalian church government has three orders of ministry (bishops, priests and deacons), it is generally agreed by most evangelicals that in the New Testament there were only two orders of government – elders (also called bishops or overseers and shepherds or pastors) and deacons. The bishop (*episkopos*) and elder (*presbyteros*) were synonymous descriptions of the same office in New Testament times (see Acts 20:17 and 28, 1 Peter 5:1-2, and Titus 1:5, 7). Even most Anglican commentators agree with this. Thus, J. B. Lightfoot writes, 'It has been shown that in the apostolic writings the two [elders and bishops] are only different designations of one and the same office'[139]. Similarly, W. H. Griffith-Thomas writes, 'There is abundant proof that the terms and

---

[139] J. B. Lightfoot, "The Christian Ministry", *The Epistles of St. Paul: Philippians*, 4th Ed., London: Macmillan and Co., 1879, p193

offices of Bishops and Presbyters were interchanged until at least the time of Clement of Alexandria' – that is till towards the end of the 2nd Century[140]. The New Testament does not present to us a hierarchical form of church organisation like that which later developed under the Episcopalian model.

Instead, the churches we read of in the New Testament were governed by a council of elders (presbyters), and were thus presbyterian. Evidence for the plurality of local church leaders is found throughout the New Testament: in Acts 11:30, 14:23, 15:2, 4, 6, 22, 23, 16:4, 20:17, 20:28, 21:18, Phil. 1:1, 1 Thess. 5:12-13, 1 Tim. 4:14, 5:17, Titus 1:5, Hebrews 13:7, 17, 24, 1 Peter 5:1, and James 5:14. Nowhere does the New Testament teach that an overseer (bishop) or pastor (i.e. shepherd) is a different person or office to that of an elder, nor is any single Priest, President, Minister, (Senior) Pastor, Teaching-Pastor, Teaching-Elder or other sole dignitary or figurehead anywhere mentioned or greeted in any of the letters to the churches. They simply did not exist in biblical churches.

However, the New Testament also presents evidence for a congregational form of church government. Congregationalism in the New Testament is visible in two main features. The first feature of congregational church government is autonomy (that is, self-government) under Christ. There was no over-arching organisation that provided a control-and-command centre for the churches. The unity of the churches in the New Testament was spiritual rather than organisational via some sort of confederation. Nowhere do we find any supra-congregational body: there are no letters written to archbishops, synods or general assemblies. Instead, the Lord Jesus Christ is the Head of the church (Eph. 1:22, 4:15; 5:23; Col. 1:18; 2:19) and His body has no earthly headquarters; its Head is in Heaven. Evidence for the autonomy of local churches is seen in Revelation 1-3, where we read of 'the seven churches in Asia' (they are not collectively addressed as 'the church of Asia'), each of which is symbolised by an individual lampstand

---

[140] W. H. Griffith-Thomas, *The Principles of Theology*, London: Church Book Room Press, 1956, p325

(not one lampstand with seven branches), and each of which is individually addressed by the Lord either in admonition or encouragement[141].

Not only is the local church autonomous in relation to other churches (i.e. free of outside control), it is also autonomous in relation to its own internal affairs, and responsible for the management of its own business. Crucially, it is the congregation – not its leaders – which is given authority over certain aspects of church government. It is the congregation which has the right to excommunicate (Matt. 18:17, 1 Cor. 5:2, 2 Cor. 2:5-6), not the elders alone. The congregation also has the right to welcome and receive new members (for the right of the congregation to dis-fellowship trumps the right of anyone else to admit someone without the congregation's approval). The congregation has the right to govern what happens with its money (Acts 6:3, 5) via the appointment of deacons – after all, it is the congregation's money they are distributing! Finally, 1 Thess. 5:12-13 tells the congregation to 'recognise those who labour among you, and are over you in the Lord …', and this verse not only encourages the congregation to approve those who are worthily exercising leadership, but implies also that the congregation should be able to express reservations about someone who is unfit to be appointed as an elder on moral, doctrinal or other spiritual grounds. This is because it is a sound principle, observed in the secular sphere as much as in the spiritual, that it is impossible to lead without the consent of those who are being led.

A second feature of congregational government in the New Testament emerges from the evidence of participatory church gatherings: the congregation is given a voice in the church gatherings. In the New Testament, the pulpit (or the microphone) was not controlled by a priest or minister, or by the elders, or by a committee, or by some external

---

[141] There is only one possible reference in the New Testament to a group of churches addressed as a united whole – 'the church throughout all Judea and Galilee and Samaria had peace, etc.' (Acts 9:31, ESV), but the manuscripts here are divided, and the fact that the vast majority of manuscripts read 'the *churches* throughout all Judea …' (as in the KJV) renders the concept of any organisational unity doubtful.

accrediting authority that trained and sent out suitable ministers. Instead, individual Christians had the right to use their spiritual gifts in the church. The church gatherings were a place where Christ's leadership of the church was exercised through the activity of the Holy Spirit speaking through the members of the body. This is not to say that the elders had no role to play. As in every other aspect of church life, the elders should take the lead in the church gatherings.

This second feature of congregational government (participatory church gatherings) explains why the congregation was given such far-reaching rights and powers in relation to the self-government of the church. The rights to excommunicate and receive, particularly, cannot be exercised without a godly, sound-minded and well-taught body of Christians. Where would we find, or how should we develop, such a body of Christians? The reason why the New Testament entrusts such responsibilities to the congregation of ordinary Christians is because it also envisages maturity among ordinary disciples through the development of spiritual gifts, scriptural knowledge and godly discernment, all of which are products of interactive church gatherings.

What shall we say about the government of New Testament churches? Were they presbyterian or congregational? Some would argue that the evidence is confused and contradictory – certain scriptures indicate a presbyterian model and others a congregational model. However, the answer is that the churches of the New Testament were *both presbyterian and congregational*. These are complementary rather than contradictory truths. Churches in the New Testament were elder-led with congregational participation.

This prevented excessive power flowing either to the leadership, with elders acting as lords instead of servant examples, avoiding the peril of an overly controlling eldership ('the dictatorship of the eldership'). At the other extreme, the biblical picture of eldership prevents excessive power flowing to the congregation, resulting in chaotic and leaderless anarchy. The biblical balance of power instead shows evidence of divine wisdom.

6. Body Life

The New Testament repeatedly pictures the church as a body, with Christ as its head.

- Romans 12:4-5 – 'For as we have many members in one body, but all the members do not have the same function, so we, *being* many, are one body in Christ, and individually members of one another'.
- 1 Corinthians 12:12 says, 'For as the body is one and has many members, but all the members of that one body, being many, are one body, so also is Christ'.
- Ephesians 1:22-23 says, 'And He put all things under His feet, and gave Him to be head over all things to the church, which is His body, the fullness of Him who fills all in all'.
- Colossians 2:19 (and Eph. 4:15-16 likewise) says, 'and not holding fast to the Head, from whom all the body, nourished and knit together by joints and ligaments, grows with the increase that is from God'.

The New Testament teaches three main truths in relation to the body. Firstly, the body teaches the unity of believers – we all belong together. Secondly, the body teaches the diversity of believers – we each have different gifts. Thirdly, and for present purposes the most important, the truth of the body teaches that we are all meant to participate, like the members in a human body; we are all necessary for the healthy functioning of the church. Each member is significant and important.

There are two particular problems Paul addresses in 1 Corinthians 12:15-26 in relation to the body. Firstly we read about some people who had a spiritual inferiority complex in verses 15 to 19. These sorts of people say 'because I'm not the eye, I'm not part of the body'. They think "I'm no good for anything" because they don't have certain spiritual gifts. This problem is approaching epidemic proportions nowadays – lots of Christians are unsure about their gifts, and lots of Christians are doing very little for God in the church or outside.

Bear in mind, too, that performing a job using a natural talent is not the same as using a spiritual gift. Someone strumming a guitar is not using a spiritual gift, nor is arranging flowers for a display, nor is it a spiritual gift to press some buttons on a computer or other electronic device in a church service. These are not spiritual gifts, although the attitude of humble service that motivates someone to perform such tasks is a spiritual gift. But even in a modern megachurch, there can only be so many people who act as ushers or musicians – and a large percentage of the rest of the congregation end up doing nothing, exercising no gifts at all. This is not what the church in the New Testament is meant to be like.

The second problem that Paul deals with is found in 1 Cor. 12:20-26. Here is the person with the spiritual superiority complex. This person thinks, "I'm too good for these people", or "I can get on fine without these people". Paul's advice in verses 25 &26 is that we should care for others, not adopt an attitude of superiority.

Do we have this second problem today? Yes, church life in the wider evangelical world is drifting ever closer to a Roman Catholic model of ministry where a few priestly professionals put on a performance for the laity seated in large auditoriums. Christianity was not meant to be a spectator sport. Of course we want good meetings, but it is wrong if we tell people they are not good enough to speak in church, so only superstars can participate.

Mind you, the same thing can happen with other gifts. Some people handle hospitality so professionally that no one else is allowed to touch it – they would just mess it all up. Such a superiority attitude can hurt Christian unity, and it can stop development and growth of others in their use of gifts. The two problems, inferiority and superiority, go together. Some people are full of excuses about why they can't possibly serve God, and others are so capable that they end up doing everything. However, such superstars only have a limited life-span; if they don't allow others to develop, the day will come when there is no one ready and able to take their place.

7. The Lordship of Jesus Christ

One last principle that the New Testament teaches is the Lordship of Jesus Christ over the church. This principle aligns with the truth of the body: Christ is the head of the church. This is seen in the verses quoted earlier in relation to the body (Eph. 1:21-22, 4:15-16, Col. 2:19) as well as Eph. 5:23 ('Christ is the head of the church'), and Col. 1:18 ('He is the head of the body, the church').

The lordship of Jesus Christ means three things, one negative, one positive, and one practical. Negatively, the lordship of Jesus Christ in the church means that no other person should be in charge of the church. The Lord Jesus said, 'But you, do not be called 'Rabbi'; for One is your Teacher, the Christ, and you are all brethren. Do not call anyone on earth your father; for One is your Father, He who is in heaven. And do not be called teachers (lit. 'leaders, guides'); for One is your Teacher (lit. 'leader, guide'), the Christ' (Matt. 23:8-10).

In his letter to the Colossians, Paul not only taught that Christ is the head of the church, but he warned the Colossians about people coming in trying to take Christ's place as Lord in the church. In Col. 2:8 Paul writes, 'Beware lest any man spoil you (or, carry you off as plunder; ESV, NASB, NIV: take you captive) through philosophy and vain deceit, after the tradition of men, after the rudiments of the world, and not according to Christ' (KJV). Men were trying to take control of the church so that it became their personal property and fiefdom.

Ray Stedman writes in his book *Body Life* about worldly authority structures with their kings, presidents, governors, generals and secretaries, and reminds us that Jesus said, 'It shall not be so among you' (Mark 10:43). Yet despite these words, down through time, the Christian church has borrowed from these worldly power structures, changed the titles to popes, patriarchs, bishops, pastors and deacons, 'and gone merrily on its way, lording it over the laity and destroying the model of servanthood that our Lord intended'.

Stedman continues, 'In most churches today, an unthinking acceptance has been given to the idea that the pastor is the final voice of authority in both doctrine and practice, and that he is the executive officer of the church with respect to administration. But surely, if a pope over the whole church is bad, a pope in every church is no better'[142].

---

[142] Ray Stedman, *Body Life*, 1995, p110

Christ is the head of the church. He is the only Chief Priest (Heb. 3:1, etc.), Senior Pastor (see 1 Peter 5:4), or leading brother (Heb. 2:11-12) that the New Testament shows any knowledge of.

Secondly, in positive terms, Christ's lordship means that He governs and control His church. How does this happen? In the New Testament, Christ directed the church through the Holy Spirit. We see the Holy Spirit's direction of the missionary movement in Acts 8 (Philip), Acts 13 (Barnabus and Paul started their first missionary journey) and Acts 16 (the Holy Spirit forbad Paul going to certain places). Equally significant are the ways the Holy Spirit directed the church in Antioch to send relief to the poor saints in Jerusalem (see Acts 11:28) and the Holy Spirit brought resolution to the issue of whether Gentiles needed to be circumcised: 'It has seemed good to the Holy Spirit and to us to lay upon you no greater burden than these necessary things' (Acts 15:28). In the letters to the seven churches in Asia (Revelation 2-3), the Lord Jesus dictated a message for each of the churches, but at the end of each church's message, we read, 'He who has an ear, let him hear what *the Spirit* says to the churches' (Rev. 2:7, 11, 17, 29, 3:6, 13, 22).

Thus, the way that Christ directed His church in the New Testament was through the Holy Spirit, and the normal way that the Holy Spirit works is through His people, through the use of our spiritual gifts, because our use of spiritual gifts is a 'manifestation' of the Holy Spirit (1 Cor. 12:7). As we see in Acts 15, the Holy Spirit's voice was clearly heard through the cumulative effect of various speakers discussing the situation at hand interactively with an attitude of expectant submission to what the Lord wished to say through the Spirit to the churches.

Thirdly, in very practical terms, Christ is seen to be Lord in the church by the place we give Him. Are we singing songs and hymns about ourselves or about Him? Are we preaching about our 'felt needs' or are we preaching Christ crucified? Are we giving Christ His rightful place as Lord in the church by remembering Him at the *Lord's* Supper? By remembering Christ in the breaking of the bread and sharing of the cup, Christ becomes the centre of the church's gathering and our thoughts about Him set the tone for the entire meeting.

Still today, then, Christ is Lord. He governs and guides his church through the Holy Spirit. In turn, the Holy Spirit works through His people whom He indwells, gifts, empowers and through whom He speaks. In turn, our participation in the church should be Christ-focused.

Hear the words of A. W. Tozer in his article, *Pragmatism Goes to Church*: 'We must acknowledge the right of Jesus Christ to control the activities of His church. The New Testament contains full instructions, not only about what we are to believe but what we are to do and how we are to go about doing it. Any deviation from those instructions is a denial of the Lordship of Christ. I say the answer is simple, but it is not easy for it requires that we obey God rather than man, and that brings down the wrath of the religious majority. It is not a question of knowing what to do; we can easily learn that from the Scriptures. It is a question of whether or not we have the courage to do it'[143].

---

[143] A. W. Tozer, "Pragmatism Goes to Church", *God Tells the Man Who Cares*, in *The Best of Tozer* Book Two, Grand Rapids, MI: Baker, 1980, p256

CHAPTER 9

OBJECTIONS TO PARTICIPATORY CHURCH GATHERINGS

Here are ten biblical and theological objections to participatory church gatherings. We will look at practical objections in a later chapter.

Didn't Paul Preach till Midnight at Troas?

If participatory church gatherings were the uniform practice of the early churches, then why do we read that Paul preached till midnight at Troas? Acts 20:7 reads: 'Now on the first day of the week, when we were gathered together to break bread, Paul, ready to depart on the next day, spoke to them and continued his message until midnight'.

This objection largely revolves around one word: Paul *preached* till midnight. True enough, some translations do use the word 'preached'. Thus, the New Jerusalem Bible says 'Paul preached a sermon that went on till the middle of the night'. The New Living Translation reads, 'Paul was preaching to them, and since he was leaving the next day, he kept talking until midnight'. However, these versions are taking some liberties in their translation of this word 'preached'.

In contrast with these translations, notice how the following versions translate this word:

- New Revised Standard Version: 'Paul was holding a discussion with them'
- The RV (and Darby): 'Paul discoursed with them',
- The ESV reads, 'Paul talked with them'.

In Greek, the verb being used here is *dialegomai*. This word carries quite a wide range of meaning. At one end of the spectrum there are verses like Acts 17:4 where we read that Paul in Athens '*reasoned* in the synagogue with the Jews ... and in the marketplace daily with those who he met there'. Now, it might possibly be argued that Paul was preaching sermons in the synagogue, but he could hardly have been doing the same thing in the marketplace, yet the same word covers both situations. It is more reasonable to think that both in the synagogue and in the marketplace, it was more of a debate that Paul was engaged in.

Another example is in Mark 9:34 where we read that the disciples 'on the road ... had been *arguing* among themselves who was the greatest'. It is hard to imagine them 'preaching sermons' about who was the greatest as they walked along the road. The words 'discussing' or 'conversing' do not even seem strong enough to capture the meaning here. Likewise, in Jude 1:9, we read that Michael was '*disputing* with the Devil over the body of Moses'. It is unlikely that the Devil, normally so quick to get His word in, was silent while Michael preached a sermon to him.

At the other end of the spectrum, this word sometimes simply means 'speak', such as in Hebrews 12:5 which reads, 'you have forgotten the exhortation which *speaks* to you as sons, "My son, do not despise the chastening of the LORD ..."'. However, even here there is the overtone of the 'to-and-fro' of discussion involved in parental discipline.

Most of the references to the word *dialegomai* in the NT are connected with Paul's evangelising in the synagogues. Paul's normal *modus operandi* was to go into the synagogues and preach Christ, however, he was inevitably met with opposition and argument. Thus, the word could be translated as 'dialoguing' or 'discussing' (Acts 19:9), 'arguing', 'reasoning' (Acts 18:19, 24:25) or 'disputing' (Acts 24:12).

It is not coincidental that *dialegomai* resembles our English word 'dialogue', for the meaning of the two words is quite similar. Thus, it seems quite reasonable to conclude that Paul was discussing as much as he was preaching that night at Troas.

In summary, the description of the scene in Troas is similar to that of the Lord Jesus in the Upper Room with his disciples in John 13-16;

there was dialogue and discussion. The fact that Paul took the lead is only natural: here was a group of new Christians who, for one night only, had the opportunity to learn from the great apostle. The normal courtesies of Christian life mean that we should extend the same opportunities to gifted visiting speakers today. It is only natural, too, that a church of new believers would be very grateful to have a more mature teacher take the lead in instructing them.

In 1 Corinthians 14, Paul was not Commending the Corinthians, but Criticizing them

Some commentators argue that the participatory church meeting was just another one of the problems that the church at Corinth was famous for. Paul was not advocating what he writes about here, but was describing the scene in shock and dismay. 1 Corinthians 14:26 is describing the actual state of affairs in the church at Corinth, but only for the purpose of outlining abuses which need to be corrected.

W. E. Vine in his commentary on 1 Corinthians 14:26 argues that the apostle Paul is not commending the Corinthians for their participation in the church gathering, but rather is criticizing them for being so forward: 'If all came prepared beforehand to exercise some form of oral ministry, there could only be confusion. Such readiness, even eagerness, to make oneself heard would lead to abuse and would endanger the testimony'[144]. Vine would probably argue that the first part of the verse should be punctuated with an exclamation mark of astonishment.

In reply, however, Paul nowhere criticizes the Corinthians for the open, free and participatory format of their meetings, as if it were a problem. Thus, there is no word of criticism or condemnation in 1 Corinthians 14:26, the verse which describes the participatory format of church gathering. Nor does Paul follow up the description of their gathering with any of the expressions he used elsewhere in the letter to correct the wayward Corinthians. There is no expression of astonishment like 'What!' (compare with 1 Cor. 6:16, 11:22, etc.), nor does Paul go on

---

[144] W. E. Vine, *First Corinthians*, London: Oliphants, 1951, p195

to suggest that the Corinthians are ignorant of important principles ('Do you not know … ?', cf. 1 Cor. 3:16, 5:6, 6:2, 9:13, etc.). There is no substance, either in Paul's word or tone, to the suggestion that Paul is criticizing the Corinthians for their participatory gatherings *per se*, that is, for their toleration of individuals participating in the church gatherings.

On the contrary, a number of verses in this chapter show that Paul wishes to encourage 'all' of the Corinthians to take part, which is the very essence of a participatory church gathering. Thus, in addition to Paul mentioning that 'each' had something to contribute (v26), just a few verses afterwards we read, in verse 31: 'for you can all prophesy one by one, that all may learn and all may be encouraged'. Likewise, in verse 5, we read, 'I wish you all spoke with tongues, but even more that you prophesied'. Verse 24 says, 'But if all prophesy and an unbeliever or an unlearned person comes in, he is convinced by all, he is convicted by all'.

William Kelly writes, 'none can deny to the assembly the fullest liberty: else it could not have been thus abused. Modern arrangements exclude not only the abuse but that liberty which ought to be; and in fact, where the Spirit of the Lord is, liberty is characteristic of His presence'[145].

Indeed, the spontaneous, Spirit-prompted nature of some of the gifts mentioned here – particularly the two main gifts mentioned throughout the chapter, prophesying and speaking in tongues – virtually requires us to understand a culture of individual spiritual responsibility and freedom of contribution as part of the ordinary church gatherings.

Paul says that the guidelines for order he gives for church gatherings here are found 'in all the churches of the saints' (verse 33). The church in Corinth was not some abnormality among the churches. Paul later says that the guidelines for order he has given in this passage are 'the commandments of the Lord' (verse 37).

Another way this objection has been phrased is to suggest that 1 Corinthians 14 is 'correctional not instructional'. But this is not true:

---

[145] William Kelly, *Notes on the First Epistle of Paul the Apostle to the Corinthians*, London: G. Morrish, n.d., p239

Paul gives instructions for how the open, participatory format should be ordered. Indeed, this objection borders on the illogical, for every attempt at correction is, to some degree, also instructional. Why would Paul (or any Christian teacher) point out the faults of God's people without attempting to show them the right way? This would be like a doctor diagnosing a disease, and then without any attempt to give the patient any remedy, showing them straight to the door. Paul's correction of the Corinthians related merely to certain limitations placed on their freedom to contribute, not to removal of this freedom, or its replacement with a different order of service. The fact that Paul does not set out some alternative 'order of service' to the free, interactive and participatory model of 1 Corinthians 14 shows that this is the model that Paul recognizes and reinforces as divinely-ordered.

Thus, Paul's correction was merely concerned with minor adjustments to the participatory model – limiting the numbers of certain contributions (tongues, prophecy), and insisting that one person speaks at a time, etc. Paul did not rebuke or correct the Corinthians for multiple members using their gifts in the church, but was instead encouraging, confirming and codifying this pattern of church gatherings. Vine (and those who repeat this argument) have invented their own narrative of Paul censuring the Corinthians' participation and imposed their own imagined scenario upon the passage.

1 Corinthians 14:26-40 is 'Descriptive not Prescriptive'

Another objection to using 1 Corinthians 14 as a basis for how we should organize our church gatherings is to say that the New Testament only *describes* what churches of the apostolic era did, rather than giving us authoritative or binding commands to obey. We are therefore not obliged to follow the example of the churches of the New Testament.

Millard Erickson writes, 'Attempts to develop a structure of church government that adheres to the authority of the Bible encounter difficulty at two points ... (Firstly), there is no prescriptive exposition of what the government of the church is to be like comparable to, say, Paul's elucidation of the doctrines of human sinfulness and justification by faith. *The churches are not commanded to adopt a particular form of church order* ... When we turn to examine the descriptive passages, we find a second problem: there is no unitary pattern'[146].

Or, for more lively language, consider the following: 'Yet another way in which we are 'unbiblical' is that we have church services, led from the front. These, we are told, were 'entirely alien to the early church'. We should have meetings as described in 1 Corinthians 14.26-40, where all present actively participate. There are serious flaws in this argument. It assumes that 1 Corinthians 14.26 is prescriptive for all churches and not just descriptive of what the Corinthians were doing. It entirely overlooks the Lord's Day meeting described in Acts 20.7-12, where one man spoke for some time. It also gives the impression that those who sing heartily and listen avidly are not actively participating'[147].

The main objection here is that 1 Cor. 14:26-40 is 'descriptive, not prescriptive'. However, this 'descriptive not prescriptive' objection is more than a little problematic; it has four flaws.

Firstly, the entire passage from 1 Cor. 14:26-40 contains no less than fourteen imperatives. That means (for those not familiar with Greek grammar), that Paul issues fourteen exhortations or commands in this passage, either encouraging certain behaviours or prohibiting certain acts. To see these imperatives in English, look out for the word 'let' in the passage (as in 'let the prophets speak', 'let your women keep silent', etc.) or the word 'should' in some other versions like the NIV ('two or three prophets should speak', etc.). There is hardly any passage in the entire New Testament with a higher concentration of commands than this passage. This is one of the most prescriptive passages in Scripture.

It is objected that verse 26 is not prescriptive, but the last clause of 1 Cor. 14:26 uses an imperative ('let all things be done to edification') which is tied to the words immediately preceding it. What are the 'all things' that must 'be done for edification', but the use of the gifts mentioned just before? Thus, verse 26 states that the listed gifts should

---

[146] Millard Erickson, *Christian Theology*, Baker Academic, 2nd Edition, p1094, emphasis added

[147] Basil Howlett, reviewing a book called *Biblical Church, A Challenge to Unscriptural Traditions and Practice*, in the April 2009 edition of the British Christian newspaper *Evangelicals Now*

be used in ways which are to be 'for edification' (and the verses which follow tell how this is managed).

The passage clearly prescribes for multiple participants to be allowed to use different spiritual gifts in the church service. Thus, following verse 26 listing a variety of gifts, verses 27ff. indicate that multiple people were allowed to participate (two or three prophets, etc.), in addition to questioning and weighing up what had been said. So, the commands in verses 27ff. give guidelines for a participatory church service involving multiple speakers using different spiritual gifts, not the one-man ministry of most denominational traditions.

Secondly, the 'descriptive, not prescriptive' objection overlooks (or deliberately ignores) 1 Cor. 14:37, which says that instructions regarding the participatory form of church life described in the preceding verses are the commandments of the Lord. 1 Cor. 14:37 governs all of the instructions from verses 26 onwards. How can a passage like 1 Cor. 14:26-40 which deals with church order not be authoritative if Paul says that what he has written are 'the commandments of the Lord'?

It seems frankly astonishing that those who profess to be submissive to Christ as Lord should say that His commandments are 'not prescriptive but only descriptive'. 1 Cor. 14:26 is descriptive, yes, but also prescriptive in that the things that happen in the church service (as described in verses 26 and following) are to be done in a certain way and according to a certain order, not according to our own imagination or human devising.

Thirdly, even if this passage were simply descriptive (which it is not), we cannot dismiss descriptive passages as if they have nothing to say to us. Apostolic practices possess abiding value and authority; they provide ongoing guidance for us still today. If we claim to be followers of Christ, we should imitate the practices of His first followers, those Christ Himself appointed as our guides (1 Cor. 11:1). We should ordinarily follow apostolic examples, particularly if the practice (1) is consistently seen throughout New Testament churches, (2) is commanded by the apostles, (3) is not merely cultural (sandals, candles, etc.), and (4) is not contrary to what is possible for us to do today. We cannot simply claim that a 'descriptive' passage of Scripture has no authority over us.

In any case, there are other ways besides 'prescriptive' or 'descriptive' that we could describe the passage. 1 Corinthians 14 says that multiple Christians (not just a 'Pastor') have the freedom or right to use a variety of spiritual gifts in the gathering of the church. 1 Corinthians 14 gives us the norm for what happened in church in Paul's day, based not only Paul's apostolic guidelines for church gatherings given in the passage, but also because this was the type of format found 'in all the churches of the saints' (1 Cor. 14:33). 1 Corinthians 14 gives authoritative guidance for how spiritual gifts are to be used in the church gatherings.

Instead of 'descriptive' or 'prescriptive', we can just as easily use these other words like 'rights', 'freedoms', 'norm' or 'authoritative guidance' to describe God's inspired instructions for church gatherings. These other words teach us that Christians can and should have a church gathering like that described in 1 Corinthians 14. None of these freedoms or rights are ever withdrawn, nor is there any other sort of church order described anywhere else in the New Testament. The passage in Acts 20 describing Paul in Troas does not contradict 1 Corinthians 14 at all, as we have just seen. Such apostolic guidelines therefore still apply today.

Fourthly, and perhaps most seriously, the objection subtly undermines the authority of Scripture. When the 'descriptive not prescriptive' slogan is applied to the New Testament generally (Millard Erickson, for example, is referring to the NT writings more generally) it has the effect of undermining what the New Testament epistles tell us about Christian life. Numerous things are commanded of God's people, many of them in relation to their church life. Of course, not everything commanded in the NT applies to us today (we do not all have to visit Damascus because Paul was told to go there after his conversion, for example), but if we are free to ignore what Paul says in 1 Corinthians 14:26-40, despite the fact that these are the 'commandments of the Lord' (v37) about church order, we are left with no way of knowing which parts of the Bible we should take as 'authoritative and binding' and which parts of the Bible we can dismiss if we happen to dislike them. If we can just pick and choose which parts of the New Testament to obey, are we any different to Thomas Jefferson who cut out the miracles from the gospels which he couldn't accept? If we can choose to ignore scriptural commandments if they don't happen to suit our denominational traditions or personal preferences, why can't we add other human ideas to Scripture in other areas, like sexual morality, the doctrine of salvation, or the nature of God? We have started to make up our own religion. The slogan 'descriptive not prescriptive' is a cancer that eats away at the authority, sufficiency and profitability of Scripture. In summary:

1. the passage in 1 Cor. 14:26-40 has perhaps the highest concentration of prescriptive (imperative) commands in the entire New Testament,
2. 1 Cor. 14:37 says that these things are the 'commandments of the Lord',
3. apostolic practices are authoritative guidelines for us today; we can and should have church gatherings like those described in 1 Cor. 14.
4. the result of this objection is to undermine the authority of Scripture and to fashion our own man-made system of worship

To argue that 1 Corinthians 14:26-40 is 'descriptive, not prescriptive' is neither sound exegesis of the text nor submissive to the Bible's authority.

1 Cor. 14 only Mandates Edification, not any Particular Model of Church Gathering

A number of commentators argue that Paul's main purpose in 1 Corinthians 14 is to stress the need for edification rather than to insist on any particular form of church gathering. This is the approach of two recent commentaries by Thiselton and Garland.

Before we turn to these, we need to notice that while arguments based on a biblical author's purpose are often illuminating, they can also be used to distort and deny what the Bible says. For example, some who argue for homosexual relationships suggest that the purpose of the Bible's prohibitions against homosexuality was simply to condemn the 'pride, fullness of food, and abundance of idleness' in Sodom (Ezekiel 16:49) or its association with idolatry, not homosexuality *per se*. Of course, this argument also requires that we ignore explicit condemnations of homosexuality elsewhere in Scripture, even in the immediate context (e.g. Ezek. 16:50, 'committed abomination').

Even if we consider less highly-charged issues, arguments from an author's purpose are often problematic. For example, if someone were to insist that Luke's purpose in writing Acts was to vindicate Paul at his Roman trial, or that Revelation was all about 'God wins', they might well be right. But, in effect, such arguments impose a straitjacket on these books and limit what we can learn from them. For example, Paul's speech to the Ephesian elders in Acts 20 about the need for teaching in church is robbed of any relevance for today, for it too is all about Paul's innocence. Even in the case of John's Gospel (where we are told the purpose is that we might believe in Christ, John 20:30-31), might it not be possible that this is simply the main purpose, and that there are also other secondary purposes in individual passages (e.g. John 13)?

These examples show that asserting an author's purpose often (a) involves guesswork, because the biblical author does not explicitly tell us his purpose, (b) insists that a passage may only have one purpose, whereas a text may have many purposes, (c) tries to deliberately exclude other possible purposes, (d) involves cherry-picking certain features in the text and ignoring others, and (e) involves pushing an agenda, rather than simply explaining the passage. Arguing from an 'author's purpose' is not only precarious, it is sometimes a way to evade something the Bible says that leaves us feeling uncomfortable[148]. We do not have access to the writer's thoughts or purposes, only their words; we cannot read minds, only the inspired Scripture. We must treat God's Word with respect and care, not imaginative flair.

In relation to 1 Cor. 14:26-40, it is obvious that Paul is saying more than simply 'edify one another', even if this is the main point of chapter 14 as a whole. To argue that the only point of this passage is edification is to overlook Paul's emphasis upon order in verses 26-40, or his allowance of interruptions in v30, or to ignore his words about women's silence in vs 34-35, or his instructions about intelligibility throughout. It also dismisses what Paul says about the wide variety of spiritual gifts that

---

[148] See the essay by Norman L. Geisler, "The Relation of Purpose and Meaning in Interpreting Scripture" in *Rightly Divided: Readings in Biblical Hermeneutics*, ed. Roy B. Zuck, Grand Rapids: Kregel, 1996, pp143-157

God has given His people and their freedom to use these gifts in church. Paul is saying a lot of things in 1 Cor. 14:26ff; we cannot simply eliminate everything else the passage teaches except edification. If God Himself has granted His people the liberty to use their gifts in church, what who has the right to take it away?

Serious commentators engaged in close and sustained analysis of the passage do not pick out one word or element from a passage and ignore anything else it says. Thiselton does not resort to this; instead, he uses another approach, arguably even more desperate, to argue that the author's sole purpose of 1 Cor. 14:26-40 is to stress the need for edification (the 'overriding aim', the 'true aim', the 'governing axiom')[149]. Firstly, he takes the radical step of rewriting verse 26 in a very different way: '*Suppose* that when you assemble together each contributes a hymn, an item of teaching, something disclosed, or speaks in a tongue, or puts the tongues language into words, the point remains: "let everything serve the building up of the community."' Instead of translating verse 26 'whenever you come together', Thiselton inserts the word 'suppose' (without any justification) to argue that 1 Corinthians 14:26 is not meant to provide a 'description of a typical gathering for worship' but is instead a hypothetical situation. He thus treats the entire passage as an imaginary scenario, not an actual account of what happened in church gatherings at Corinth. Secondly, Thiselton argues that 'each one' having something to contribute to the meeting (v26) does not 'woodenly' mean 'each one'. He does not explain why the word 'each' cannot take its normal meaning, or even tell us what it does mean here, and he ignores other evidence in the chapter that shows that 'all' (v31) of the brethren were encouraged to participate. Having imposed his own reconstructed, imaginary scenario upon the passage, Thiselton stresses little other than that church should be edifying and intelligible.

Thiselton's approach thus proceeds as follows: (1) re-write the inspired words of Scripture to suit himself, (2) so as to make the passage a hypothetical, not an actual, scenario, (3) argue that the words of the

---

[149] A. C. Thiselton, *The First Epistle to the Corinthians: A Commentary on the Greek Text*, NIGTC, Grand Rapids, MI: Eerdmans, 2000, p1133

passage do not mean what they say, so that it is not true that 'each one' can use their gifts, (4) so as to transfer the emphasis to one element, edification, to the exclusion of any other lessons. Lastly, Thiselton takes aim at anyone arguing for the alternative, i.e. straightforward, understanding of the passage (that 'each one', v26, is free to use their gifts in the church gatherings) by saying they are guilty of reading the verse 'too readily in accordance with their own church traditions'[150] – i.e. imposing their own modern ideas back on the passage!

Here is a prime example, not only of how to abuse Scripture, but of how uncomfortable some people are with the plain meaning and the obvious implications of the participatory nature of biblical church worship in 1 Cor. 14:26-40.

Garland takes the same approach as Thiselton. He offers very little in the way of original commentary, but follows Thiselton's every false-step, encouraging the idea of rewriting verse 26 with 'suppose', arguing that 'each' does not mean 'each', and that we have here a hypothetical scenario rather than a real description of what is happening in Corinth. However, at least Garland titles this section, 'Regulations for Worship and Concluding Instructions on Spiritual Gifts', stating that 'gatherings in which each person could make a contribution under the guidance of the Holy Spirit need some ground rules'[151]. By so doing, he admits that we have in 1 Cor. 14:26-40 instructions about how church gatherings are to be run. By contrast, Thiselton titles this section with the vague heading, 'Controlled Speech and Building Up', seemingly reluctant to admit any relationship with or authoritative guidance for church gatherings in Corinth or today.

To sum up: whereas some commentators attempt to place all the emphasis in 1 Cor. 14:26 upon edification to the virtual elimination of what is said about the free exercise of gifts, by contrast, in Paul's version of 1 Cor. 14:26, the verse is about multiple things: (1) freedom for participation, (2) order and (3) edification (among others).

---

[150] A. C. Thiselton, *1 Corinthians: a Shorter Exegetical and Pastoral Commentary*, Grand Rapids, Eerdmans, 2006, p246

[151] David E. Garland, *1 Corinthians*, BECNT, Grand Rapids, MI: Baker, 2003, pp655-7

Participatory Church Gatherings do not apply today because the miraculous gifts described in the early church do not exist today

Charles Hodge in his commentary on 1 Corinthians argues as follows: 'Although there were officers in every church, appointed to conduct the services and especially to teach, yet as the extraordinary gifts of the Spirit were not confined to them or to any particular class, any member present who experienced the working of the Spirit in any of its extraordinary manifestations, was authorized to use and exercise his gift. Under such circumstances confusion could hardly fail to ensue. That such disorder did prevail in the public assemblies in Corinth is clear enough from this chapter. To correct this evil is the apostle's design in this whole passage. It was only so long as the gifts of tongues, of prophecy, of miracles, and others of a like kind continued in the church that the state of things here described prevailed. Since those gifts have ceased, no one has the right to rise in the church under the impulse of his own mind to take part in its services'[152].

We could rephrase Hodge's objection as follows: '1 Corinthians 14 deals with the gifts of speaking in tongues and prophesying, but because we no longer have these gifts, the picture presented in 1 Corinthians 14 of open and participatory church gatherings does not apply today'. However, leaving aside the fact that there are no church 'officers' mentioned in Corinth, and Hodge's equally unwarranted statement that such officers conducted the services of New Testament churches, the fact remains that even if certain spectacular gifts have ceased, this does not diminish the relevance of 1 Cor. 14 to church life today because 1 Corinthians 14 is not simply about the gifts of tongues and prophecy.

There are many other gifts and verbal spiritual contributions to the church gatherings mentioned in 1 Cor. 12-14 including teaching (14:6, 19, 26), exhortation (v3), knowledge (v6), revelation (v6, 26), exhortation (or encouragement, v3), comfort (v3), singing (v15), praying (v15), giving thanks (perhaps in connection with the Lord's Supper, v16), a psalm (v26), judging prophecies (v29, 30), asking questions (v35), a word

---

[152] Charles Hodge, *1 & 2 Corinthians*, Edinburgh: Banner of Truth Trust, 1983 reprint of original 1857 commentary, pp300-301

of wisdom (12:8), a word of knowledge (12:8) and discerning of spirits (12:10 – 'discerning' here is the same root word used in 14:29 for 'judging' prophecies). Most of these ways of speaking are still operative today, so we cannot dismiss 1 Corinthians 14 as only applying to a charismatic ministry, or to the apostolic era when certain more spectacular gifts were active.

It does not logically follow that other gifts of the Spirit should cease to be freely exercised in church just because two or three have ceased to exist. Should we not still be allowed to encourage and exhort, or teach, or exercise discernment, or ask questions, or share insights into divine truth, or give thanks or sing? Where else in the NT are these apostolic freedoms taken away? Where are we told that only one person may preach per Sunday service? The idea that multiple participants should be freely able to use their spiritual gifts in church is not the least dependent on every single one of the gifts in NT times still being operative.

Furthermore, in the present author's opinion, there is a sense in which prophecy still occurs today. Not in the dubious sense in which some Christians claim to have a 'word from the Lord', a practice which even some charismatic theologians are now cautioning against[153]. Instead, consider the following commentators' definitions of prophecy:

- **F. F. Bruce**: 'the declaration of the mind of God in the power of the Spirit'[154].
- **J. I. Packer**: 'the essence of the prophetic ministry was forthtelling God's present word to his people, and this regularly meant application of a revealed truth rather than augmentation of it. . . . Any verbal enforcement of biblical teaching as it applies to one's present hearers may properly be called prophecy, for that in truth is what it is'[155].
- **A. C. Thiselton**: 'On the level of vocabulary alone, prophecy may denote a gift or activity as broad and general as declaring or telling

---

[153] See Wayne Grudem, *Systematic Theology*, Leicester: IVP, 1994, pp1040-1

[154] F. F. Bruce, *1 & 2 Thessalonians*, p127

[155] J. I. Packer, *Keep in Step with the Spirit*, New York: F. H. Revell, 1984, p215

forth the revealed will of God. . . . Since Paul explicitly defines the aim of prophetic speech as "to edify, exhort, and encourage, it coincides therefore to a large extent with what we call a sermon today"'[156].

- **John Stott**: prophecy is to 'know and speak God's mind and will'. . . . Certainly, therefore, there are today no apostles . . . and no prophets comparable to the biblical prophets . . . Nevertheless, once the uniqueness of the biblical prophets (and apostles) has been conceded, we should be ready to add that there are today secondary and subsidiary kinds of prophetic gift and ministry. For God undoubtedly gives to some a remarkable degree of insight either into Scripture itself and its meaning, or into its application to the contemporary world, or into his particular will for particular people in particular situations'[157].
- **William MacDonald**: 'In its primary NT sense, to prophesy meant to speak the word of God. The inspired utterances of the prophets are preserved for us in the Bible. In a secondary sense, to prophesy means to declare the mind of God as it has been revealed in the Bible'[158].
- **J. Ramsay Michaels** (writing about the expression in 1 Peter 4:11, 'If any man speak, let him speak as the oracles of God') says, 'In effect, Peter is broadening traditional understandings of prophecy so as to include all the teaching and exhortation that goes on in connection with Christian worship. "Whoever speaks" (and therefore not just Christian prophets in a technical sense) should speak as if delivering the very oracles of God'[159].
- **James Denney**, (after giving examples in the NT where prophecy involves foretelling, e.g. Agabus in Acts 11), states that the meaning of prophecy was not limited to this: 'the prophet was a man whose

---

[156] A. C. Thiselton, *1 Corinthians: a Shorter Exegetical and Pastoral Commentary*, Grand Rapids: Eerdmans, 2006, p201-2
[157] John Stott, *The Message of Thessalonians*, p127-8
[158] William MacDonald, *Believers Bible Commentary*, p2043
[159] Michaels, *1 Peter*, 250

rational and moral nature had been quickened by the Spirit of Christ and who possessed in an uncommon degree the power of speaking edification, exhortation and comfort. In other words, he was a Christian preacher, endued with wisdom, fervor, and tenderness; and his spiritual addresses were among the Lord's best gifts to the Church. Such addresses, or prophesyings, Paul tells us, we are not to despise'[160].

The biblical data shows prophecy to be more than simply foretelling the future, but also forth-telling the mind, will and truth of God. Consider the following references from both Testaments:

- Acts 2:17-18 says: 'And it shall come to pass in the last days, says God, that I will pour out of My Spirit on all flesh; your sons and your daughters shall prophesy, your young men shall see visions, your old men shall dream dreams. And on My menservants and on My maidservants I will pour out My Spirit in those days; and they shall prophesy'. There is a sense in which all of God's people are prophets.
- In Exodus 7:1, Aaron is called Moses' prophet, whereas in Exodus 4:16 Aaron is called Moses' spokesman. 'Prophet' here seems equated with 'spokesman'.
- In Deuteronomy 18:18, Moses is told by God, 'I will raise up for them a Prophet like you from among their brethren, and will put My words in His mouth, and He shall speak to them all that I command Him'. Notice: God says that He will put His words in the mouth of the prophet: a prophet is God's mouthpiece or spokesman.
- Abraham is called a prophet in Gen. 20:7, and the patriarchs collectively are called prophets in Psalm 105:15, not particularly because they made notable predictions or proclamations, but because they were God's representatives among the people.

---

[160] James Denney, "The Epistles to the Thessalonians", in *The Expositor's Bible*, ed. W. Robertson Nicoll, London: Hodder and Stoughton, 1902, Baker Books 1982 reprint of 1903 US edition, p355

- The Hebrew Bible includes the historical books of Joshua, Judges, Samuel and Kings in the section called the Prophets, because 'the history of Israel was, in itself, a revelation of God'[161].
- In 1 Chronicles 25:1-3, the musicians in the Temple were to 'prophesy with harps, stringed instruments and cymbals' (verse 1), Asaph 'prophesied according to the order of the king' (verse 2), and Jeduthun 'prophesied with a harp to give thanks and to praise the LORD' (verse 3). This prophetic music ministry was not always a spontaneous outburst; it happened at the 'order of the king'. The regular praise and thanks in the temple was prophetic: it declared the truths of God's character and mighty acts.
- The name Barnabus means 'son of prophecy' in its original Aramaic, but is translated into Greek as 'son of encouragement' (Acts 4:36). It identifies prophecy with encouragement, and thus equates prophecy with a gift that most would still say occurs today.
- Revelation 19:10 says that 'the testimony of Jesus is the spirit of prophecy'. The central message of the prophet is above all a witness to Christ. The corollary of this verse is that all Christians are in one sense prophesying by testifying to Christ.

The word 'prophecy' means more than foretelling the future. While there are many references to prophets in the Old Testament either foretelling the future, or having direct revelations from God or even having their own personality overwhelmed and controlled by the power of the Holy Spirit (e.g. Saul prophesying naked in 1 Sam. 19:23-24), however, in addition to these references, there are other passages which present a broader understanding of prophecy: forth-telling the mind, will and truth of God that met the need of the moment. The prophets prefaced their message with, 'Thus says the LORD' and prophecy often involved proclamation as much as prediction.

Prophecy in the New Testament is a spiritual gift in the narrow sense of the term (Romans 12:6, 1 Cor. 12:10, Eph. 4:11), a gift of the very

---

[161] H. L. Ellison, *Men Spake from God, Studies in the Hebrew Prophets*, Exeter: The Paternoster Press, 1966, p15

highest order (1 Cor. 12:28, Eph. 2:20), a foundational gift of the church that only some people possessed. But it also has a broad definition: being God's spokesman or representative or declaring God's praise or message. Thus, there are two senses in which the word prophecy is used in Scripture, a broad, weak sense and a narrow, strong sense. In the New Testament there are certain people who were specially gifted by the Holy Spirit to be prophets (the strong sense). However, secondly, just as people in the Old Testament prophesied when the Holy Spirit came upon them so, with the coming and indwelling of the Holy Spirit in the New Testament, all of God's people are in a weak sense of the term 'prophets', God's representatives and spokesmen.

This double-sense of the word should not surprise us, for we see the same thing with most gifts. Just as there is the gift of an evangelist (Eph. 4:11), yet all Christians should evangelise, and there are gifts of faith (1 Cor. 12:9) and giving (Rom. 12:8), while all Christians believe and should give, so it is true of prophecy. While in New Testament times there were people with the special gift of prophecy who were part of the foundational stage of the church, laying down the deposit of truth for all time, there is also a sense in which all Christians prophesy by speaking for God, either to believers or non-believers.

I suggest that we see these two senses of the word 'prophecy' being used in 1 Corinthians 11-14. We see the strong sense when we read about the gift of prophecy in 12:28-29 where Paul lists prophets immediately after apostles in importance. But we also see the word used in a broad and general sense:

- 1 Cor. 11:4-5 speak about men (and women) 'praying or prophesying', and the two terms cover the whole range of ways a person can claim to have a relationship with God, either by speaking to or for Him. That is, prophesying seems to be used here in the broad sense of 'speaking for God to men' in contrast with praying which consists of 'men speaking to God'.
- 1 Cor. 12:3 says, 'Therefore I make known to you that no one speaking by the Spirit of God calls Jesus accursed, and no one can say that Jesus is Lord except by the Holy Spirit'. This verse occurs at

the beginning of a chapter dealing with spiritual gifts; its purpose is to show that all of God's people possess God's Spirit, not just those with extraordinary gifts. God's Spirit (or Breath) speaks audibly through His people as they testify that Jesus is Lord. All Christians are, in this way, His mouthpieces and His spokesmen.

- In 1 Cor. 14:3, Paul says, 'he who prophesies speaks edification and exhortation and comfort to men'. Prophecy is here described in the broadest of terms; it builds up, stirs up and cheers up. These are activities normally associated with teaching, exhortation and words of comfort. Paul is talking about the ongoing pastoral needs of the church here, not the once-for-all foundational apostolic deposit of truth.
- In 1 Cor. 14:3, and throughout the chapter, prophecy is contrasted with speaking in tongues. The contrast is set up in the verse before: no one understands someone speaking in tongues. But while speaking in tongues is unintelligible, prophecy seems to encompass every sort of intelligible spiritual contribution in the church.
- Most of the references in 1 Cor. 14 speak of prophecy in the weaker sense of the term. Thus, Paul associates prophecy with 'teaching' three times explicitly, 'edification' seven times (in various forms of the word), as well as the words 'learn' and 'ignorance'. In verse 31, he says, 'you can all prophesy one by one, that all may learn and all may be encouraged'. Notice: not only does prophecy result in learning and encouragement (which would equate it with the results of teaching today), but it is said to be something done by all (not just a few specially gifted 'prophets').
- In verses 24-25, Paul describes a visitor coming into the church gathering and being convicted by the words of the prophets. The 'secrets of his heart are revealed', he falls down and acknowledges that 'God is truly among you'. Paul again is describing the normal, ongoing pastoral and evangelistic situation in the church here, rather than the foundational deposit of truth. We still experience this in our church life sometimes today as God's Word speaks to a personal situation in a way that nobody else knows about. For example, the author once had someone who was angry with him come into

- church, only to hear another speaker encourage God's people to put things right with other believers. The next time this man came to church, another speaker talked about forgiveness. God spoke to the man without the speakers knowing that there was a problem.
- Even in verses where a distinction is made between prophecy and other intelligible gifts, there seems to be a great deal of overlap between them. For example, verse 6 says, 'what shall I profit you unless I speak to you either by revelation, by knowledge, by prophesying, or by teaching?' Here prophecy is distinguished from other gifts, however prophecy is always dependent upon some form of revelation, and also involves some truth content (i.e. knowledge) which is passed on to others (i.e. teaching). The terms prophecy, revelation, knowledge and teaching are therefore overlapping, partly synonymous terms.

It is hard to avoid the conclusion that Paul is using the term prophecy in 1 Cor. 14 primarily as a counterfoil and contrast to speaking in tongues, and thus covering in a broad and general sense a number of ways that people can 'speak for God' in intelligible ways that result in God's people being edified. It would appear to include the normal ways in which people attempt to teach or preach in church today. Therefore it would seem inappropriate to dismiss this chapter as inapplicable to today's church[162].

---

[162] Space forbids a detailed treatment of Grudem's influential, charismatic view of prophecy (*The Gift of Prophecy in the New Testament and Today*, Wheaton, IL: Crossway, 1988). Suffice to say that Grudem's view has several good points (prophecy in 1 Cor. 14 was not equal in authority to Scripture for it had to be judged) as well as several problems (prophecy in the NT is not the same as in the OT - despite the same word being used, apostles = prophets in Eph. 2:20, Agabus was mistaken in Acts 21:10-11, Grudem's definition of prophecy as a spontaneously delivered direct revelation, sometimes partially mistaken – based largely on one solitary verse, 1 Cor. 14:30 – but did prophets only receive revelation once a week, during church?). His objectors point out these problems but tend to argue that NT prophets were infallible and that 1 Cor. 14:29-30 describes *prophets* being judged (not their prophecies), despite the fact that there

It is Inconsistent to put 1 Cor. 14 into practice but not have Speaking in Tongues

1 Corinthians 14 encourages Christians to speak in tongues. In verse 5, Paul says he wished all the Corinthians spoke in tongues, and in verse 39 he says, 'do not forbid to speak in tongues'. Obviously, modern-day charismatic Christians believe in speaking in tongues and allow this in their church gatherings. It would seem inconsistent for them to believe in speaking in tongues and *not* follow the guidelines given in this chapter for how they are to be exercised in church.

But what about Christians who do not believe that speaking in tongues occurs today? Would it be inconsistent for them to practice participatory church gatherings based on 1 Corinthians 14 and yet not allow speaking in tongues? Would this not be another case of someone taking a 'pick and mix' approach to the Bible, adopting those things he feels comfortable with and ignoring others equally scriptural?

The present author does not believe that speaking in tongues (in the biblical sense of the term) happens today. This is not because he thinks that there is some Bible passage that clearly tells us that tongues ceased with the apostles. Virtually all evangelicals now agree that 'when that which is perfect' of 1 Cor. 13:10 does not refer to the completed canon of Scripture or the end of the apostolic age, but to being in Christ's presence when we will see Him 'face to face' and 'know just as I also am known', 1 Cor. 13:12[163].

The present author does not believe that the gift of tongues that we find in the New Testament (technically called xenoglossia: the

---

is no mention of false-prophets being excommunicated in 1 Cor. 14, and other passages about prophecy teaching us to 'test all things' (1 Thess. 5:19-21, 1 John 4:1). It seems better to agree with Grudem that prophecy in 1 Cor. 14 was not infallible, and with his objectors that the gift of prophecy (i.e. the strong sense of the term) used in the church's foundation to give us the deposit of truth and spoken of in this way in Eph. 2:20, 4:11, etc. has passed away.

[163] Even the most ardent cessationists like John Macarthur hold this to be the true interpretation of the passage; see *Strange Fire: the Danger of Offending the Holy Spirit with Counterfeit Worship*, Nashville, TN: Thomas Nelson, 2013, p148-9

miraculous ability to fluently speak a foreign language that has never been learned, like the apostles in Acts 2) is operative today. Most charismatic Christians today have abandoned this claim too, because early charismatic missionaries who thought they were 'speaking in tongues' in Chinese, Finnish, etc. were not understood by native speakers. Instead, charismatics today argue they are speaking in a 'heavenly language', a 'private prayer language', or 'Holy Ghost language', not a known foreign human language. However, there are four problems with this type of 'speaking in tongues'. Charismatics may find it difficult to consider or accept criticism, claiming that the experience vindicates itself, however, we need to be prepared to 'test all things' (1 Thess. 5:21).

Firstly, charismatics claim that this second sort of speaking in tongues (technically known as glossolalia) has biblical support because (a) 1 Cor. 13:1 speaks of the tongues of *angels* as well as men, (b) 1 Cor. 14:2 tells us that the person speaking in tongues 'does not speak to men but to God', and (c) such tongues needed to be miraculously interpreted by someone with a special gift (1 Cor. 14:5) – i.e. they could not be interpreted by an ordinary person who knew this foreign language, like in Acts 2. Therefore, it is claimed, the speaking in tongues found in 1 Cor. 14 is different to that found in Acts 2.

However, the New Testament does not envisage two different types of 'speaking in tongues', nor is there any good evidence that 1 Cor. 14 presents a different type of miraculous tongues-speech to Acts 2. The claim that someone is speaking in an angelic language (1 Cor. 13:1) is unconvincing. As someone has said, "If you claim to speak in the language of angels, you prove it!" If we have no evidence of modern Christians miraculously speaking in ordinary foreign human languages (like in Acts 2), then why should we believe the claim to be able to speak in the most exalted, angelic, languages? Argument (b), that a person speaking in tongues 'does not speak to men but to God' (1 Cor. 14:2), applies equally to an *unknown* foreign human language as much as to a heavenly language. That is, ordinary Greek-speaking listeners in Corinth would not have understood someone speaking in a Chinese 'tongue' anymore than someone today who speaks only English would be able to, and thus the Chinese tongues-speaker in Corinth would not have been speaking to men, but only to God. Therefore this argument does not prove that the language in 1 Cor. 14 is a heavenly one. Argument (c), that the 'heavenly' tongue needed to be miraculously interpreted (not just translated by a native speaker) is again unconvincing because either unknown language (Chinese or angelic) would need to be miraculously interpreted if no one knew it naturally.

Several verses in 1 Corinthians 14 (10, 21, 22) seem to point to the fact that miraculously-spoken foreign human languages are under consideration: verse 10 speaks about 'languages in the world', verse 21 borrows a quote from the Old Testament to argue that God uses foreign human languages to get His message across (in the OT context, this was the language of the Assyrians bringing God's judgement on Israel), while verse 22 says tongues are a sign to unbelievers (not for God, or simply for the ecstasy and encouragement of the speaker).

A second problem with modern 'tongues' is that numerous pagan cultures around the world practice exactly the same thing as charismatics in their religious rites (e.g. voodoo cults, African tribes, Tibetan monks[164]) – even atheists can produce it. Non-Christian cults and non-Christian teachings also claim validation from speaking in tongues: Roman Catholics claim glossolalia enhances their worship of Mary, Mormons are more convinced in their false religion because they 'speak in tongues' and even liberal theologians are confirmed in their unbelief of Scripture via glossolalia. These facts render the claim that tongues are a manifestation of the Holy Spirit untenable.

Thirdly, scientific studies of modern tongues-speakers further cast doubt on charismatic claims. Researchers have found no evidence of known human languages among those claiming to speak in tongues. Nor does glossolalia bear any resemblance to real language, either in its range of sounds or grammar. It instead consists of only a few vowels and consonants in repetitive combinations with simulated foreign accents. An article entitled 'Behavioral Science Research on the Nature of Glossolalia'

---

[164] George J. Jennings, "An Ethnological Study of Glossolalia", *Journal of the American Scientific Affiliation*, March 1968

described it as 'partially developed speech'[165]. The linguist Professor William Samarin wrote, 'There is no mystery about glossolalia. Tape-recorded samples are easy to obtain and to analyze. They always turn out to be the same thing; strings of syllables, made up of sounds taken from among all those that the speaker knows, put together more or less haphazardly but which nevertheless emerge as word-like and sentence-like units because of realistic, language-like rhythm and melody. Glossolalia is indeed like language in some ways, but this is only because the speaker [unconsciously] wants it to be like language. Yet in spite of superficial similarities, glossolalia is fundamentally *not* language. All specimens of glossolalia that have ever been studied have produced no features that would even suggest that they reflect some kind of communicative system'[166]. Samarin elsewhere defined it as 'unintelligible babbling speech'[167]. William Welmes, professor of African languages at UCLA wrote, 'I must report without reservation that my sample does not sound like a language structurally . . . The consonants and vowels do not all sound like English (the glossolaliac's native language), but the intonation patterns are so completely American English that the total effect is a bit ludicrous'[168].

A fourth problem with 'speaking in tongues' arises from the quality of the 'interpretations' given, many of which are bland and shallow, being often just attempts to give the 'sense of the meeting' without any interpretation of the actual words of the tongues-speaker, and thus essentially 'words from their own heart' (Jer. 23:16). The gold-standard test of speaking in tongues is found in Acts 2: non-Christian native

---

[165] *Journal of the American Scientific Affiliation*, September 1968

[166] William J. Samarin, *Tongues of Men and Angels*, New York: Macmillan, 1972, p227

[167] William J. Samarin, "Variation and Variables in Religious Glossolalia", *Language in Society*, ed. Dell Haymes, Cambridge: Cambridge University Press, 1972, pp121-130. These words were followed by more sophisticated linguistic analysis: 'unintelligible babbling speech that exhibits superficial phonological similarity to language, without having consistent syntagmatic structure and that is not systematically derived from or related to known language'.

[168] *Christianity Today*, Nov. 8, 1963

speakers acknowledging that a person who has never learnt their language nevertheless speaks it fluently. Such proof would establish the miraculous, supernatural character of speaking in tongues. But charismatics are reluctant to allow speaking in tongues to be put to a simpler test: recording someone speaking in tongues and getting multiple people to give independent 'interpretations' of the same recording. There is very little evidence that modern 'interpretation' is genuine, and if the 'interpretation' is a pretence, then what is the 'tongue'?

This all points to one conclusion: modern Christians who 'speak in tongues' are not doing the same thing as what happened in the book of Acts or in the church in Corinth. It is not the spiritual gift mentioned in the Bible. It is just 'barnyard babble'.

It is for these reasons that the author does not believe that the biblical gift of speaking in tongues occurs today. The author is a *de-facto* cessationist: the gift ceased at some point in history, probably towards the end of the apostolic age, once it had fulfilled its purpose as a sign of God's judgment upon the Jewish people and the gospel being taken to all the Gentile nations. Speaking in tongues was a divine 'gift'; the Holy Spirit gave it 'according to His own will' (Heb. 2:4), which means that He was free to cause it to cease once it had fulfilled His purpose. Modern-day speaking in tongues is not miraculous, whereas the biblical gift was. It is not from the Holy Spirit; it is counterfeit worship. The author would be open to claims of speaking in tongues if it was shown to be the real thing, if it was something that was truly from God. All Christians believe that God *could* cause people to speak in tongues today – He is the Living, Almighty God who does as He pleases in heaven and on earth. But equally, 1 Cor. 14:29 and 1 Thess. 5:21 teach us to 'test the spirits', not to gullibly accept things that are neither edifying nor from God. Therefore it is perfectly consistent for Christians to hold to what the Bible teaches about participatory church gatherings without accepting anything and everything that is claimed to be a spiritual gift.

The New Testament Evidence is Confused and Contradictory

We have already quoted Baptist theologian Millard Erickson who argues that 'there is no prescriptive exposition of what the government of the church is to be like', and so 'we have little choice' but to 'build on . . . descriptive and narrative passages'. He goes on to say that here 'we find a second problem: there is no unitary pattern'. There is so much variation that we cannot discover an authoritative pattern. Lastly, 'even if it were clear that there is one exclusive pattern of organization in the New Testament, that pattern would not necessarily be normative for us today. It might merely be the pattern which was, not the pattern which must be'[169].

The objection that the New Testament displays no unitary pattern of church organization owes much of its modern popularity to B. H. Streeter in his 1929 book, *The Primitive Church*, where it was argued that some New Testament churches were congregational and charismatic (i.e. Spirit-prompted gifts were used by the congregation) while others were Presbyterian (i.e. elder-led), and yet others were episcopal (Streeter argued that James functioned as a monarchical bishop)[170]. C. K. Barrett, a Methodist Minister and Professor of New Testament at Durham University in England similarly wrote, 'A church order that claims to represent the one true apostolic form of the church will not only fail to do justice to the variety found in the New Testament, it will run the risk of being more apostolic than the apostles'[171].

However, as we have earlier argued in the chapter on biblical principles behind participatory church gatherings, it is clear that church government in the New Testament era did not involve episcopacy (monarchical bishops): James is nowhere given the title of bishop (let alone sole-bishop), and we should not try to invent such offices or organizational structures if they are not found in Scripture.

Also clear is the fact that church government in New Testament times contained features of both congregationalism and presbyterianism: there is abundant evidence of both (a) the participatory, Spirit-led use of gifts and (b) the shepherd-care of elders. The practical effect of certain

---

[169] Millard J. Erickson, *Christian Theology*, 2nd Ed., Grand Rapids, MI: Baker, 1998, pp 1094-5.
[170] B. H. Streeter, *The Primitive Church*, New York: Macmillan, 1929
[171] C. K. Barrett, *The Signs of an Apostle, The Cato Lecture 1969*, Carlisle: Paternoster, 1996, p88

people taking the most active roles in teaching and preaching in participatory church gatherings would inevitably be to make these people the spiritual guides of the church. The 'pastors' (i.e. shepherds, Eph. 4:11) would thus be involved in both feeding and leading their flocks. In other words, in the 'charismatic communities' of the New Testament, the gifts and offices of feeding and leading overlap. Leadership and government are mentioned alongside other spiritual gifts in Romans 12:6-8 and in 1 Cor. 12:28; they were not just offices, but spiritual gifts. These two features of church life (congregationalism and presbyterianism) are not evidence of confusion and contradiction. They existed alongside each other in a complementary fashion and are evidence of biblical balance: the active participation of the congregation under the guidance and care of elders.

Furthermore, the claim that the New Testament presents a picture of variety and confusion stands in direct contradiction to what Paul said in 1 Cor. 14:33 ('as in all the churches of the saints') about the apostolic uniformity of church organisation, government and practice. Streeter's arguments provide no solid reasons for dismissing the New Testament as authoritative, and adopting some extra-biblical plan. The New Testament is both clear and our sufficient guide for church life today.

The New Testament Provides 'Principles, not Patterns'

It is commonly argued that the New Testament provides no authoritative blueprint, pattern or template for church organisation. Evangelical writers frequently state that the New Testament does not tell us how to 'do church'. Instead, the New Testament gives us general principles to follow.

Bruce H. Leafblad, Emeritus Professor of Church Music and Worship, writes, 'Many of the aspects of modern worship may be traced to the biblical era and to the biblical documents themselves. However, what the Scriptures do *not* provide the church is important to note. For example, the New Testament nowhere sets forth a fixed order for Christian worship to be observed by all churches. . . . Overall, the Scriptures don't seem to have as keen an interest in the "packaging" of worship – that is, in its forms and formats – as in its essence and its integrity. So down through the ages of Christian history the church has had the task of translating the biblical materials into "ordered" worship experiences since no such order is provided in the New Testament itself"[172].

Wayne Grudem writes: 'The sufficiency of Scripture ... does not mean that the Bible answers all the questions that we might think up. . . . There will of course be some times when the answer we find is that Scripture does not speak directly to our question. (That would be the case, for example, if we tried to find from Scripture what "order of worship" to follow on Sunday mornings, or whether it is better to kneel or perhaps to stand when we pray, or at what time we should eat our meals during the day, etc.) In those cases, we may conclude that God has not required us to think or act in any certain way with regard to that question (except, perhaps, in terms of more general principles regarding our attitudes and goals). But in many other cases we will find direct and clear guidance from the Lord to equip us for "every good work" (2 Tim. 3:17)'[173].

Rob Warner frames the objection this way: '*Denominational imperialism* assumes that a single and definitive church order can be read off the pages of the New Testament and applied to the church in every generation and culture. The New Testament is assumed to provide not merely the authoritative guiding principles, but also the definitive blueprint for church structure and life. We therefore turn to someone from another denomination and say, with ecumenical graciousness, 'You worship God in your way, and we'll worship him in his way'. Like men staring down a well and seeing their own faces reflected below, the founders and advocates of each new denomination stare into the Bible and all too often find their own structures to be the exclusive, legitimate pattern for the apostolic church. Those who disagree have frequently been assumed to lack intelligence, integrity or spiritual illumination . . .The result of denominational imperialism is the imposition of fixed and

---

[172] "Evangelical Worship", in *Experience God in Worship*, ed. Michael Warden, Loveland, CO: Group Publishing, 2000), p95, emphasis in the original
[173] Wayne Grudem, *Systematic Theology*, Leicester: IVP, 1994, p131

inflexible requirements, whereas the New Testament reveals liberty, variety and pragmatic flexibility in Church life and order'[174].

Both Grudem and Warner argue that the New Testament only provides 'principles' for Church life; it does not provide a 'pattern' or direct instructions. However, the idea of 'principles' is problematic in some respects. For example, homosexuals would argue that the principle of love overrides what the letter of Scripture says about marriage, arguing that they should be able to marry. Similarly, egalitarians like Gordon Fee argue that the principle of Spirit-gifting is more important than gender: 'The real question is, Which comes first, gender or gifting? What [opponents of women in ministry] are trying to tell me is that gender comes above gifting. How can that be? The Spirit gives the gifting. If a woman stands and prophesies by the Spirit, and men are present, does the Spirit not speak to them? Come on! How dumb can you get?'[175]

Fee forgets the fact that in 1 Cor. 14, Paul repeatedly tells us that the principle of Spirit-gifting does not automatically license someone to speak. People speaking in tongues are told to be silent if there is no one to interpret (v28), and people prophesying are told to be silent if something is revealed to a listener (v30). Similarly, the fact that women possess spiritual gifts does not set aside what the Bible says about women in church: they are to be silent, for it is a disgrace for a woman to speak in church (v34-5).

It becomes obvious from examples like these that it is possible to use 'principles' as a pretext for ignoring what the Bible actually says, playing off one principle against another to make the Bible say whatever we want. If we get to pick and choose which 'principles' the Bible teaches, then we can do whatever we like. For example, while some Christians might suggest the principle of expository Bible teaching is important, we could easily imagine others arguing that 'getting the crowds in' is the most important business of the church, and that they need to do 'whatever it takes', even if that means video clips and drama team

---

[174] Rob Warner, *21st Century Church*, Eastbourne: Kingsway, 1999, pp79-80
[175] Julian Lukins, "A Professor with Spirit", an interview with Gordon Fee in *Charisma Magazine*, 9/1/2010

productions instead of preaching. Liberal theologians would tell us that the principle of 'social justice' is more important than Scripture. Others might suggest that fellowship is the most important principle, and rather than listening to Bible teaching at church on Sundays, instead decide to spend time drinking coffee with friends, or going water-skiing. Others might suggest the 'principle of praise' (charismatic disco-churches), or perhaps the 'principle of spirituality' (trendy hipster churches with their prayer labyrinths and prophetic art classes).

Who gets to decide which 'principles' are important? How shall these principles be justified? Christians who accept the Bible as God's inspired and authoritative Word cannot take a pick-and-mix approach to the 'principles' it gives us. Unless we are content with pure pragmatism (whatever works), then surely we must be open to all the Bible teaches, not just what we find more personally fulfilling or fashionable or expedient or traditionally acceptable. In other words, we need to be prepared to accept whatever God says in the Bible.

Grudem's claim that the Bible says nothing about an 'order of service' is only half true. The New Testament provides no 'order of service'; instead, the New Testament presents the exact opposite of an 'order of service', a church service that is open to the leading of the Spirit of God, participatory, and with a great deal of freedom for the believers to exercise their gifts. It is true that there is no mention of any 'order of service' that we are familiar with, whether elaborate and liturgical or a more contemporary 'program'. Such services bear little resemblance to the picture of church life painted in the New Testament. But this is because the Bible envisages a church gathering that is very different to the sorts of services modern churches are familiar with.

It is true that the Bible does not give exhaustive directions about what we must do in church (it does not tell us, for example, what time we must meet, or what hymnbook to use, or what Bible passages to preach upon at various times of the year). The Bible provides us instead with a simpler template for how to organize our church gatherings, a blueprint centred on 1 Cor. 14:26-40 and backed up by references to the same pattern elsewhere throughout the New Testament. It was a form of church gathering that was uniformly found throughout the apostolic churches, nor is any other type of church gathering known to the New Testament. The description is accompanied by apostolic insistence that such guidelines are the commandments of the Lord.

Our problem is not a lack of biblical information; the problem is our denominational blind-spots, our tenaciously-held traditions, our commitments to pragmatism, our fascination with the latest fashions, and our desire to lean on our own understanding instead of trusting in the Lord (Prov. 3:5). God's Word is sufficient for church life, as for any other area of Christian life. God has given *everything* we need to know 'for life and godliness' (2 Peter 1:3). The Holy Spirit was given to teach the apostles 'all things', so they would be 'led into *all* truth' (John 14:26, 16:13). Paul preached 'the whole counsel of God' (Acts 20:27). Jude could say that we have 'the faith once for all delivered to the saints' (Jude 1:3). God in His wisdom has provided all that we need to successfully navigate the life of faith. This includes Church life as much as any other area of Christian living, for the New Testament is far from silent in the matter of church gatherings. The problem is our reluctance to study, trust and obey what the Bible says.

Just because they did it in NT times, does this mean that we have to?

I was once speaking to a Christian friend, a church elder, who asked, 'just because the Bible describes it happening like this in those days, does this mean we have to do things the same way today?' Another way of rewording this question is as follows: Is the New Testament still authoritative over us today? In some ways, I think this is the most important question of all.

Evangelical Christians believe that the Bible is inspired, authoritative, clear and sufficient[176]. We turn instinctively to Scripture for

---

[176] That is, evangelicals believe that the Bible is inspired in the sense that it's very words are God's, Spirit-breathed words (2 Tim. 3:16). By the authority of Scripture, evangelicals mean that we should believe and obey what the Bible teaches. Under the heading of clarity, evangelicals believe we can understand what Scripture is saying (with God's Spirit's help, prayerful patient study and

establishing our doctrinal beliefs about God, the Person of Christ, and salvation, or practical subjects like marriage, prayer, or giving. On these subjects, the Bible is our go-to book, it has the last word, and it is the supreme authority. Even when we run into difficult questions on these subjects, we do not push the Bible to one side or say it is confused, unhelpful, out of date, or 'merely Paul's opinion'. We agree with J. C. Ryle when he wrote, 'Let the Bible, the whole Bible and nothing but the Bible be the rule of our faith and practice'. We claim to accept 'the whole counsel of God' (Acts 20:27).

But it is a curious fact that when the subject changes to church life, the same evangelicals who spring to the defence of the inspiration, authority, clarity and sufficiency of Scripture in other matters suddenly turn around and treat the Word of God as if it were just another voice in a crowded, noisy market-square of competing ideas. Thus, to ask whether we have to do things the way the New Testament says we should is really to question whether Scripture is authoritative for us today. Here we have a case of double-standards: when the subject is church worship, the same Christians who champion the authority, clarity and sufficiency of Scripture everywhere else, suddenly make an about-turn and question, dilute or deny these doctrines.

C. H. Mackintosh wrote, 'men must either deny that the Bible is the Word of God, or admit its sufficiency and supremacy in all ages, and in all countries–in all stages and conditions of the human race. Grant us but this, that God has written a book for man's guidance, and we argue that that book must be amply sufficient for man, no matter when, where, or how we find him'[177].

Another more theological way this objection is worded is to argue that participatory church gatherings were found in the infant, developmental phase of the church, until more mature patterns of church government and order were instituted. It is argued that participatory

---

interaction with other believers). Finally, the Bible is sufficient in that it provides all that we need to know for salvation and godly living.

[177] C. K. Mackintosh, "The Bible: Its Sufficiency and Supremacy" in *The Mackintosh Treasury: Miscellaneous Writings*, Neptune, NJ: Loizeaux Brothers, 1976, p17

church gatherings are most clearly seen in churches where there was not yet any established government under elders and deacons (1 Corinthians and 1 Thessalonians). Therefore, participatory church gatherings are the infant, developmental phase of church life in the New Testament. It follows that, while the church in early apostolic days was characterized by the power and presence of the Holy Spirit, such Christianity was always destined to give way to more mundane and mechanical arrangements. Even a fire cannot burn with its initial intensity forever, but must eventually die down. Just as the apostles themselves were a temporary, foundational phase of the church, so church life developed and outgrew its early structures and adopted more mature and settled forms, just as a child outgrows its infant clothing. B. H. Streeter argued a 'doctrine of development'; that 'the history of Catholic Christianity during the first five centuries is the history of the standardization of a diversity having its origin in the Apostolic age'[178].

There are two things that can be said in reply. Firstly, it is true that the early apostolic churches – like all churches – went through a period of growth from infancy to maturity. The early stages involved congregational participation in worship, and once there had been a suitable period of growth and maturity, elders and deacons were appointed. However, this picture of participatory congregational involvement with leadership by elders is consistently found throughout the New Testament, from beginning to end. Elders appeared very early on in Acts (chapter 11) and even in 'charismatic' Thessalonica we find evidence of emerging leadership (1 Thess. 5:12-14), so that eldership was not some late development. Similarly, both features persist to the end of the New Testament era. Thus, we find evidence of participatory church gatherings in the Pastoral Epistles and in Peter's epistle, where we also find evidence of government by elders. Participatory church gatherings were not just a feature of infant churches, or churches without government by elders; they were found also amongst mature churches.

Secondly, the New Testament gives no expiration date for apostolic forms of church government or gatherings; nor does it describe or

---

[178] Streeter, *The Primitive Church*, p30

anticipate, let alone legislate for, 'more mature' forms. Peter and John both sign their letters simply as (fellow) elders in 1 Peter 5:1 and 2 and 3 John, not as archbishops, showing that there was no development beyond these forms of church organisation in the New Testament. On the contrary, we repeatedly find warnings of future departure from the 'faith once for all delivered to the saints' (Jude 3) throughout the later epistles. The history of the post-apostolic church is the history of the adoption of innovations that denied and undermined what the New Testament teaches. For example, we see the rise of monarchical bishops claiming special authority nowhere granted to them in the New Testament, and ruling as lords over God's people, which the New Testament condemns in the clearest language. The developments of the post-apostolic church were not progress at all, but decline and disobedience.

W. E. Vine writes, 'The question arises whether what is therein revealed [that is in the New Testament] was intended to be complete and permanent, or simply introductory and subject to modification. Either the Scriptures, God-breathed and divinely preserved, give us a full revelation of the mind of God for our instruction, or we are left to the notions and propaganda and dictates of men, with all the bias of their natural ideas and inclinations; in other words, we are left to be the subjects of ecclesiastical tyranny and of misguided human tradition. The Scriptures themselves testify to their completeness and finality, as a divine revelation. "The faith," the body of Scripture doctrine, was "once for all delivered to the saints" (Jude 3, R. V.). That "once for all" is a plain statement. A confirmatory intimation is provided in the apostle Paul's exhortation to Timothy to guard the good deposit of the truth and to commit what he had received to faithful men that they might in their turn be able to teach others the same (1 Tim. 1:13; 2:12). No fresh article of faith was to be revealed. What had been taught must be handed on from generation to generation without addition, diminution or modification. In church matters, as in other respects, the teaching of the New Testament is complete as a revelation of the will of God. While no ecclesiastical code, no list of doctrines, no formal set of regulations were issued, what is presented in the Word of God is uniform and consistent throughout, in matters both of doctrine and of practice, and has been proved sufficient under all conditions, however varied they may be, whether from the racial or any other point of view"[179].

"I'm Not Convinced"

There is a certain sort of Bible scholar who will review this book and conclude, "I'm not convinced". No alternative expositions of the relevant New Testament passages will be offered, nor any rebuttal of the deductions drawn from these passages in favour of participatory church gatherings. Or if there are counter-arguments, they will be a rehash of some of the flimsy objections surveyed in this chapter: 1 Corinthians 14 involves 'criticism not commendation', or that it is 'correctional not instructional', or that it is 'descriptive not prescriptive', or that the New Testament presents 'principles, not patterns'. Instead of careful, in-depth examination of key New Testament passages, the dismissal of participatory church gatherings will be brief, accompanied by a few shallow and simplistic slogans.

Readers need to be aware that there is a certain sort of academic Bible scholar who it is very hard to convince by *any* amount of biblical argumentation. This sort of academic agnosticism is not confined to the question of participatory church gatherings. For example, it will not matter how many references to believers baptism by immersion are shown from the New Testament or how many passages are produced to show that churches of the New Testament period were governed by a body of elders, such scholars will reply "I'm not convinced" if they prefer a different model of church government or if they belong to a denomination which practices baptism differently.

Now, some academic biblical scholars simply have a diminished view of the authority of Scripture – they shrug their shoulders at anyone who treats the actual words of Scripture as inspired and determinative. Others have a deeply-ingrained attachment to their denominational tradition, or their ecclesiastical position, and view with extreme prejudice any idea that might threaten it.

---

[179] "The Origin and Rise of Ecclesiasticism and the Papal System", *The Collected Writings of W. E. Vine*, Nashville, TN: Thomas Nelson Publishers, 1996, p356

But for some scholars, the problem lies elsewhere: they are reluctant to give a simple, straightforward answer to any debated question. They have consulted so many commentaries and considered the different viewpoints on so many contentious issues that they are constitutionally incapable of giving an unqualified opinion on any disputed point. Consequently, they consider it a mark of sophistication to be unsure of many things that the Bible teaches. This attitude is nowadays labelled 'post-modernism' with its denial of absolute truth or objective morality and its 'deconstruction' of texts by raising problems and pointing out difficulties. But underlying it is the age-old rebellion against the exclusive and authoritative truth-claims of Christianity.

What a difference between these learned scholars and the child-like faith of which Christ spoke. By contrast, newly-converted Christians who are keen to please God only have to see a truth in Scripture, and they are quick to humbly obey it. Once they learn of the practices of the first Christians in the New Testament, they instinctively desire to imitate their example. These are the sort of Christians that God Himself takes pleasure in: 'On this one will I look; on him who is poor and of a contrite spirit, and who trembles at My word' (Isa. 66:2).

The lesson from all this is simple enough: unless someone saying "I'm not convinced" is able to give a substantial reason, a good knock-down rebuttal that explains why participatory church gatherings are not biblical, or why the Bible is not authoritative over us today, their opinion can safely be ignored.

Conclusion

In this chapter we have looked at a number of objections to the idea of participatory church gatherings. Some of them are sincere questions from honest enquirers, but others are better described as attempts to run from the truth of God's Word, hermeneutical tricks of those unwilling to accept what Scripture says. In the words of Søren Kierkegaard, 'The matter is quite simple. The Bible is very easy to understand. But we Christians are a bunch of scheming swindlers. We pretend to be unable to understand it because we know very well that the minute we understand, we are obliged to act accordingly. Take any words in the

New Testament and forget everything except pledging yourself to act accordingly. My God, you will say, if I do that my whole life will be ruined. How would I ever get on in the world? Herein lies the real place of Christian scholarship. Christian scholarship is the Church's prodigious invention to defend itself against the Bible, to ensure that we can continue to be good Christians without the Bible coming too close. Oh, priceless scholarship, what would we do without you? Dreadful it is to fall into the hands of the living God. Yes it is even dreadful to be alone with the New Testament'[180].

---

[180] Søren Kierkegaard, *Provocations: Spiritual Writings of Søren Kierkegaard*, ed. Charles E. Moore, Farmington, PA: Plough, 2002, p201

CHAPTER 10

Practical Reasons for Participatory Church Gatherings

Church as a Performance

Two female lead singers (in thigh-high skirts) up on stage invited the congregation to stand and worship God, and the words for *Amazing Grace* came up on the screen. The band played the old familiar tune, but the lead singers started in such a sophisticated, syncopated way that nobody in the audience was able to join in and sing along. After their 'duet', and a set of a few more songs, there was a clumsy attempt at communion in a novel way and then the collection. After that, it was time for the message, and the lights went dim. The Bible passage contained one of the most sobering scenes of divine judgment from the Old Testament but the Pastor tried his best to keep the tone upbeat, even throwing in the odd joke as he proceeded through the sermon.

There were about a dozen things that I was uneasy about, but the combination of them all in one service left me shaken. I'm not going to list them all; I admit that some of them had more to do with personal preferences than biblical principles. My one over-riding impression was that the whole affair seemed like a performance. It was the small details as much as the big things, like killing the lights before the message (as if we were in a theatre) so we couldn't read our Bibles, and the congregation not being able to participate in singing *Amazing Grace*. I remembered what I had read somewhere: evangelical Christianity has become part of the light entertainment industry.

D. A. Carson, writing about the dangers of a 'consumer mentality in the heart of mainstream evangelicalism' says this: 'Perhaps the most damning evidence comes in the little things. When church music directors never fail to tell their choirs to "go backstage" to get ready, it is not hard to discern the tentacles of the entertainment industry controlling our vocabulary and our thoughts. . . . When churches advertise themselves in the newspaper with lines like, "We feature entertaining worship" – an exact quote, I am afraid – one scarcely knows whether to laugh or weep'[181].

Alan Wolfe writes that modern evangelicalism in America has 'so strong a desire to copy the culture of hotel chains and popular music that it loses what religious distinctiveness it once had ... The truth is there is increasingly little difference between an essentially secular activity like the popular entertainment industry and the bring-'em-in-at-any-cost efforts of evangelical megachurches"[182].

Jim Cymbala writes, 'People have lowered the standards in a vain attempt to make churches look more successful than they really are. The sermons have to be uniformly positive, and the services can't go longer than 60 minutes. Even then, church is inconvenient for some, especially during the football season. Showing up at church is so inconvenient that soon people will be faxing in their worship! . . . The truth is that "user-friendly" can be a cover-up word for carnality. The same people who want sixty-minute worship services rent two-hour videos and watch [sporting] games that run even longer. The issue is not length, but appetite. Why the misplaced desire? Seriously, what will our children and grand-children grow up experiencing in church? Extended times of waiting upon the Lord will be totally foreign to their experience. There will be no memory bank of seeing people reach out to God. All they will recall are professionally polished, closely timed productions'[183].

Church gatherings among Jesus' first followers were nothing like a 'performance'. Nor, by the way, were they anything like the staid and

---

[181] D. A. Carson, *The Gagging of God: Christianity Confronts Pluralism*, Zondervan, 1996, p465-6

[182] Alan Wolfe, *The Transformation of American Religion: How We Actually Live Our Faith*, New York: Free Press, 2003, p257

[183] Jim Cymbala, *Fresh Wind, Fresh Fire*, Grand Rapids: MI, Zondervan, 1997, 2003, p132-3

traditional service of old-fashioned Protestantism with its hymn, prayer, hymn, sermon, pattern. Instead, the church was an interactive community of people that provided mutual encouragement, where the members met together to use their spiritual gifts to build each other up.

Eduard Schweizer writes of the early church as follows, 'The togetherness of the church and its services is not that of a theatre audience, where one or several paid actors act on the stage while everybody else is looking on. Each one takes part with his special gift … the body of Christ is not a body of soldiers in which one sees at best the neck of the preceding person … it is a body consisting of members living in their mutual addressing, asking, challenging, comforting, sharing of Christ and his gifts'[184].

There are other problems with the modern 'church as a spectator-sport' model. It raises questions about authenticity; just like any other piece of theatre, the more 'performance' is involved, the more we suspect that participants are putting on a mask and acting a part. The more powerful and polished we make our church services, the less they reflect the reality that we are, at best, weak and broken sinners dependent upon the power of God to fulfil His purposes in the world. It also raises questions about the church's relationship to the world; if Christ has called His followers to be counter-cultural (read the Sermon on the Mount), then how is it that the public face we present is becoming more and more like the world's entertainment industry?

But for some people, perhaps the most worrying issue is that the Hollywood Performance model of church is not actually working.

The Pragmatic Approach to Church Life is not Working

Instead of a biblical approach to church practice ('what does the Scripture say'), modern evangelicalism has largely adopted a pragmatic approach ('whatever seems to work'), justified by arguing that the New Testament provides no authoritative instructions, guidelines or patterns for church gatherings. This not only turns a blind eye to the fact that the

---

[184] Eduard Schweizer, "The Service of Worship", in *Neotestamentica*, Zurich: Zwingli, 1963, p335-36

New Testament describes church services; it is also a denial of the authority and sufficiency of Scripture. It allows us to adopt and adapt whatever church practices we, in our human wisdom, think will see the church grow. As a result, we are free to combine some biblical ideas about church while ignoring others, mixing some traditional practices with other trendy fads in a syncretistic fashion to produce a product that we hope will 'do the job'.

The irony is that the pragmatic approach ('whatever works') is not working. We are going backwards, having an ever diminishing effect evangelistically, and losing the 'culture wars'.

Gary Gilley, writing in *This Little Church went to Market*, says, 'it doesn't take a mathematician to realize that if the percentage of Americans going to church has remained constant, yet mega-churches are popping up almost weekly, then the giant churches are largely being populated by folks funnelling in from small churches. Just as the major retailers are killing mom-and-pop department stores, chain restaurants and groceries are doing the same things in their respective venues, and the Mall has demolished 'downtown', so the mega-churches are doing a number on the small church. But large does not necessarily mean better, and when all the numbers are tallied, overall church attendance (on a percentage basis) is not increasing despite the methods championed by these mega-churches'[185].

There have been literally thousands of megachurches planted in the United States in the last few decades, yet the number of people going to church is lower now than ever before. The percentage of people going to Church on an average Sunday in the West is not growing or staying constant; it is in dramatic decline. Just as the 1990's in Britain saw a decline of one million people attending Church on any given Sunday, so the same decline is happening in the United States. Protestants shrunk from over 70% of the US population in the late 1950s to under 50% in 2012, mainly as a result of the decline of the so-called Mainline or Liberal denominations (Lutherans, Methodists and Episcopalians), who

---

[185] Gary Gilley, *This Little Church Went to Market*, Darlington: Evangelical Press, 2005, p41

went from over 30% in the 1970s to less than 15% in 2012. However, evangelicals have also declined from their high-water mark of over 30% in the late 1990s to 24% in 2012. The American Christian pollster George Barna reckons that church attendance in the USA is in the process of falling off a cliff. Millions of 'born-again' Christians in the USA have stopped attending church in the last few years.

Churches built on pragmatism love metrics. They need to measure whether the plan is working by keeping track of all sorts of numbers. For such churches, the ABCs are Attendance, Buildings and Collections: how many bodies are sitting on seats, how big is the building and how much money is the church taking in. Unfortunately, the reality is that the corporate model of Church growth is not paying off. The numbers are not adding up, they are going down.

The Convenience Culture of Modern Consumer Christianity

One of the great changes that has occurred in the evangelical church scene over the last few decades has been the increasing importance of pragmatism over theology and biblical faithfulness, and consequently the elevation of style over content. We might call it the Aestheticization of Christianity, the triumph of art over substance.

Church marketing consultant Richard Southern encourages churches to make, 'an essential paradigm shift, putting the needs of potential customers before the needs of the institutional church. [People] think of churches like they think of supermarkets, they want options, choices and convenience. . . . Protestant megachurches have become the evangelical answer to Home Depot, marketing such services as worship, child care, a sports club, 12-step groups, and a guaranteed parking space'[186].

One of the results of pragmatism in the church is that modern Christians tend to think of going to church in the same way they think of going to a restaurant: you pay a little for the privilege, and if the service is good you might come again (but if not, you will go somewhere else next time). Admittedly, modern Christians don't exactly pay very much to

---

[186] Richard Comino and Don Lattin, "Choosing My Religion", *American Demographics*, April 1999, p63

attend church (from 1968 to 2001 the giving of the average church member in the US declined from 3.1% of income to 2.66%)[187], but just giving up some time to attend church is now considered a sacrifice. Church has become another consumer convenience, catering to our spiritual needs.

David Wells writes, 'Allowing the consumer to be sovereign in this way in fact sanctions a bad habit. It encourages us to indulge in constant internal inventory in the church no less than in the marketplace, to ask ourselves perpetually whether the "products" we are being offered meet our present "felt needs". In this environment, market research has found that there is scarcely any consumer loyalty to particular products and brands anymore. The consumer, like the marketer, is now making fresh calculations all the time. And so it is that the churches that have adopted the strategy of marketing themselves have effectively installed revolving doors. The pews may be full, but never with the same people from week to week. People keep entering, lured by the church's attractions or just to check out the wares, but then they move on because they feel their needs, real or otherwise, are not being met'[188].

Haddon Robinson writes, 'Too often now when people join a church, they do so as consumers. If they like the product, they stay. If they do not, they leave. They can no more imagine a church disciplining them than they could a store that sells goods disciplining them. It is not the place of the seller to discipline the consumer. In our churches we have a consumer mentality'[189].

The reality is that churches are competing against each other to attract a floating population of Christian (and perhaps the odd non-Christian) 'consumers', each trying to out-do each other by offering more convenience and comfort ('one service', parking, etc.) or by promoting a celebrity preacher, or the best music or social interaction. It is a sad

---

[187] John L. and Sylvia Ronsdale, *The State of Church Giving through 2001*, Champaign, IL: Empty Tomb, 2003, p.12

[188] David Wells, *God in the Waste Land*, Grand Rapids, MI: Eerdmans, 1994, p75

[189] quoted in Marlin Jeschke, *Discipling in the Church: Recovering a Ministry of the Gospel*, Scottsdale, PA: Herald Press, 1988, p143

reflection on the shallowness of many Christians today that it takes nothing more than a crowd to draw a crowd. Small to medium sized churches are in survival mode as they battle to retain members. Instead of seeing people converted, most Western church growth nowadays is the result of transfers. Should Christianity really be about sheep-stealing or 'shuffling the pack'?

Someone has called it McChurch; church has become a business, and church life is full of the methods of modern middle management: surveys, statistics, marketing and mission statements. Or maybe a better way to describe modern Church life is Convenience Store Christianity. Some people nowadays consider themselves members of a church, despite only attending once or twice a month. Some churches put on multiple, different types of services, 'to cater to every taste'. Churches are bending over backwards to attract and keep their customers, to be ever more accommodating.

We are doing a Poor Job of Producing Disciples

The problem goes deeper than just the decline in numbers: modern Western consumer churches are not doing a very good job of producing mature disciples.

William MacDonald wrote in his book *True Discipleship*: 'True Christianity is an all-out commitment to the Lord Jesus Christ. The Savior is not looking for men and women who will give their spare evenings to Him – or their weekends – or their years of retirement. Rather He seeks those who will give Him first place in their lives'[190].

Discipleship is at the very heart of what Christ taught about being His follower. Christ repudiated the numbers game, and while He regularly drew great crowds, He also repeatedly turned away from such fair-weather followers, instead investing His energy in training his true disciples. Christ made discipleship the goal of His Great Commission. He gave His Church the job, not of trying to get people to 'make a

---

[190] William MacDonald, *True Discipleship*, Kansas City: Walterick Publishers, 1975, p5

decision', but of making disciples: 'Go therefore and make disciples of all nations' (Matthew 28:19).

Christ set out the terms of discipleship in His Sermon on the Mount: Christ-like, righteous living in dependent faith upon God. Being a disciple of Christ is difficult – it was not for nothing that Christ climbed the mountain with his followers before delivering this manifesto. Towards the end of the Sermon, Christ said, 'Narrow is the gate and difficult is the way which leads to life, and few there be who find it' (Matthew 7:14). Christian discipleship involves hardship and difficulty – how is it then that we have turned Christianity into a pleasurable hour sitting in a padded seat being entertained by professionals?

Just how poor a job modern evangelicalism is doing in producing disciples is seen in the results of surveys. In 1987, American pollster George Gallup reported, "There's little difference in ethical behavior between the churched and the unchurched. There's as much pilferage and dishonesty among the churched as the unchurched. And I'm afraid that applies pretty much across the board: religion, *per se*, is not really life changing."[191]

In 1991, William Hendricks stated, 'The Princeton Religion Research Center has measured the impact of religion on day-to-day work. Comparing the 'churched' with the 'unchurched' on a wide range of behaviors like pilfering supplies (stealing), overstating qualifications on resumes (lying), calling in sick when not sick (lying and stealing), and overstating tax deductions (lying, stealing, and cheating), the center finds 'little difference in the ethical views and behavior of the churched and the unchurched.' What differences there are 'are not significant or are of marginal significance."[192]

In his 2005 book, *Revolution*, George Barna says about the 32% of Americans who describe themselves as 'born-again' (that is, they claim that they have made a personal commitment to Jesus Christ and believe that when they die they will go to heaven because they have confessed their sins and accepted Jesus Christ as their Saviour):

---

[191] George Gallup, "Vital Signs", *Leadership*, Fall 1987, p. 17
[192] William Hendricks, *Christianity Today*, Nov. 25, 1991

- only 9% of 'born-again' Christians have a biblical worldview: that is, they believe that the Bible is accurate in its teachings, that Jesus lived a sinless life, that absolute moral truth exists, that Satan is real (not symbolic), that all believers have a responsibility to share their faith with others, that salvation is by God's grace, not works,
- the likelihood of a married couple who are born-again Christians getting divorced is the same as couples who are not disciples of Christ.
- the typical born-again believer will not lead a single person to faith in Christ during their lifetime
- few 'born-again' Christians define success in spiritual terms. Most describe success in terms of professional achievement, family happiness or material prosperity
- born-again believers spend far more time watching television, listening to music, reading books or discussing hobbies or leisure interests than reading the Bible
- the only time 'born-again' Christians generally worship God is in church

Now, there are many causes for the current worldliness and carnality of modern evangelicals. But Frank Viola identifies one of the problems causing the epidemic of spiritual infantilism: 'The modern clerical system is a religious artifact that has no biblical basis. This system has allowed the body of Christ to lapse into an audience due to its heavy reliance on a single leader. It has turned church into the place where Christians watch professionals perform. It has transformed the holy assembly into a center for professional pulpiteerism supported by lay-spectators. Perhaps the most daunting feature of the clergy system is that it keeps the people it claims to serve in spiritual infancy. Because the clergy system usurps the Christian's right to minister in a spiritual way during corporate gatherings, it ends up debilitating God's people. It keeps them weak and insecure. Without question, many – if not most – of the people who are part of the clergy profession love God's people and desire to serve them. Many of them sincerely want to see their fellow brethren take spiritual responsibility. (Numerous clergy have expressed their frustration with not seeing their congregations take more responsibility. But few of them have traced the problem to their own profession.) Yet the clergy profession ends up disempowering and pacifying the believing priesthood. This is the case regardless of how uncontrolling the person who fills the clergy position may be. Here's how it works. Since clergy carries the spiritual workload, the majority of the church becomes passive, lazy, self-seeking ("feed me"), and arrested in their spiritual development'[193].

Christian Smith puts it this way: 'The clergy profession is fundamentally self-defeating. Its stated purpose is to nurture spiritual maturity in the church – a valuable goal. In actuality, however, it accomplishes the opposite by nurturing a permanent dependence of the laity upon the clergy. Clergy becomes to their congregations like parents whose children never grow up, like therapists whose clients never become healed, like teachers whose students never graduate. . . . the actual effect of the clergy profession is to make the body of Christ lame. This happens not because clergy intend it (they usually intend the opposite) but because the objective nature of the profession inevitably turns the laity into passive receivers'[194].

The modern evangelical version of church is producing a generation of pew-potatoes. But spiritual health, like physical health, depends not only on getting a good diet, but also getting plenty of exercise[195].

Why Christians Reach a Point where Growth Stalls

Worse yet, it is not simply that many Christians remain spiritual babies. Even the spiritually mature are dissatisfied. Bill Hybels of Willow Creek Community Church (weekly attendance: 20,000), one of America's most successful mega-churches, described what he called the 'Wake-up Call of my Adult Life' in 2007. Releasing the results of a survey of Willow

---

[193] Frank Viola, *Reimagining Church*, Colorado Springs, CO: David C. Cook, 2008, p160

[194] Christian Smith, "Church Without Clergy", *Voices in the Wilderness*, Nov/Dec 1988

[195] Read through 1 Timothy 4 (and particularly verses 6 and 7) to see the way that Paul tells Timothy to maintain spiritual health.

Creek's membership called REVEAL, Hybels said that the church scored highly among 'seekers' and new Christians. However, Hybels was shocked by the reaction of the mature Christians. Many described themselves as 'spiritually stalled' or dissatisfied with the role of the church in their spiritual growth.

Before we jump to criticize mega-churches, there are two points that need to be clarified to better understand the survey. Firstly, the survey was conducted in 30 churches. Greg Hawkins, one of Willow Creek's leaders, in a comment at *Out of Ur*, Christianity Today magazine's blog, said: 'the findings are based on thirty churches besides Willow. In all thirty churches, we've found the six segments of REVEAL's spiritual continuum, including the Stalled and Dissatisfied segments. And these churches aren't all Willow clones. We've surveyed traditional Bible churches, mainline denominations, African-American churches and churches representing a wide range of geographies and sizes'. Thus, the problem is not confined to mega-churches. Lots of churches have spiritually mature Christians who feel that their church is not really helping them to grow anymore.

Secondly, in addition to its 'seeker-sensitive' evangelistic services, Willow Creek provides Bible teaching at its week-night classes for mature Christians, as well as small groups for fellowship and outreaches for ministry activity. In other words, Willow Creek is really little different to most evangelical churches, just bigger. Its believer-oriented activities are of a high class and, in all probability, better than found in the average evangelical church. It seeks to provide everything that is needed for salvation and Christian growth. Yet, the ones who should be the most spiritually responsive are not making progress nor are they satisfied with what their church is providing for them. The survey says as much about the culture of evangelical churches in general as it does about the mega-churches.

So, what did Hybels and Hawkins identify as the problem? They argue that attendance at the church's programs is not enough. Getting involved in the church's programs (by attending church services, listening to Bible teaching, being part of a small group and getting involved in some ministry activity) did not result in mature Christians feeling a sense of spiritual fulfilment or growing in their walk with Christ.

What did Hybels and Hawkins decide was missing from these Christians' lives? Here is Hybels' suggestion: 'We made a mistake. What we should have done when people crossed the line of faith and become Christians, we should have started telling people and teaching people that they have to take responsibility to become 'self-feeders'. We should have gotten people, taught people, how to read their bible between services, how to do the spiritual practices much more aggressively on their own'.

Hybels is not the only person telling us that the modern Western experience of Church is leaving many serious Christians feeling unsatisfied. In George Barna's 2005 book, *Revolution* (sub-titled, *Worn out on Church? Finding Vibrant Faith beyond the Sanctuary Walls*) he tells how millions of Americans who call themselves 'born-again' are leaving the church. Barna's book is not without some serious problems (for example, he abandons the idea that church fellowship is an important part of the Christian life; in fact, he says of church: 'we made it up'!). However, the book gives an important insight into why so many people are leaving the American evangelical church scene. Of course, there are spiritual slackers leaving church because golf on Sunday morning seems more attractive. But Barna also shows that there is another group of people who are leaving for an altogether different reason. These people have left the church because they realised that the spiritual growth they were experiencing in their lives was the result of them being involved in some other Christian activity – homeschooling, para-church ministries, workplace fellowships, etc. By comparison, 'the experience provided through their church' (even churches that 'have biblical preaching, people coming to Christ and being baptized, a full roster of interesting classes and programs, and a congregation packed with nice people') 'still seems flat'[196]. Here's the revelation in *Revolution*: church is *not* what is leading to spiritual growth and transformation in the lives of most American Christians.

---

[196] George Barna, *Revolution*, Carol Stream, IL: Tyndale House, 2005, p14

Barna: 'If the local church were the answer to our deep spiritual need, we would see two things. First, people who were most heavily involved in a Christian congregation would be more spiritually developed than others. Second, churched Christians would increasingly reflect the principles and characteristics Scripture tells us are the marks of Jesus' true disciples'[197]. Barna's research shows that this is simply not the case.

Thus, the problems with modern Western consumer, convenience, spectator Christianity go beyond the numbers. Western Christianity is failing to produce disciples whose lives are distinctively different from unbelievers. But even among those who consider themselves to be mature Christians, there is only so much growth that sitting on a seat on Sunday or being involved in a fellowship group will provide. Despite the fact that various Bible passages assert that the teaching of God's Word will bring people to spiritual maturity in Christ (Col. 1:25-29), so that we may grow up in all thing into Him who is the Head, Christ (Eph. 4:11-6), yet our modern Western experience of church is failing to live up to its biblical billing.

Why is this? There comes a point in a Christian's growth where a person needs to become a 'self-feeder', in Bill Hybels words. But, of course, this really only ever happens in conjunction with something else: when people start teaching God's Word and ministering to others rather than sitting and listening.

Christians are not experiencing God in Worship

In his book, *The Seven Habits of Highly Effective Churches*, George Barna speaks about another problem, the fact that many Christians are not experiencing God in worship: one-third of church-going adults have never experienced God's presence. One-half of regular churchgoing adults admit they have not experienced God's presence at any time during the past year. The younger the adult, the more likely they are to state that God is a distant, impersonal reality for them. Why no experience of God? Barna gives the following reasons (pp83-95):

---

[197] Barna, *Revolution*, p30

- Millions of adults who frequently attend church believe that the purpose of attending is to have a pleasing experience.
- There is no desire to confront sin in their lives
- No idea of worship: 'among the two-thirds who attend church services regularly but could not provide a proper definition of worship, some of the more common guesses were that worship is "attending church", "being a church member", and "believing that God exists". The most common answer, though, was "I don't know"
- 'Most adults attend worship services with one person in mind: themselves'
- Only one out of three church attenders believe that preparation for worship prior to going to church is important. By contrast, when people take the time to read the Bible, pray or engage in other exercises designed to prepare them for worship prior to arriving, worship is more likely to occur.
- People consider that it is the church's job to make worship happen: 'How many people attend church services almost daring the church to get them to worship?'
- Expect God to meet with you: if people expect to encounter God, they have more passion, energy and joy in worship[198].

Notice particularly two things Barna says about the need for prior preparation for worship. Number One: we cannot think that it is the church's job (or other people's) to make worship happen. Allied to that is the second observation: if we want to experience God in worship, it requires us to prepare spiritually. In other words, worship requires our individual participation in the process.

Pastoral Burnout

Not only are ordinary Christians dissatisfied with their spiritual growth, the modern evangelical church scene faces a huge problem with its clergy: burnout.

---

[198] George Barna, *The Seven Habits of Highly Effective Churches*, Ventura, CA: Regal Books, 1999, pp83-84

In her book *Mad Church Disease: Overcoming the Burnout Epidemic*, Anne Jackson tells the story of her ministry burn-out as a church's Director of Communication and Media, working a hectic seven-day week, managing two creative teams producing services in a church that was bursting at the seams. Eventually her health broke down due to high stress levels, but it wasn't just her physical and mental health that suffered, or her marriage. Once she had returned to work from hospital, one of the associate pastors asked her a question: "Does working at this church interfere with your communion with Christ?" Jackson says, 'I sat in my chair, stunned. With nothing left to do but say what both of us were thinking, I replied, "Yes". But how could it? How could working in a church with an amazing staff, serving a wonderful community, *all for God*, interfere with my own relationship with my Father? I didn't have the answer. But I knew, beyond a shadow of a doubt, that I was so wrapped up in doing, I had forgotten how to simply be. How to be a child to a Father. How to be a vessel he can use. How to be a wife to my husband. How to be a light in a dark world. My friend's question haunted me for weeks'[199].

In the Foreword to her book, Craig Groeschel said that at a particularly low time in his ministry, he listened to Bill Hybels speaking, who confessed that 'the way I was doing the work of God was destroying the work of God in my life'. Groeschel commented: 'someone had finally put words to what I felt so deeply. The way I was doing the work of God was destroying the work of God in me'. Groeschel concludes: 'something is wrong with the way many ministers minister'[200].

Marcus Honeysett, a Baptist minister, and instrumental in forming the organisation Living Leadership in the UK writes, in a 2009 article titled, *A Church Leadership Crisis?*, 'I believe that the percentage of people leaving Christian leadership (humanly-speaking) prematurely is at an epidemic rate, especially in the 45-55 age group. Stress-related illnesses are sky high, and high levels of family stress are leading to increased

---

[199] Anne Jackson, *Mad Church Disease: Overcoming the Burnout Epidemic*, Grand Rapids, MI: Zondervan, 2009, p38
[200] Jackson, *Mad Church Disease*, p6

marriage breakdown rates among leaders. Numbers falling to sexual temptation seem to be increasing. A friend recently told me that this merely reflected the population at large in any profession. That may be so, but it is irrelevant, because we need our Christian leaders to be the strongest of heart and the most energised in the gospel as they call people to come and die with Christ'[201].

Rick Lewis writes, 'Research being conducted in Australia shows Christian leaders dropping out of ministry at an alarming rate. One outstanding expert in this field is Dr. Rowland Croucher, of John Mark Ministries. He estimates that in Australia there is one ex-pastor for every currently serving pastor; about 13,000 at the present time. My own informal survey of people involved in ministry supervision in the UK, Canada and the United States indicates that dropout rates for those countries are similar. Roy Searle, a former President of the Baptist Union in the UK, told me in a personal conversation that dropout rates for evangelical and charismatic leaders in particular are quite phenomenal …. But the crisis is not confined to those who drop out. A large percentage of those who remain in ministry suffer from various degrees of stress and burnout. Analysis of the National Church Life Survey published in Australia in 2001 covering 4,500 senior ministers, pastors and priests has findings that are sobering indeed. It reveals that burnout is a major feature in the lives of nearly a quarter of all congregational leaders. In addition, a further half are bordering on burnout. When half of our Christian leaders drop out and only one in four of those who remain are doing well, we have a serious crisis on our hands'[202].

The problem is that not only do most clergy nurture a spiritually-dependent and immature laity, they are literally burning themselves out, physically and spiritually, trying to do it.

Frank Viola writes, 'Just as serious, the clergy system warps many who occupy clerical positions. The reason? God never called anyone to

---

[201] Marcus Honeysett, "A Church Leadership Crisis?", in *Partnership Perspectives*, Jan 2009, p21
[202] Rick Lewis, *Mentoring Matters: Building strong Christian leaders, Avoiding burnout, Reaching the finishing line*, Oxford: Monarch Books, 2009, p70

bear the heavy burden of ministering to the needs of the church by himself. Yet regardless of the spiritual tragedies the clergy profession engenders, the masses continue to rely on, and insist upon it. For this reason the so-called laity is just as responsible for the problem of clericalism as is the clergy. If the truth be told, many Christians prefer the convenience of paying someone to shoulder the responsibility for ministry and shepherding. In their minds, it's better to hire a religious specialist to tend to the needs of God's people than to bother themselves with the self-emptying demands of servanthood and pastoral care'[203].

People Learn and Grow Best by Participating

We have already looked at the Learning Triangle earlier in the book and what it teaches: that people learn little by listening to sermons, that they learn well by discussion in groups and they learn best by teaching themselves.

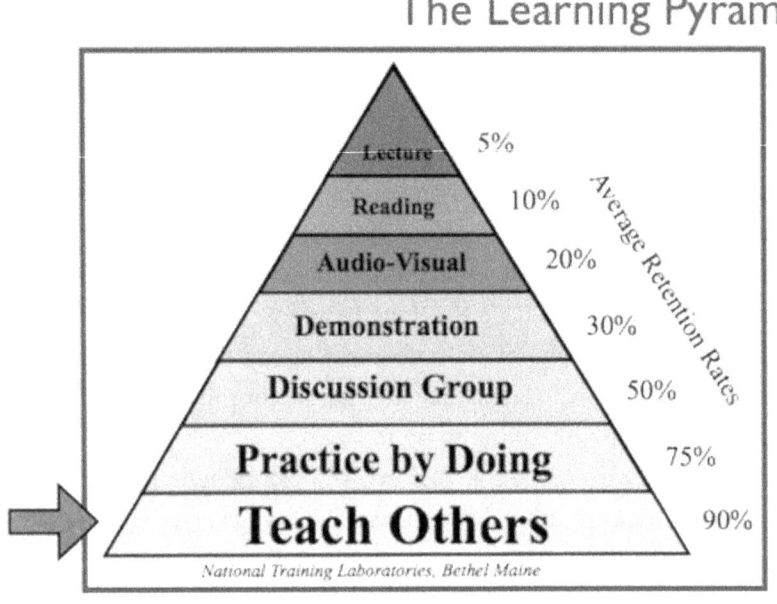

---

[203] Frank Viola, *Reimagining Church*, p160-1

The lessons for church life are two. If we were sincerely interested in getting people in our congregations to grow and become more like Christ, we would:

1. Include stimulating discussion straight after our sermons so that people would remember a lot more about the subject.
2. Try as quickly as possible to get people involved in teaching others the Word of God – for that is the very best way for them to grow themselves.

In other words, we would encourage participation in church gatherings by questions and opportunities for teaching.

If we think about the way most churches teach the Word of God and contrast it with the way that other educational organisations in the world work, the result is embarrassing. In church, one person gives a monologue for about half an hour, once or twice a week. The audience sit and listen in silence and then they go home, where very few of the audience seriously study their Bible in the intervening week.

Contrast that with school, where children are never expected to sit and silently listen to a half-hour lecture (at least, not since Victorian times). Instead, students are expected to interact with what the teacher is saying and articulate an understanding of the lesson material in their own words. Other learning strategies include homework and examinations. Even university education, which still uses the lecture format for many subjects, will usually include time for questions and discussion. If nobody has a question, the lecturer will have a 'plant' ready with a prepared question.

Similarly, while vocational training (for example, learning to be a builder or a nurse) was once entirely 'on-the-job', nowadays there will be a combination of lectures and practical experience. All learning involves information-delivery, but the information has to be put into practice. This is probably the most important type of education, at least insofar as it relates to Christian growth, because it directly compares with what is involved in being a disciple. A disciple means a learner, not in the sense of someone whose head is filled with information, so much as an apprentice, someone who is learning through practice to perform a task to the same standards as the master-craftsman. This is what it means to be a disciple of the Lord Jesus Christ. It is not sufficient to be someone who simply believes in Him – we are called to become like Christ. The life-learning process of becoming like Christ is what He requires of anyone who wants to follow Him. It is not (simply) about listening to lectures.

Here are twelve advantages of interactive Church life:

- people learn truths at a much deeper level if they discover them for themselves
- people remember truths much better if they have to articulate them for themselves
- people learn through asking questions, as well as hearing answers
- people sometimes never hear the right answers until they ask the right questions
- preachers find out which parts of their messages were not well understood from people's questions
- people have their mistaken ideas corrected when they articulate these misconceptions
- preachers sometimes say things that need to be corrected, and people learn the truth this way
- different people have different perspectives on some biblical subjects and their contributions add to everyone's understanding
- as iron sharpens iron, so truths that are taught can be refined and stated in a more careful way through discussion
- theological truths are often multi-faceted (for example, Christ is both God and man, salvation is by faith not works, yet our faith shows itself in works, etc.) and discussion offers the opportunity to properly balance truths
- controversial or debatable questions generate interest among listeners
- questions mean that the speaker has to have matters very clear in his own mind

Participation increases Productivity

Participation not only produces increased benefits in an educational institution. It also has benefits in the business world.

In the modern business world, companies which are part-owned by their employees are growing in number and tend to be more successful, competitive, innovative and sustainable. Because they are co-owners, employees tend to take greater pride in their work, give better customer service, be more committed, productive, consulted, have better well-being, and increased job-satisfaction. The Employee Ownership Association in the UK claims that 'independent research suggests that a combination of shared ownership and employee participation delivers superior business performance'[204]. For example, John Lewis Partnership, the largest employee-owned company in the UK (with about 90,000 staff-partners) is one of the most successful retailers in the country.

In the US, nearly 10% of the private sector workforce is employed in some form of Employee Stock Ownership Plan (ESOP). Employees working in such conditions enjoyed higher pay, greater well-being, more involvement in decision-making, better job-security and had more trust in the management[205]. In the 2010 General Social Survey, adults who worked for companies with an ESOP were one-third to one-fourth as likely to have been laid off in the prior year as compared to those without an ESOP[206].

It's all pretty obvious: increased ownership and participation results in increased profits and satisfaction. As John Maxwell puts it: 'The key to making others feel valued in a group or on a team is to invite

---

[204] http://employeeownership.co.uk/what-is-employee-ownership/employee-ownership-benefits/

[205] Joseph R. Blasi and Douglas L. Kruse. *Shared Capitalism at Work: Employee Ownership, Profit and Gain Sharing, and Broad-Based Stock Options* (National Bureau of Economic Research Conference Report). Chicago: The University of Chicago Press, May 2011.

[206] General Social Survey, National Opinion Research Center, 2010

participation. The smartest person in the room is never as smart as all the people in the room. Input creates synergy, buy-in and connection'[207].

The principle of shared ownership and participation should not be a foreign idea to the Christian. This is the way the New Testament describes the church: as a body with each member having an important role to play and a spiritual gift to use.

---

[207] John Maxwell, *Everybody Communications, Few Connect*, Nashville, TN: Nelson, 2010, p45

CHAPTER 11

PARTICIPATORY CHURCH GATHERINGS AND THE LORD'S SUPPER

What is the relationship of participatory church gatherings to the Lord's Supper? In this chapter we will look at four subjects:

1. The priority of the Lord's Supper
2. The fact that the Lord's Supper only formed part of the church's gathering
3. Practicalities related to the Lord's Supper recorded in the New Testament
4. Putting it all together: how the Lord's Supper intersects with participatory church gatherings.

But before we look at these subjects, we must address two small matters, one theological and one terminological. Firstly, we are not going to delve into a discussion of the theological issues surrounding the Lord's Supper. There are four views: the Roman Catholic view (Transubstantiation: the bread and wine turn into the body and blood of Christ), the Lutheran view (Consubstantiation: Christ is present 'in, with and under' the elements), the Reformed view (Christ is spiritually present in the elements), or the Memorial view (the emblems graphically picture Christ's death and aid our memory). The author holds to the Memorial view and also believes that Christ is spiritually present at the Lord's Supper – not in the bread or wine – but among His people. However, our discussion in this chapter is more concerned with practical considerations.

Secondly, we need to deal with the issue of terminology. There are a number of names used to describe the ordinance, some found in the Bible and some not. Catholics refer to Eucharist, which comes from the Greek word *eucharisto* (meaning to 'give thanks'), used in Matthew 26:27, Mark 14:23, Luke 22:19, and 1 Cor. 11:24. This word describes how the Lord gave thanks for the bread and the wine before sharing them. One term commonly used in churches today is 'Communion', which means 'sharing' or 'fellowship'. It is taken from 1 Cor. 10:16-17 where Paul writes, 'The cup of blessing which we bless, is it not the communion [i.e., sharing, fellowship] of the blood of Christ? The bread which we break, is it not the communion [sharing] of the body of Christ? For we, though many, are one bread and one body; for we all partake of that one bread'. Paul does not use the word 'communion' here as a title for the ordinance, but rather to describe what happened: the early Christians shared the one loaf of bread and drank from the common cup to symbolize their unity.

There are a number of ironies associated with these two terms. Firstly, while preferring the term 'communion' today, many churches have (paradoxically) abandoned the symbolism of actually sharing from the one loaf and one cup as the New Testament describes. Secondly, by using long-winded religious jargon like Eucharist and Communion, an element of mystery and ceremony has been added to something that was originally very simple.

The term 'the Lord's Supper' is mentioned in 1 Cor. 11:20 ('Therefore when you come together in one place, it is not to eat the Lord's Supper'), and contrasts the ordinance with the fellowship meal of the Corinthians in verse 21: 'each one takes his own supper'. The term 'the Lord's table' is used in 1 Cor. 10:21 to contrast partaking of the Lord's Supper with eating food offered to idols: 'You cannot drink the cup of the Lord and the cup of demons; you cannot partake of the Lord's table and of the table of demons'. From the verse it is apparent that 'the Lord's table' refers to the same thing as the 'Lord's Supper' – the verse connects the 'table of the Lord' with the 'cup of the Lord' and contrasts both with the cup of demons and the meat served on the demon's table in the idol-temple.

The most difficult term to deal with is 'the breaking of bread'. This expression refers to a number of related things:

1. It refers to the physical act of breaking open a loaf of bread (see Lam. 4:4, Matt. 14:19, 15:36, Luke 24:30, Acts 27:35)
2. Hence, it refers to sharing a common meal (see Luke 24:35), because on all the occasions listed above, bread was broken at the start of a normal meal.
3. In ancient times, bread was broken in mourning for the dead (see Jer. 16:7, Ezek. 24:17, Hos. 9:4) at a funeral wake.
4. Hence it also refers to the Lord's Supper which commemorates Christ's death (Matt. 26:26, Mark 14:22, Luke 22:19, Acts 2:42, 1 Cor. 10:16)

The difficulty with the term 'breaking of bread' arises in certain passages in the New Testament where it is not clear whether the term refers to sharing a normal, common meal, or partaking of the Lord's Supper. The two passages where this occurs are in Acts 2:42-46 and Acts 20:7-11. We will return to them later.

The Priority of the Lord's Supper

It seems clear that the Lord's Supper was a priority in the churches of the New Testament. We see this primarily in three passages.

In Acts 20:7, we read about Paul coming to Troas: 'Now on the first day of the week, when the disciples came together to break bread'. This verse shows us that the Lord's Supper was the main purpose (although certainly not the only one) for their gathering. The church in Troas did not come together for the 'Preaching of the Word' – they came together to break bread. In our day of celebrity-cult Christianity, most churches in Troas' position would be advertising that their purpose in coming together was to hear a message from Paul, the outstanding apostle, theologian, preacher, missionary statesman and Bible expositor. But the church in Troas did not even set aside the Lord's Supper because of Paul's visit this weekend. The early church gathered together in honour of Christ, not its preachers or leaders. They made the remembrance of His death a priority and a central feature of their meeting.

Secondly, 'the breaking of bread' is mentioned in Acts 2:42 as one of the priorities of the early believers in Jerusalem. The verse literally reads, 'they continued steadfastly in the apostles' teaching, and in the fellowship, and in *the* breaking of *the* bread, and in the prayers'. The use of the two definite articles in the expression, 'the breaking of the bread', signifies that the breaking of bread here was more than a way of describing an ordinary meal. It was instead *the* particular meal comprised of *the* particular bread. The fact that 'fellowship' had already just been mentioned, which would surely include hospitality around the table, makes the mention of 'breaking of bread' superfluous if it were simply a reference to eating. This verse mentions notable Christian activities, including apostolic teaching and prayers, amongst which 'eating' would hardly be considered a Christian activity of the highest order (non-Christians eat together too). Observance of the special meal instituted by the Lord was therefore a matter of first importance for the early Christians in Acts 2.

Thirdly, it is interesting to notice the order of topics dealt with by Paul in his letter to the Corinthians. Paul deals with the subject of the Lord's Supper in 1 Cor. 11 before he comes to speak about the use of spiritual gifts in chapters 12-14. He writes, 'Now in giving these instructions I do not praise you, since you come together not for the better but for the worse. For *first of all*, when you come together as a church, I hear that there are divisions among you' (11:17-18). Notice the words, 'first of all'. They signify that the abuses at the Lord's Supper, which Paul goes on to address, were a subject of first importance. This is because the Lord's Supper is a matter of first importance.

Indeed, 1 Corinthians 11:20 implies that the main purpose of the church's gathering is the Lord's Supper, for Paul writes that the Corinthians had substituted something else in place of the remembrance of Christ: 'Therefore, when you come together in one place, it is not to eat the Lord's Supper'. The implication is, '*you* (the word is emphatic) do not come together *with the purpose of* eating the Lord's Supper, (although they should have), *but rather so that you can eat your own food*' (cf.

Alford[208]). There are various alternative ways that we could possibly interpret this verse:

- as a question: 'when you come together, is it not to eat the Lord's Supper?'
- as a moral warning: '*in your present state*, you ought not to eat the Lord's Supper'
- as a rebuke: 'your selfish eating does not amount to an instance of the Lord's Supper'
- as an explanation: 'your factionalism prevents you from unitedly eating the Lord's Supper').

But all of these different interpretations retain the emphasis upon the *purpose* of the gathering: the reason for the gathering was to eat the Lord's Supper.

Despite the priority that the New Testament places upon the Lord's Supper, the modern evangelical church largely neglects it. The early Christians 'devoted themselves' (Acts 2:42, NIV) to the 'breaking of bread', but this hardly describes the situation in the modern evangelical world. While it seems that churches in New Testament times observed the Lord's Supper as part of their weekly gathering, some modern churches only have the Lord's Supper a few times a year, and then only as a staid and shallow ritual.

When Paul was recounting the institution of the Lord's Supper, he twice uses the word 'often': 'In the same manner He also took the cup after supper, saying, "This cup is the new covenant in My blood. This do, as *often* as you drink it, in remembrance of Me". For as *often* as you eat this bread and drink this cup, you proclaim the Lord's death till He comes' (1 Cor. 11:25, 26). The word 'often' does not specify that we should 'break bread' every week, but it does suggest frequency, not rarity. However, in the modern evangelical church, it would be more honest to change the wording of these verses to read, 'as seldom as you eat this bread and drink this cup'.

---

[208] Henry Alford, *The Greek Testament*, Vol. 2, London: Rivington, 1852, p540

It is true that we are not commanded to observe the Lord's Supper every week, but the same could be said of attending church every week – the New Testament does not command it. The reason is simple: the New Testament rarely resorts to commands, because it assumes we are eager to please God, to remember Christ, to meet together and to encourage one another. In 1 Corinthians 16:2 Paul told the disciples to take up a collection on the first day of every week, and this presumes not only that the Christians were together when it was taken (for accounting purposes), but also that the church gathering on the first day of the week had become a settled institution of the Christian church. The apostolic institution still applies today.

Some argue, on practical grounds, that having the Lord's Supper too frequently leads to diminished appreciation. As the old proverb says, familiarity breeds contempt. Or, to put it the other way, if it is observed occasionally it becomes more special and precious. However, it would be a strange husband who said the same thing about kissing his wife – that doing it less often makes it more special. Someone has amended the old proverb to say that familiarity only breeds contempt with contemptible things. Our Lord Jesus asked us to remember Him, and as He elsewhere says, 'if you love me, keep my commandments'; if we love Him, we will do so often, not try to find reasons to lessen its frequency. In fact, the Lord's words take the form of a command: 'Do this in remembrance of Me'.

In summary, it would seem that the Christians in the New Testament met together to remember the Lord in the breaking of bread on the first day of the week, the Lord's Day (Acts 20:7, 1 Cor. 16:2), continuing the Lord's own resurrection tradition of meeting with the disciples on the first day of the week (John 20:1, 26). The Lord's Supper was not held once a year, or once every few months, but was something the early Christians *continued steadfastly* (Acts 2:42) in observing, *'when they came together'* (1 Cor. 11:17). I. Howard Marshall summarizes the biblical evidence as follows: 'In line with what appears to have been the practice of the early church in the New Testament the Lord's Supper should be celebrated frequently in the church, and there is good reason for doing so on each Lord's Day'[209].

The Lord's Supper was Only Part of the Church's Weekly Gathering

There are three occasions in the NT where we find a description of the Lord's Supper, firstly, at its institution on the night the Lord was betrayed, secondly in Troas in Acts 20, and thirdly, in 1 Corinthians 11 and 14. In all three instances, it is important to notice that it was not simply a meeting for remembrance, but included teaching, exhortation and edification.

At the institution of the Lord's Supper, Christ gave thanks for the bread and wine, passed them to his disciples to share and then they sang a hymn. For the rest of the time, perhaps for an hour or two, the Lord was teaching His disciples about practical spiritual matters (John 13-16).

We see the same picture in the second passage in Acts 20:7-11 when Paul visited Troas. There 'on the first day of the week, when the disciples came together to break bread (i.e. to have the Lord's Supper), Paul, ready to depart the next day, spoke to them and continued his message until midnight'. Again we see that the vast majority of the time involved teaching and preaching (a more literal translation would be 'dialoguing') till midnight (just like the Lord dialogued with his disciples in the Upper Room in John 13-16).

Thirdly, when we come over to 1 Corinthians, we find Paul writing about the church gatherings. He uses the same expression 'when you come together' to refer to both the Lord's Supper (1 Cor. 11:17, 18, 20, etc.) and the participatory style of edification that occurs in church (1 Cor. 14:26-40). Paul does not add a special rider ('when you come together *for teaching, or for edification*') in chapter 14 as if this was a second, different meeting, or speak about it occurring on some other occasion ('when you come together *for your midweek teaching meeting*'). There is no hint that there are two different occasions when the church

---

[209] I. Howard Marshall, *Last Supper and Lord's Supper*, Grand Rapids, MI: Eerdmans, 1980, p155

gathered, once for remembrance of Christ, and again for edification using spiritual gifts. Paul uses the exact same expression 'when you come together' on both occasions without any further distinction or explanation, which suggests that it was at exactly the same gathering as the Lord's Supper that the various gifts mentioned in chapters 12 to 14 were to be exercised.

In summary, then, we see that the weekly gathering in the early church involved both the Lord's Supper and the use of spiritual gifts for building up the believers in their faith. It involved 1 Corinthians 11 as well as 1 Corinthians 14. It was Christ-focused as well as edification-oriented. Bible teaching was not relegated to some other time in the week when only the most dedicated were able to attend.

The church's weekly gathering was not just a 'remembrance meeting', a meeting for 'worship only'. Some Christians, keen to give Christ His rightful place in the church, and reluctant to treat the Lord's Supper as an occasional event, remember Christ weekly but leave no time for the exercise of spiritual gifts. However, a remembrance-only church meeting is nowhere found in God's Word. Others leave a short, token time for a word of exhortation after the Lord's Supper. However, the early Christians did not leave a short period for a 'little word' after the worship-time, a brief ten minute period left over for encouraging teaching. Instead there was opportunity for multiple participants to use different gifts to edify the church by teaching and by exhortation, as well as opportunities for follow-up discussion and questions based on these messages. There were also hymns of praise and prayers of thanksgiving or petition interspersed throughout the meeting. The time for edification must have easily been equal to or greater than the time for remembrance, if we allow the New Testament evidence to be our guide. The church's weekly gathering was a conference with multiple speakers, a spiritual feast every week. No wonder the early Christians grew so quickly, both in knowledge and in number.

In addition, we learn from 1 Cor. 11:17-34 that the church at Corinth (as in other places) shared a fellowship meal together. Therefore, it seems safe to conclude that the church's main weekly gathering involved all of these elements, a fellowship meal, the Lord's Supper and a time for ministry using spiritual gifts.

Some, particularly in the house-church movement, would argue that the fellowship meal *was* itself the Lord's Supper. However, this seems highly unlikely, for Paul writing to the Corinthians, while reinforcing the priority and importance of the Lord's Supper, suggested that the fellowship meal should be abandoned if it was causing so many problems. In 1 Cor. 11:22 and 34, Paul said that the individual church members should eat at home if they could not eat together without division and disgraceful behaviour. Thus, the fellowship meal is non-essential and able to be dispensed with, while the Lord's Supper is of prime importance. In addition, when Paul recounts the institution of the Lord's Supper in verses 23-26, only bread and wine are mentioned as being shared in remembrance of the Lord's death, not a full meal. Similarly, in verses 27-28, when Paul warns against people partaking of the Lord's Supper unworthily, only bread and wine are mentioned: 'Therefore whoever *eats this bread* or *drinks this cup of the Lord* in an unworthy manner will be guilty of the body and blood of the Lord. But let a man examine himself, and so let him *eat of the bread* and *drink of the cup*'.

Therefore, we conclude that the Lord's Supper was an integral part of the church's weekly meeting, but only a part – not the whole.

The Practicalities of the Lord's Supper

Here we look at how the Lord's Supper was held from the New Testament evidence. While the record is not detailed, yet we discover interesting information from Scripture.

One feature common to all the references to the Lord's Supper is that it seemed to be held in the evening. This is seen at its institution in the gospels, in Acts 20 at Troas, and at Corinth where it was associated with 'supper' (1 Cor. 11:21), the evening meal. This would have meant that the Lord's Supper was a less public affair than other meetings for evangelism or systematic instruction, like we find in the temple courts in Jerusalem (Acts 2-5), in the synagogues, or in the school of Tyrannus in Ephesus (Acts 19:9). This is not to say that unbelievers were not allowed to come to the Lord's Supper (see 1 Cor. 14:23-25), but simply that the atmosphere was more private than the other gatherings.

The gospel records of the institution of the Lord's Supper describe it as a very simple affair. The Lord offered a short prayer of thanks for the bread and cup (separately), gave a brief explanation as to their significance, and passed them to the disciples to share. There was no 'quiet hour' of readings, prayers and hymns of thanksgiving. We need not insist that the remembrance of the Lord in our present situation must be as brief and simple as it was at the institution of the feast. In fact, we would expect Spirit-filled Christians to be overflowing with thankful adoration for Christ and what He has done. Seeing the disciples did not yet understand the significance of what was happening, it may have been the case that their remembrance became deeper and more extended post-Pentecost. On the other hand, the time the Lord spent instructing and teaching his disciples about practical spiritual matters after the supper was lengthy as well as participatory, with questions from different disciples. There is no reason why Christians today have any less need of lengthy, practical encouraging teaching at the meeting of the church. We see this same pattern of an extended time of edification in other places in the New Testament too.

We are not told anything about how the Lord's Supper was held in Acts 2:42. But there is another verse in the same passage which some have suggested refers to the Lord's Supper. Acts 2:46 says 'so continuing daily with one accord in the temple, and breaking bread from house to house, they ate their food with gladness and simplicity of heart'. Is this referring to the Lord's Supper or simply an ordinary meal? Some would argue that the expression 'breaking bread' in v46 simply refers to sharing ordinary meals, and perhaps that is what is being referred to. However, consider the practicalities of how the early church in Jerusalem conducted the Lord's Supper. Was it practically possible for 10,000 believers (there were '5000 men' by Acts 4:4) to meet together collectively in one place to observe the Lord's Supper? To hold the Lord's Supper for 10,000 believers in one place would be a logistical challenge. Where would they have met – in the Temple courts, with the possible Jewish opposition, as they did for apostolic preaching and teaching (Acts 3:11, 5:12, 21, 42)?

Would they have all shared from the 'one loaf' and 'cup', symbolically demonstrating their unity in Christ (1 Cor. 10:16-17)? How long would it take simply to pass round the bread and wine for 10,000 people? How would such a meeting have been profitable: would anyone hear prayers without amplification in the open air in a public space? The idea that a meeting for 10,000 people would have been participatory is unlikely. The impracticality of such a gathering, and the fact that we nowhere read of it, suggests that the early believers instead met together in smaller numbers for the Lord's Supper, and probably in homes or locations like the 'upper room' where the Lord instituted the ordinance, where it would have been far more logistically possible, private, practical, profitable and participatory (pardon the alliteration). Thus, even if Acts 2:46 is not referring to the Lord's Supper, it was probably in home-meetings (Acts 12:12) or 'upper room' gatherings that the Lord's Supper was held.

When we come to Acts 20 in Troas, there are again questions of a practical nature. Most commentators argue that the Lord's Supper was put off until midnight by Paul's extended time of teaching, and was observed after Eutychus' restoration to life, followed by a meal and more conversation (so Chrysostom, Gill, Ellicott, Alford, and most modern commentators). John Stott writes, 'Then he (Paul) went upstairs again and broke bread and ate, sharing in both the Lord's Supper and the fellowship supper, which had evidently not been served previously'[210]; F. F. Bruce comments on verse 11, 'it was after midnight ... when they carried out the purpose for which they had met'[211].

However, other commentators hold that the 'breaking of bread' happened at the beginning of the evening, and the 'breaking of bread' mentioned in v11 at midnight is an ordinary meal (so Adam Clarke, Jamieson, Fausset and Brown, and, apparently, Matthew Henry). One piece of evidence that supports this view is the fact that the four Greek participles in verse 11 are all in the singular, not the plural: 'Now when he had *come up*, had *broken* bread and *eaten*, and *talked* a long while, even till daybreak, he departed'. It is only Paul who is spoken of here as eating.

---

[210] John Stott, *The Message of Acts*, BST, Leicester: IVP, 1990, p320.
[211] F. F. Bruce, *The Acts of the Apostles: the Greek Text with Introduction and Commentary*, London: The Tyndale Press, 1952, p372, 374

Albert Barnes says about v11, 'Had taken refreshment. As this is spoken of Paul only, it is evidently distinguished from the celebration of the Lord's Supper'; he quotes Bengel: 'This breaking of bread was the particular act of Paul, when about to set out on his journey, and was distinct from that which had occurred the day before, Acts 20:7'.

It seems unlikely that the Lord's Supper was held after midnight in Troas for the following reasons. The church would not have had a meal very late in the evening every week; the fellowship supper would be held at the normal time for meals, at the start of the evening, after which the breaking of bread and sharing of the cup followed. *Contra* Stott, it would seem unlikely that the Christians would have ignored or omitted to serve the fellowship meal at the beginning of the evening when everyone was naturally hungry. A midnight Lord's Supper would also seem to devalue the ordinance; leaving something so late is hardly giving it a place of priority. This would conflict with the earlier statement that the breaking of bread was the purpose of their gathering. Partaking of the Lord's Supper after Eutychus' restoration also makes it seem a hurried afterthought; the description in verse 11 reads as if it were a very perfunctory matter, not an act of deep devotion. It would be hard to imagine how the sacred supper would not have been overshadowed by the shock and distraction of the accident which had just happened. It would seem more appropriate for everyone to have taken a break after Eutychus' fall, for Paul to have taken something to eat or drink after a long evening of teaching and in view of his travels the next day, and that those who needed to go home would have done so at this point[212].

On the other hand, if the Lord's Supper occurred at the beginning of the evening, before Paul's preaching, then we are again faced with the problem that we lack any detailed description of the practicalities of the Lord's Supper. We are given no answers in Acts 20:7 to questions like how long the actual remembrance time lasted, whether it was liturgical or participatory, and (if participatory) what sort of contributions were

---

[212] Commentators who argue for a midnight Lord's Supper are also influenced by the presence of the article in verse 11 in certain early manuscripts: 'when he ... had broken *the* bread'. However, the majority of manuscripts omit the article.

normally considered appropriate, or how many people took part in it. Did it consist simply of someone giving thanks for the bread and the cup and the sharing of the elements, or did it consist of an hour of readings, prayers of thanksgiving and hymns about Christ's death? We do not know, because we are left in almost total silence as to what actually happened at the Lord's Supper here.

When we come over to 1 Corinthians, we are again given only limited information about how the Lord's Supper was conducted. Just like the institution of the Supper in the gospels at the Passover, and at Troas in Acts 20, the Lord's Supper was connected with a fellowship meal in Corinth, suggesting that the 'breaking of bread' occurred at the beginning of the meeting straight after the meal.

It would seem that the Lord's Supper was participatory in nature. Paul Barnett, in his commentary on 1 Corinthians 14:26 mentions something in passing that is worth considering: 'In [1 Cor. 14] verse 26 Paul gives us a window into the 'meeting together' of this apostolic congregation. He does not say that these elements [i.e. speaking in tongues, prophesying, teaching, psalm-singing, etc.] also occurred at the Lord's Supper (see on 11:17-34), though it is a reasonable assumption that they did'.

While the argument falls short of proof, it does indeed seem 'a reasonable assumption' that Lord's Supper was participatory for a number of reasons:

1. In view of the fact that at the main church gathering, comprising the Lord's Supper and the edification of the saints, the edification-time was participatory in nature, we may presume that the Lord's Supper was similar in nature, seeing they were part of the one meeting, and in the absence of any instructions to the contrary being set out in the New Testament.

2. The reference to 'giving of thanks' by a brother in 1 Cor. 14:16 possibly refers to someone giving thanks for the bread or cup at the Lord's Supper. Alternatively, it could simply refer to someone giving thanks to God while speaking in tongues during the participatory use of spiritual gifts. Either way, it would appear that believers ordinarily

had the opportunity to give thanks to God in the church gatherings without specially being invited or appointed to do so.

3. We read of no church minister, elder or deacon responsible for officiating at the Lord's Supper in 1 Cor. 11:17-34 (or anywhere else in the NT). Paul does not direct his remarks about the need to rectify the abuses at the Lord's Supper at Corinth to some specially-designated official or minister within the church.

4. Paul nowhere sets out a special liturgy or order of service for the Lord's Supper, other than simply restating what the Lord said and did when He instituted it, which functions as a template for how it should happen.

5. The final reason for a participatory Lord's Supper, virtually amounting to proof, is that because the Lord's Supper was followed by a time of participatory edification, there would have been an opportunity for anybody to engage in worship and thanksgiving for the person and work of Christ during this 'open time'. If then, for the sake of argument, the meeting started with the briefest of Lord's Suppers (simply the bread and wine being shared) and no opportunity was allowed for anyone to participate in praising God or giving thanks or sharing a Scripture or a hymn before the bread and wine, there would still be opportunity for open participation after the bread and wine. Any Spirit-filled person with heart-felt appreciation for Christ would find it hard not to use this opportunity. Therefore, we conclude that an opportunity for participation at the Lord's Supper must have occurred, either before or after the bread and wine.

Howard Marshall, summarising the evidence about the Lord's Supper says: 'The New Testament says nothing about who should conduct or celebrate the sacrament, and there is no evidence whatever that anything corresponding to our modern "ordination" was essential. The celebration of the sacrament today should not be confined to those ordained to the ministry by the laying on of hands but should be open to any believer authorized by the church to do so'[213].

---

[213] Marshall, *Last Supper and Lord's Supper*, p155

From the foregoing evidence, we may offer the following conclusions:

- The Lord's Supper was a more private meeting than other gatherings for evangelism or public instruction; the Lord instituted it in an 'upper room'.
- The Lord's Supper was usually held in the evening
- The Lord's Supper only constituted part of the meeting – there was also an extended time for edification
- The Lord's Supper was probably held at the beginning of the meeting.
- The Lord's Supper was most probably participatory

We are given no answers to questions like how long the remembrance lasted, or how many people took part publicly. We have no warrant for insisting on either a short or lengthy time of remembrance or an elaborate and highly regulated order of service – the Bible nowhere gives us any evidence of this happening. In the gospels we have the inauguration of the Lord's Supper, which involved a very short and simple service. In the book of Acts we have only brief mentions of the Lord's Supper – not exhaustive descriptions of what took place. In 1 Corinthians the reference to the Lord's Supper takes the form of correction rather than exposition of any particular pattern. We are given no indication that the Lord's Supper need be a lengthy and elaborate event in any of these passages. Some Christians may be familiar with a certain form and ceremony when celebrating the Lord's Supper, and might argue that such ceremony is only 'natural', or 'orderly', or 'spiritual', or 'beautiful', or even 'heavenly'. But this is not the same thing as being biblical, and the fact that something is 'natural', 'orderly', or 'heavenly' does not mean that it is spiritually beneficial. Someone might say that it would be impossible to over-indulge in the worship of God, however in Corinth the tongues-speakers who delighted in speaking to God (1 Cor. 14:2, presumably in worship and praise), needed to be told not to over-indulge in worshipping in such a 'spiritual' and heavenly way. Paul was forced to limit their participation so that the meeting would not be dominated by worship, but instead there would be plenty of time for edifying teaching as well. A meeting entirely given to worship was considered spiritually unbalanced and unhealthy.

Putting it all Together in the Church Gathering

How should we incorporate the Lord's Supper in a participatory church gathering? How do we balance the remembrance of Christ at the Lord's Supper with the opportunity for the participatory use of spiritual gifts for the edification of the church? How do we arrange affairs so that neither of these activities consists of token half-measures or perfunctory rituals? How do we arrange our church gathering so that it is both biblically faithful and spiritually beneficial?

Some would argue for a church gathering governed by strict rules, whilst others would argue for maximum freedom. For an example of a meeting governed by strictly ordered rules, consider Watchman Nee's rather strange idea of an ideal celebration of the Lord's Supper. 'The meeting for the breaking of bread as a remembrance of salvation naturally falls into two sections. Before the breaking of the bread is the section for the Son; after the bread is broken it becomes the section for the Father. The first portion is the Lord's; the second portion is God's … So in the first section, all our prayers and hymns and praises should be directed to the Lord … After the bread is broken, the second section of the meeting begins. The Lord does not desire that we come to Him and stop there. He wants us to go on to the Father… Our accepting of the Son is but half of salvation; the Father's accepting us is the other half. Consequently, after the bread is broken, we should come to the Father. We should begin to praise God the Father. … Brothers and sisters, He who leads us in the meeting is the Holy Spirit, and the leading of the Holy Spirit is not contradictory to the principle of salvation. The Holy Spirit will lead us first to the Son and then to the Father. Let us learn to follow His leading and go the Father after having broken the bread… For this reason, all the hymns and prayers in the second part are centred on the Father. We do not follow our own dictates but are so led by the

Holy Spirit. I believe if the Holy Spirit has His free way with us, He will undoubtedly lead us in this manner'[214].

Watchman Nee here advocates the Lord's Supper in a carefully ordered format. He envisages a 'worship meeting' all on its own, as opposed to the Lord's Supper being simply part of the church's gathering, as we find in the New Testament.

Consider another example of a highly-ordered service, as described and then critiqued by William McRae writes: 'One of the simplest orders of service is the meeting in which the saints focus only upon the person and death of Christ before the bread and cup are passed. After the emblems, believers are permitted to minister regarding the resurrection or present ministry of our Lord or to exhort the other believers. In a recent issue of a Christian magazine this order of service was strongly advocated. The writer said: 'In such a meeting the ministry, fellowship, and worship are centered on the Lord Jesus Christ and are under the leadership of the Holy Spirit. The introduction of evangelism or intercession is out of place. Personal testimony or experience, however soul-stirring it might be to the speaker, should be avoided unless it contributes to the contemplation of Christ. When the Lord's Supper has been observed and the worship and ministry portion has been concluded, a suitable prayer could close the meeting. At this time all necessary announcements, business reports, correspondence and other assembly affairs may be presented. While this detail is not spelled out in Scripture, it seems only fitting that we don't allow the temporal affairs of the assembly to intrude on the contemplation of our blessed Lord whom we gather together to worship. "This do in remembrance of Me."'

McRae comments: 'This statement shows a remarkable misunderstanding of New Testament principles. How right he is that no such detail is given in Scripture! His system is all humanly devised. I find it almost unbelievable that one would speak of "the leadership of the Holy Spirit" in a meeting where we have spelled out what can be done, and when it can be done. Could there be a better illustration of

---

[214] Watchman Nee, *Assembling Together*, New York: Christian Fellowship Publishers, 1973, pp53-56

quenching the Spirit than this? The writer quotes our Lord's words: "This do" and applies them to the meeting. This careless bit of exegesis has led to great confusion. Isn't the Lord here speaking of the bread and cup and not of the entire meeting? In the meeting of the church the believers did remember Him in this fashion, but that is not all they did. Note carefully that it was not exclusively a worship meeting. Do not misunderstand me. I am not saying that such a meeting is wrong. Surely there is liberty for such a worship service if it is so desired. But a purely worship service is not the New Testament meeting of the church. In the New Testament meeting of the church there was no settled format whatsoever'[215].

McRae argues that the church's gathering involved both the Lord's Supper as well as a time for the use of gifts by multiple members of the congregation. The church's gathering was not solely for remembrance – it also involved edification. In addition, McRae argues that there should be no settled format whatsoever in the church's meeting. It is a meeting with maximum freedom for the Holy Spirit to lead in whatever direction at whatever time. But, logically-speaking, there are three places in the meeting where the Lord's Supper could occur. It could occur right at the beginning, midway through the meeting, or at its end.

1. <u>At the end</u>: the problem with a meeting in which the Lord's Supper occurs right at the end is as follows. In the present author's experience, if the bread is broken right at the very end of the meeting, everything beforehand tends to be a mixture of sometimes unrelated and disjointed matters. One brother might offer a prayer of thanksgiving for Christ and His work, anticipating the Lord's Supper, after which another might relate a story about something that happened during the week or bring an encouragement from the Scriptures. The solemnity of thoughts about Christ's sufferings might be followed by something quite trivial. The problem is not simply that the meeting jumps between the sublime and the

---

[215] William McRae, *The Meeting of the Church*, Dallas: Believers Chapel Booklet, 1974, 2001

ordinary; it is pulling in two different directions. There is constant jumping between the two sometimes abruptly diverging tracks, and this means that neither track is able to be fully developed for the benefit of God's people.

2. <u>In the middle</u>: a second option is to have the Lord's Supper in the middle of the meeting, preceded by worship and remembrance, and followed by edification. One danger here is of setting a fixed time at which the bread and wine are shared, for sometimes the worship time might drag on wearily till this point when the need is for a longer period of encouraging teaching (or vice versa). In many churches that have the Lord's Supper in the middle of the meeting, the worship-time associated with the Lord's Supper is extended and drawn out, while there is comparatively little time for edification. This is very different to the New Testament picture we find in 1 Corinthians 14 where there are multiple speakers using a variety of gifts for edification. If a church decides to have the Lord's Supper in the middle of the meeting, it needs to leave enough time for edification, so that multiple speakers can teach and encourage the church, as in 1 Cor. 14.

3. <u>At the beginning</u>: lastly, there is the option of having the Lord's Supper right at the beginning of the meeting. This seems to have been the way that things happened in the New Testament, for at both the institution of the Supper in the gospels, and in 1 Corinthians (and, in all likelihood in Troas in Acts 20), the church shared a fellowship meal at the beginning of the evening. The bread and wine for the Lord's Supper seem to have been shared at the end of this meal and this presumably was the pattern followed in Acts and 1 Corinthians. In a meeting starting with the Lord's Supper, there would be opportunity for worship and thanksgiving for as long as the Spirit led after the partaking of the bread and wine and, sensitive to the Spirit, the church could then move into edifying teaching and encouragement.

In contrast to the suggestion of maximum freedom, I suggest that there seems to be some order in the church gathering in the New Testament. The Lord's Supper and the time of edification seem to have been distinct parts of the meeting, rather than the meeting jumping between worship and practical encouragement. As we have seen from the various passages in the New Testament dealing with the Lord's Supper, the breaking of the bread seemed to occur at the beginning of the meeting, before the time for the edification through spiritual gifts. Whichever way we put together these parts of the meeting, there needs to be three things: (1) a time of reverent remembrance, (2) sufficient time for the practical encouragement and teaching of the church, and (3) a sensitivity to the leading of the Holy Spirit.

It would appear that the New Testament balances both principles of freedom and order. There is no prescriptive outline for how the meeting is to be held – for it is led by the Spirit, and there was freedom for God's people to use their gifts in it – yet it seemed to follow a simple order in which the Lord's Supper preceded the edification time.

Balancing Freedom and Order

How do we balance the meeting's twin aims, remembrance of Christ and edification of the saints, and twin guidelines, freedom and order?

a. In relation to Time:

It should be obvious that an essential requirement for balancing the twin needs of worship and edification is that there is sufficient time for both. Is it really possible to talk about the leading of the Spirit when everything is governed by a clock on the wall? On the one hand, freedom means not restricting meetings within narrow time-confines. On the other, meeting times need to be scheduled sensibly so that they do not run up against natural needs (like travel requirements or meals).

In the church at Corinth, Paul put a limit on the number of people speaking in tongues and on those prophesying. This was necessary so that the meeting would not be completely dominated by people speaking in tongues. In the case of prophecy, which was edifying, the limit seems to have been applied so that the meeting did not go on too long.

Should not the same principle be applicable in other situations? For example, at the Lord's Supper, what would be the benefit of singing six or seven hymns that dragged the meeting out for an hour, limiting the opportunity for other spiritual gifts to be exercised? Some hymns are beautiful and profound, it is true, but after two or three, the impact of devotionally powerful lines is blunted.

Similarly, there are some churches where virtually every brother feels he must offer a prayer of thanksgiving before the bread and wine are shared. Some brothers only spiritually defrost an hour into the meeting, and then wish to thank God in prayer, but the result is that the Lord's Supper drags on for an hour, and there is little time for any other spiritual gift to be exercised.

From the New Testament evidence, the Lord's Supper was simple and thankful, not elaborate and elongated. The First Supper lasted only as long as it took for the Lord to give thanks for the bread and wine, and for the apostles to share them. There is no record of the Lord encouraging all the apostles around the table to share a scripture, thought, song or prayer in His honour. We have no biblical evidence for the idea of 'a quiet hour' devoted to the Lord's Supper, where virtually every brother must share something in worship – either a hymn, a thought or a prayer. The Lord's Supper should not be allowed to go on so long that there is not sufficient time for the equally-important edification of the saints by multiple speakers.

b. In relation to Order of Service:

We have seen that there appears to be a general pattern in early church gatherings, a 'default' order of events, in that the Lord's Supper seemed to come first before the exercise of gifts for edification. Even though there are no 'hard and fast rules' about the matter – Paul did not say we have to have the Lord's Supper first – still it seems that this was the norm.

Allow me to suggest some reasons for such an order. By putting the Lord's Supper first in time, we emphasize its importance and priority in the church meeting. Secondly, by putting the Lord's Supper first, we let it set the tone for the rest of the meeting – the tremendous truths it teaches about Christ's death, our salvation, and our unity in Him, will colour the rest of the gathering. Thirdly, putting the Lord's Supper first gives Christ His rightful place as Lord. The church is not a fan-club for gifted preachers, a Corinthian celebrity-cult. We gather to Christ Himself, and acknowledge Him as Lord.

Yet beyond this simple pattern of the Lord's Supper followed by the exercise of spiritual gifts, we should be careful not to insist on some fixed and rigid order in relation to what happens in the meeting. A formal, set order of service is one way to quench the Spirit. But it is very easy to get stuck in ruts through sheer laziness or spiritual dullness, so that the meeting always starts the same way, or that one person does exactly the same thing every week. There should be freedom for the Holy Spirit to lead in the meeting.

c. In relation to Gifts

The Holy Spirit should be allowed to be sovereign, to lead and direct in the church gathering. This means that different spiritual gifts will be exercised, at the Lord's Supper as much as in the time of edification which follows it. Spirit-led participation will result in a variety of contributions. When this principle is ignored, the Lord's Supper can become very predictable and stale, but freedom means there is opportunity for different contributions (hymns, prayers, bible readings, testimonies, expositions, etc.). For example, it is possible to celebrate the Lord's Supper with an unwritten rule that the most exalted contribution is a prayer of thanksgiving, so that the Lord's Supper virtually amounts to one long prayer meeting. If the apostle Paul himself were to visit such a meeting, he might well ask where such an order of service came from, for it certainly was not from his writings, which specifically warn about the importance of variety.

Some believers who practice a participatory Lord's Supper believe that it is out of place for anyone to read from Scripture during the Lord's Supper, their rationale being that we should have done our scripture-reading before we come together. While it is true that we should prepare our hearts before we come to the Lord's Supper, the idea that we cannot read Scripture during the breaking of bread leads to the anomaly that it is perfectly acceptable to read and sing the uninspired words of human hymn-writers, but not to read and meditate upon the inspired Word of God.

Because it is true that a prayer in which someone's heart overflows in thanksgiving and praise worships Christ in a most spiritual and worthy fashion, this is no reason to introduce rules stating that all other contributions (like reading the Bible) are to be frowned upon. The result of a No-Bible-Reading rule, in some cases, has been that prayers at the Lord's Supper, instead of being filled with Scripture, consist of well-worn phraseology, repeated week after week, so that the remembrance becomes stale, predictable and unspiritual. Others offer lengthy three-point devotional sermons disguised as prayers, which are indeed preferable to prayers that wander all over the place with no direction or end. Such dedication to scripture memorization and sermon preparation is to be encouraged, but the effect would have been perhaps even more profitable had the Bible actually been read to establish the three points being expounded. The New Testament allows for a variety of contributions, but if man-made rules only allow for certain contributions (e.g. prayers and hymns), then one of the purposes of participatory church gatherings has been defeated.

d. In relation to Other Saints

'Let all things be done for edification' said the apostle in 1 Cor. 14:26, yet instead of edifying our fellow-saints, it is possible to continually criticise and frown upon the contributions of others (even if only inwardly) when they do not conform to our conceptions of how the meeting should run or the order it should follow. Instead of encouraging others for sharing a contribution, or finding something that is Christ-honouring in it and dwelling upon that, some Spirit-quenchers act like policemen and pull down others, not only spoiling their own worship by their sourness of spirit, but discouraging others from participating as well. Freedom means that we must display a gracious and patient attitude towards our fellow-saints and their contributions to the meeting as they feel led by God's Spirit.

CHAPTER 12

WOMEN'S PARTICIPATION

In this chapter, we look at a number of important passages that deal with women's participation in church gatherings.

1 Corinthians 14:34-35
Let your women keep silent in the church gatherings, for they are not permitted to speak; but they are to be submissive, as the law also says. And if they want to learn anything, let them ask their own husbands at home; for it is shameful for women to speak in the church.

1 Corinthians 14:34-35 says that women are not to participate by publicly speaking in church. The response of some Christians is to try to 'explain away', or reinterpret these verses. However, their meaning seems clear and plain. In fact, just to make sure we don't mistake his message, Paul says that women are not to speak in the church service five times:

1. **Positively**: 'Let your women keep silent in the church gatherings'
2. **Negatively**: 'for they are not permitted to speak'
3. **Foundationally**: 'but they are to be submissive, as the law also says'
4. **Illustratively**: 'and if they want to learn anything, let them ask their own husbands at home'
5. **Emphatically**: 'for it is shameful for women to speak in the church'

That is, Paul tells us that women cannot speak in the church gatherings: 'let your women keep silent'. Then he says it again, because some people need to hear things twice: 'they are not permitted to speak'. Then he tells us why they cannot: because of the foundational principle of the relationship of the sexes established at creation in the Old Testament, in which we find ordained the woman's submission to her divinely-appointed head, the man. Then he uses an illustrative example, a case-in-point, to show the extent of the prohibition – they are not even allowed to ask a question (and therefore, reasoning from the lesser to the greater, they are forbidden to preach, pray, etc.). Then he concludes by using the strongest possible language to condemn women's participation: it is a disgrace for women to speak in the church.

It is hard to imagine how Paul could have made his meaning any plainer but, undaunted, increasing numbers of novel attempts have been made to reinterpret Paul's words.

A. Some dismiss Paul as a grumpy old bachelor, or his words here as those of a typical male chauvinist. This denies the fact that these words were not simply Paul's, but God's, written under the inspiration of His Spirit.

B. Some argue that women in apostolic times did not have access to education, and were forbidden to speak in NT churches on this account. However, Jesus' twelve disciples were hardly educated men, and nowhere does Paul say that participation in the church is dependent upon someone's level of education. This objection ignores the biblical and theological reasons given in the NT for women's silence.

C. Some argue that the word 'speak' here means to 'chatter', and simply forbids ladies talking in the background. But the word 'speak' is used over twenty times in 1 Corinthians 14, and on every occasion it refers to publicly addressing the congregation. We cannot change the meaning of the word in two verses (34-35) to refer to 'chatter in the background'. When the author was a boy and played games in the street, he used to sometimes try to tweak the rules to make the games better. Some other children got quite angry at this, and said, 'you can't change the rules half-way through the game'. Neither can we change the meaning of the word 'speak' midway through the chapter to suit ourselves. C. K. Barrett writes: 'It is true that the verb [*laleo*] does in Classical Greek bear the meaning 'to chatter', and it would be understandable that Paul should wish to stem the outburst of feminine loquacity; but in the New Testament, and in Paul, the verb normally does not have this meaning, and is used throughout chapter xiv (verses 2, 3, 4, 5, 6, 9, 11, 13, 18, 19, 21, 23, 27, 28, 29, 39) in the sense of inspired speech'[216]. Note carefully: in context, 'speak' does not mean to cough, sing, tell the children to sit still or say 'Amen', nor does it forbid any of these things.

D. Others have more recently argued that the women are merely prohibited from asking public questions or 'judging prophecies'. In other words, women can pray and prophesy in the church, but they cannot sit in judgment on messages delivered in the church or interrogate the preacher, for it is argued that this would be to assume a position of authority that is not appropriate for women. Professor David Gooding asks, 'Why mustn't they [question the prophets]? Well, the view that was given to me at one stage was that some of these women might be married; and if their husband was one of the prophets, under the guise of questioning they might be wanting to bring him down a peg or two. . . . if they started to speak they might interweave a little teaching and thus usurp authority over their husbands, and that wouldn't do in public either. What about the unmarried women? They wouldn't be wanting to bring their husbands down a peg or two, would they? Is it just the unmarried women, then, who are to speak in this context, not the married ones? But that would be absurd, wouldn't it? Here's a senior Christian woman with years of spiritual experience behind her, and she mustn't question? Whereas some newly converted bright young thing of seventeen may, who scarcely knows where to find the Gospel of John? It sounds a bit odd to me. At any rate, if those were the reasons Paul would say so. When he says 'it is shameful' (1 Corinthians 14:35), and they mustn't ask a question, he gives the reason. Not that it would be shameful for a woman to question a

---

[216] C. K. Barrett, *A Commentary on the First Epistle to the Corinthians*, HNTC, New York, 1968, p332

prophet; simply 'it is shameful for a woman to speak in church"[217]. The argument that 'speak' refers to 'judging prophecies' would be more reasonable if these verses prohibiting women speaking followed immediately after verse 29 where we read about 'judging prophecies'. However, the intervening verses (vs30-33) are not about 'judging', for in vs 30-33 Paul has returned to the subject of prophesying, and this is the immediate context for verse 34-35. Verse 34 says nothing about 'judging prophecies': it says the women are to keep silent, for 'they are not permitted to *speak*' and, to repeat, the word 'speak' in this chapter means to publicly address the congregation, usually by exercising a spiritual gift. Reading 'judging prophecies' into the word 'speak' in verses 34-35 is thus unwarranted[218].

E. Others argue that the words prohibiting women speaking are not Paul's at all, and that he is quoting (in astonishment) a Corinthian slogan, but only to correct it. However there is no evidence in the verses to confirm this idea (e.g. Paul does not say, '*it is actually reported* that some of you say', like he does in 5:1, nor does he refer to this as a question they asked him in their letter, as in 7:1, nor does he use language like 1 Cor. 15:35: '*but someone will say*'). This suggestion is groundless. The fact that this is the third limitation upon the freedom to speak in church (tongues-speakers are to 'keep

---

[217] David W. Gooding, transcript from *The Christian Philosophy of Man: Eight Studies from 1 Corinthians on the Order of Churches in Light of the Gospel*, Myrtlefield House, 1994

[218] Gordon Fee summarizes the problems with the idea that 'Paul is prohibiting women judging prophecies': '(1) the extreme difficulty of being so far removed from v. 29 that one wonders how the Corinthians themselves could have so understood it; (2) the fact that nothing in the passage itself even remotely hints of such a thing; and (3) the form of v. 35, "if they wish to learn anything," which implies not "judging" their husbands' prophecies but failing to understand what is going on at all. Furthermore, despite arguments to the contrary, it is less than convincing that "discerning" the prophetic utterance of a husband is to sit in authority over him in a greater way than by a prophetic utterance. That seems to make the dependent, and therefore lesser, item (discerning prophecies) more significant than prophecy itself' (*The First Epistle to the Corinthians*, p704).

silent' if there is no interpreter in verse 28, prophets are to 'keep silent' if something is revealed to someone else in verse 30, and women are to 'keep silent' in verse 34) suggests not only a logical progression in the chapter, but also that it is Paul's own train of thought and words.

F. Some argue that these verses were never written by the apostle Paul at all, but were added centuries later by some scribe as he copied out Paul's letter, and that these words interrupt Paul's thought-flow with foreign ideas. However the verses are in perfect keeping with Paul's subject: 'speaking' in church, and being 'silent' (vs28, 30, 34). The biggest problem with this objection is that there is no textual evidence for it: not one single Greek manuscript omits these verses, and although there are three manuscripts from the eccentric Western manuscript tradition which place these verses later in the chapter, this is no proof that the verses were originally absent. Even if a textual ancestor of these three (related) manuscripts did not contain these verses, it's testimony is opposed by the overwhelming majority of other families of manuscripts and early language versions which included these verses. Nowhere else in the NT do textual critics omit two whole verses upon zero Greek manuscript evidence.

G. Some argue that Paul's prohibition related to some local problem, perhaps arising from local Corinthian customs or sensitivities, which happily no longer applies to us. However, Paul tells the believers to observe the uniform practices of the Christian churches ('as in all the churches of the saints', verse 33) rather than to observe the customs of Corinth. Paul bases the distinction between the sexes on the Law (not only because of creation, 1 Tim. 2:13ff., but see also Lev. 27, Num. 30, etc.), not local issues. Some suggest the local situation might have involved a problem inside the church, maybe involving women teaching false-doctrine. However, Paul neither mentions an issue of heresy being promoted by women, nor is there any reason, if this were the case, why he should ban all women speaking. If there were problems of a doctrinal nature, the judging process (verse 29b) would be expected to handle them and the women who were not teaching heresy should have been allowed to carry on teaching.

None of these attempts to 'explain away' the verses offer a clear and compelling case. The meaning of the verses is straightforward enough (except that here it clashes with modern politically-correct sensibilities). The fact that there are so many wildly different 'explanations' of 1 Cor. 14:34-35 suggests that the simple answer is best: women are not to publicly speak in the church gatherings. Advocates of women's public ministry, finding 1 Cor. 14:34-35 unhelpful, turn to other verses to argue that women can speak in church.

1 Corinthians 11:5 and Galatian 3:28

1 Corinthians 11:5 mentions women praying and prophesying without any hint of censure, and (it is argued) this occurred in the church gatherings. However, to that to assume that the context in 1 Cor. 11:2-16 is the church gatherings is unwarranted[219]. The key expressions 'when

---

[219] B. B. Warfield writes, 'There is nothing said about church in the passage or in the context... There is no reason whatever for believing that "praying and prophesying" in church is meant. Neither was an exercise confined to the church' ("Paul on Women Speaking in Church", *The Presbyterian*, October 30, 1919). David Gooding argues that neither in OT or NT times would women have audibly prayed or prophesied in formal temple or synagogue services, although women like the prophetess Anna (Luke 2:36-38) did so outside these formal worship services (so too the prophets Elijah, Elisha and Jeremiah). Gooding suggests that early Christians followed this Jewish custom. He writes, 'On the point that prophesying took place as much, or more, outside the church as inside – and therefore 1 Corinthians 11:2-16 is not necessarily and primarily concerned only with behaviour in the church – it is perhaps significant that the phrase, 'when you come together' is first mentioned at verse 17 and then frequently after that (11:18, 20, 33; 14:23, 26)', *Paul's Teaching about Women in 1 Corinthians Chapters 11 and 14*, Belfast: Myrtlefield House, 2019, p6. J. N. Darby writes, 'We are not as yet come to the order in the assembly. That commences with verse 17' (*Synopsis of the Books of the Bible*, Vol. 4, Kingston-on-Thames: Stow Hill Bible and Tract Depot, 1958, p175). For the same view, see also W. E. Vine, *First Corinthians*, Oliphants, 1951, p147, R. C. H. Lenski, *1 and 2 Corinthians*, Minneapolis, Augsburg Fortress, 1963, pp436-7, W. MacDonald, *Believers Bible Commentary*, Nelson, 1995, p1785, Alexander Strauch, *Biblical Eldership*, Littleton, CO: Lewis and Roth, 2nd Ed., 1988, p221,

you come together' and 'in [the] church[es]' are absent in 1 Cor. 11:2-16, although mentioned seven times each in the sections of the letter dealing with church gatherings (1 Cor. 11:17 – 14:40). Someone might argue that 1 Corinthians is all about 'church life', but certain sections (like those dealing with Christians taking each other to court or sexual relations in marriage) are not dealing with church gatherings *per se*. The onus of proof rests with those who argue that the church gatherings are in view in 11:2-16, however many commentators simply assume (or assert) that the church gatherings are in view in 11:5[220]. OT prophets (and prophetesses) prophesied in various locations (under palm trees, in king's palaces, in prison cells, on their death beds, etc.), both publicly and in private conversations (see 1 Kings 17:17ff., 2 Kings 8:7ff., 13:14ff., Jer. 38:14ff., etc.) and both to Gentile idolaters as well as to the people of God. There is no good reason to assume that prophecy, whether by men or women, must occur in Christian or congregational settings. An audience of one is sufficient – and there are situations beside the church gatherings where such occurred in the Bible. Thus, the evidence that the church gatherings are in view in 1 Cor. 11:2-16 is lacking, and based on a false assumption about 1 Cor. 11:4-5, *viz.* that prophecy must occur in the church gatherings. The argument that 1 Cor. 11:5 permits women to prophesy and pray publicly in the church does not provide a reasonable exposition of 1 Cor. 14:34-35 – it just sets up an apparent contradiction based on a false assumption.

Galatians 3:28, it is argued, does away with gender distinctions in the Christian church. However, in context, Galatians 3:28 is talking about who may be saved, not who may speak in church. Galatians 3

---

and the examination of this issue by Malcolm Horlock, "Studies in 1 Corinthians 14, Appendix", *Precious Seed*, Vol. 58.4, 2003.

[220] For example, F. F. Bruce in *1 and 2 Corinthians*, (London: Marshall, Morgan & Scott, 1971), p104, writes, 'That there was liberty in the church (for it is church order, not private or domestic devotion, that is in view here) for women to pray or prophesy is necessarily implied by Paul's argument'. In addition to assuming what needs to be proved (a church setting), Bruce finds the women's silence in 14:34-35 "strange" and offers no real explanation either of 14:34-35 or the apparent contradiction between those verses and 11:5 (ibid, p135-6).

teaches that all people – Jews, Gentiles, slaves, free, men and women – are sinners and all may be saved through faith in Christ, irrespective of race, and without gender-specific religious ceremonies like circumcision. Conversion does not abolish gender distinctions, or our nationality or social standing; an employee does not become a CEO upon salvation. If conversion abolished gender distinctions, homosexuality would be okay, whereas the NT condemns it in the plainest terms. This verse does not say that gender differences or roles cease after we come to Christ.

Women's Silence in 1 Timothy 2

Paul's instructions about the place of men and women in the church are found in 1 Timothy 2. After telling the men to take the lead in prayer in the first eight verses ('I will therefore that the men (lit. 'males') pray everywhere', verse 8), Paul turns to the woman's place in verses 11-12, writing: *Let a woman learn in silence with all subjection, and I do not permit a woman to teach or to have authority over a man, but to be in silence.*

These verses are controversial nowadays and hotly debated. They appear to state that women should be silent and not hold positions of authority (like elders or deacons, which the next section of the letter deals with) in the church. Notice the way that the two verses set this out.

1. Firstly, verse 11 states it positively: 'let a woman learn in silence with all submission'.
2. Then, verse 12 states it negatively: 'I do not permit a woman to teach nor to have authority over a man, but to be in silence'.

To understand these verses, it is important to place them in their context. The chapter starts with Paul writing about one form of public participation in the church (prayer: 'Therefore I exhort first of all that supplications, prayers, intercessions, and giving of thanks be made for all men', verse 1), and concludes with another (teaching, verses 11-12). However, the emphasis in the second half of the chapter is not on teaching, *per se*, but rather the differing roles of men and women in public participation in the church. Hence, in verse 8, Paul says, 'I will therefore that the men (lit. 'males') pray everywhere'. He moves on from here to state in verses 11 and 12 that the women are to learn in silence and not teach.

Another way to plot the flow of Paul's argument in the second half of the chapter is to observe that women are to be characterised by modesty in their clothing (verses 9-10). This same thought of modesty is carried over into the following verses (11 and 12) in which the related concept of submission is enjoined in relation to authority and teaching in the church. Modesty in clothing is matched by meekness in position and participation in the church.

Leaving aside, for the moment, the matter of the silence of women, what do we learn about participatory church gatherings from this chapter? It is interesting to note that there is nothing anywhere stated here (or anywhere else in 1 Timothy for that matter) about any particular people who have been appointed to the duties of public prayer or teaching. In the Old Testament, the priests carried out these functions, but here in the New Testament there is no 'special' or 'holy' class of Christians who are to perform these functions in the church. C. K. Barrett writes, 'Apparently all male members of the church had an equal right to offer prayer, and were expected to use their right' (*The Pastoral Epistles*, p. 54). With teaching, similarly, there is no restriction placed or guidelines offered about who may exercise the right to teach in the church, except for what is stated here in relation to the silence of women. Apparently all men had the right to publicly participate in the church gatherings. This passage thus reinforces what we have learnt elsewhere about the participatory nature of church gatherings in the Pastoral Epistles.

Turning to the matter of women's silence, there are four debated issues:

1. What does 'silence' actually mean in verse 11?
2. Who or what are the women to be in submission (v11) to?
3. Do the words 'I do not permit' (v12) imply either a personal or a temporal limitation on the prohibition?
4. What does the expression 'to have authority' (v12) mean?

What does 'silence' mean?
The word 'silence' (Gk. *hysuchia*) is used twice, at the beginning of verse 11 and end of verse 12, and seems to be the dominant motif in the two verses. However, 'silence' can mean two things: 'quietness, calm, tranquillity', i.e. the absence of dispute, argument or troublemaking (see earlier in this very chapter, 1 Tim. 2:2, for this meaning) or 'silence' in the more absolute sense of refraining from speaking or making noise.

Some would argue that verse 11 is saying that the women are not to be disputatious or argumentative in relation to what was being taught in the church. That is, Paul is not enforcing a blanket-ban on women speaking in the church, but simply arguing against women speaking in a way that is argumentative and rebellious. This would explain the end of the verse where we read that they are to 'be in submission'. However, it would not explain why only the women should be submissive to what it being taught in church.

On the other hand, the themes of the chapter (prayer at its beginning and teaching its end), would appear to indicate that, in context, silence here means refraining from public participation in these two activities. This would explain why verse 8 says that 'the males' are to pray – because the women are to be 'silent' – and why verse 12 enjoins silence a second time, in contrast with teaching. Paul appears to repeat himself so there can be no doubt about what he is saying. There seems to be no reason not to take the word 'silence' in its normal sense of 'not speaking'.

Who or what are the women to be 'in submission' to?
The absence of any object of the submission leaves us with questions. Is the submission to the men? Or to the teaching in church? Or to God?

The submission does not appear to be to God – why would it not say that the men have to submit to God also? To encourage Christian submission to God generally seems uncalled for in this context. There is nothing in the immediate vicinity about any issue with insubordination towards God. If there was some difficulty of submitting to God's will, for example, because of present hardships, Paul's tone would presumably be more sympathetic (cf. submission to suffering in 1 Peter). The fact that the passage does not mention submission 'to God' would appear to argue against this being Paul's intended meaning.

Neither does the submission appear to be to 'teaching' in the church generally, for Paul does not specify what sort of teaching the women should submit to. As we have already seen, there was plenty of false-teaching going on in Ephesus, and Paul would hardly be saying that women should submit to false-teaching as well as true.

Verses elsewhere in the New Testament (1 Pet. 3:1, Eph. 5:22, Col. 3:18, Titus 2:5) show that wives are to submit to their husbands. The connection with 'submission' in 1 Cor. 14:34 is particularly telling here. In both passages, submission is required of a specific gender (women) in a particular setting (the church). Nor does the passage specify that certain women are the special target of Paul's directive here – all women are to be submissive. Some suggest that certain high class or newly converted women were causing problems in the church. However, Paul does not mention that any particular women – whether untaught, heretical or socially prominent – were causing some specific problem in the church. The idea is contradicted by the fact that Paul requires submission of all the women generally, not just some supposed troublemakers.

The verses that follow immediately supply the reason; Paul goes on to write about how Adam was formed first before Eve and how Adam was not deceived but Eve fell into transgression (verses 13-14). In other words, this is not a local Ephesian problem, but an issue that goes back to Creation and the Fall. The specificity of the submission (women, not men; all women, not some) indicates that women are to be submissive because of their gender and for no other 'special' reason. The text supplies all the explanation we need without recourse to some speculative scenario: the submission is gender-based, the women to the men.

Finally, 'all' submission indicates the extent of the injunction - to the point of silence in the church: no praying, teaching or public participation in the church.

What do the words 'I do not permit' mean?
Some would argue that the present tense use of 'permit' here implies that Paul is saying 'I do not permit at the present time'. In other words, while

there is at present a limitation upon women teaching, it allows for women to teach at some later time. Philip H. Towner says 'the grounds for this are lacking'. He elaborates in a footnote: 'Other commands that are binding in nature or universal are expressed in the present tense (1 Cor. 7:10, 1 Thess. 4:1, 10; 5:14)'[221].

Some have also argued from this that Paul is only expressing his personal opinion: J. B. Phillips translates the expression, 'Personally, I don't allow ...'. However, Paul uses personal language throughout 1 Timothy and particularly in this chapter: 'I urged you ... to remain' (1:3), 'this charge I commit to you' (1:18), 'I exhort first of all' (2:1), 'I desire therefore that the men pray everywhere' (2:8), 'I do not permit' (2:12), 'I desire the younger widows marry' (5:14). Yes, Paul is giving personal advice – it is personal correspondence, after all – particularly in view of some of the difficulties faced by Timothy, but this in no way diminishes the apostolic and therefore authoritative nature of that guidance.

What does the expression 'to have authority' mean?

There is little difficulty in understanding the word 'teach' in 1 Tim. 2:11-12. However, there is great debate over the words 'to have authority'. The words 'to have authority' translate the Greek word *authenteo*, which is only used here in the New Testament. The basic meaning is 'to act on one's own', (hence the word was used occasionally in ancient times to describe committing suicide), but more generally, it means 'to assume a stance of independent authority'. Towner writes: 'as the studies have shown, the word group covers a range that can be broadly categorized as follows: to rule/reign; to control/dominate; to act independently; to be the originator of something; to murder. From this range, most interpreters settle within the area of "the exercise of authority"'.

However, Christian egalitarians who believe that women should be allowed to teach in church argue that the word is best translated as 'to dominate someone'. Hence they suggest that the problem was not Christian women teaching *per se* (for that was perfectly acceptable), but

---

[221] Philip H. Towner, *The Letters to Timothy and Titus*, NICNT, Grand Rapids, MI: Eerdmans, 2006, p217

doing so in a way that was domineering, or lording it over others, and thus displaying an unchristian spirit[222]. However, even if we accept the translation 'dominate' for 'have authority', what this interpretation has done is to subtly change the actual words of Scripture: instead of women being told not 'to teach or dominate the men', egalitarians have substituted 'teach *in such a way as* to dominate the men'.

The verbal sleight-of-hand is not the only problem here, although in itself it should alert us to the fact that the interpretation is somewhat forced. There is a further fly in this interpretation's ointment: why are the women told not to domineer over the *men*? If the problem is just a domineering spirit, why does Paul not simply ban a domineering spirit? Why does he instead ban women domineering over men, make no mention of women domineering over other women, and why does he only ban women teaching in a domineering way, but say nothing about men doing the same thing? Paul's instructions are full of gender-specific language here, and it is precisely this sort of language that the feminist interpretation provides no explanation for, without recourse to speculative story-telling that finds no support in the actual words of Scripture (e.g. high-class ex-pagan-priestesses teaching in church in an arrogant and haughty way).

In any case, teaching is itself an exercise of authority. Christian teaching is not an academic subject without practical implications. It involves telling other people what to believe and how to behave. There is no such thing as Christian teaching which does not in some sense 'lay down the law'; anybody who teaches is claiming to be an authority of some sort. There is always going to be some sort of authority exercised in the church: the authority of God's truth.

In conclusion, instead of twisting Paul's words to avoid what their plain meaning would seem to dictate, once again the simple answer is best: Paul is saying that women are not allowed to teach in the church.

---

[222] See for example, Linda Belleville, "Teaching and Usurping Authority" in *Discovering Biblical Equality: Complementarity without Hierarchy*, eds. R. W. Pierce and R. M. Groothuis, Downers Grove, IL: IVP, 2005, pp 205-223.

One final, practical, objection is worth considering: if people learn best by participating, does not women's silence limit women's growth? Maybe, but the learning benefit from discussion after a sermon is not limited to the questioner but extends to the whole group, while the New Testament encourages women to teach outside the church gatherings (e.g. Aquila and Priscilla taking Apollos aside and teaching him, Acts 18:26; older women teaching younger, Titus 2:3; women evangelising, Phil. 4:3; as well as teaching their children, 2 Tim. 3:15).

Modern evangelical willingness to compromise on this issue is curious, and shows how easily biblical convictions are surrendered under pressure from modern society. The church must reject society's call for the abolition of gender differences, and stand up for the divinely-created plan of different roles for men and women.

Strong churches are built on spiritually strong families. Church and family life are closely related, and the NT calls for male leadership in both spheres (Eph. 5:23-33, 1 Pet. 3:1-7). For both families and churches to be strong, men must take spiritual leadership. Women are to 'ask their own husbands at home' (1 Cor. 14:35) not only so that homes are places of Christian discussion and learning, but also so that men teach their families. Church life is meant to reinforce the role of husbands and wives in the home; the principle of male headship is not to be undermined in church by women leading and men being silent. Participatory church gatherings encourage men to contribute publicly in the church, and this requires personal spiritual health and leadership in the home. Churches where men are not expected to participate, or where the women do most of it for them, do not encourage men to be the leaders God called them to be, in the church or in the home. Instead, they institutionalize men's natural spiritual laziness and add to the image of Christianity as a religion for old ladies.

CHAPTER 14

HOW NOT TO HAVE PARTICIPATORY CHURCH GATHERINGS

In this chapter, we will look at nine ways that it is advisable NOT to have participatory church gatherings.

We will see that it is possible for a church to have services which implement some features of participatory church gatherings, but these services do not truly match the biblical picture of church gatherings we have considered in the first half of this book. As a result, they also fall short of producing the full benefits flowing from such gatherings. The result, in the long term, is not the healthy spiritual church growth that the New Testament describes. The problem with most of these types of meetings is not with what they do, but with what they omit or neglect to do.

The point of this chapter is not to say that a church cannot have some of these sorts of services we will describe. Some of them will doubtless produce some spiritual benefits. They may even be useful as interim measures for a church transitioning to the biblical picture of church gatherings. Instead, the point of this chapter is simply to state that these are half-way-house versions of the biblical pattern, and that as compromises, they will not result in long-term spiritual blessing. Therefore, if someone wishes to argue that these so-called (but really sub-biblical forms of) participatory church gatherings do not work in real life, the fault should not be attributed to what the Bible teaches. As we will see, the reason most of these services are not as beneficial as they could be is that they do not fully implement what the Bible says. It is the conviction of this author that doing things biblically produces spiritual benefits: God's wisdom works. But if we ignore the biblical picture and pursue our own form of humanly-devised church gatherings, we really have no right to complain that they don't work, or that they don't produce spiritual growth, or that they result in confusion and disaster.

Devaluing the Lord's Supper

As we have seen in the previous chapter, the Lord's Supper was a central feature of the gathering of the church every week in the New Testament. We see this is Acts 2:42 where it is one of four things the early Christians 'continued steadfastly' in (or 'devoted themselves to', NIV), and in Acts 20:7 and 1 Cor. 11:20 where it is described as the purpose of the gathering. The Lord's Supper was also (it seems likely) participatory in nature, just like the rest of the meeting.

Many churches today, however, have devalued and de-emphasized the Lord's Supper. It has become a minor, insignificant, and peripheral part of church life, celebrated on an occasional basis – once a month, once a quarter, or perhaps even once a year at Easter. It might be given a 5-10 minute slot in a service, but it is hardly soul-stirring or deeply affecting. To put it bluntly, in the modern evangelical world, the Lord's Supper has become an inconvenience. It is mere tokenism, and amounts to little more than a nibble of bread and a sip of drink. The end result is that the Lord's Supper becomes a mere perfunctory ritual, with little heart or feeling, a lifeless routine, sterile and irrelevant.

In fact, the Lord's Supper is in the process of becoming obsolete in modern evangelical church life. Many larger churches have simply scrapped it altogether, arguing that it is not only spiritually shallow, but logistically difficult with the crowds attending, and that there are better ways to spend fifteen minutes than by passing round bread and wine.

Instead of having a participatory Lord's Supper like in the New Testament, churches have substituted other arrangements:
- Letting one person conduct the Lord's Supper. The idea here is that it is hoped that by this person having put their own preparation into the effort, the Lord's Supper will retain some freshness, reality and spirituality. But the problem is that, for everyone else in the congregation, spiritual preparation is not required. Spiritual worship depends on personal preparation of heart; it is difficult to transfer a heart of worship from one person to another, or from a leader to the

congregation, from the ambient atmosphere, or from the music of a 'worship band'. The effect of the Lord's Supper performed by one person upon the members of the congregation is again minimal and fleeting.

- Organising the Lord's Supper, so that a committee draws up a program or sets out a liturgy for the service, with several people appointed to pray or read the Bible or announce a hymn. The Lord's Supper thus becomes like an infants' school assembly, with people reading their prepared lines off slips of paper. However, the Lord's Supper requires spiritual feeling, freshness and personal reality, and it is doubtful that press-ganging people into reading lines is really going to achieve this.
- Bringing the Lord's Supper to life by incorporating some gimmicks into it. Thus, it is possible to get people to do something different each time the Lord's Supper is held: standing up while partaking of the bread and wine instead of sitting down (or vice versa), walking out the front, or splitting into groups to walk to the four corners of the building, putting up some nice pictures on a screen while it is happening, or accompanying the Lord's Supper with special music. These gimmicks simply cover up the fact that there is a spiritual void underneath.

Whenever the Lord's Supper is programmed, or reduced to a liturgy, or left to one person, or has some gimmicks incorporated into it, or reduced to a ten-minute slot, or held monthly, quarterly or yearly, these are all signs that a church is struggling to make the Lord's Supper meaningful. Many churches just give up, and it is abandoned. If a church feels compelled to retain the Lord's Supper, it is held as a ritual obligation, not as a means of enriching God's people. Instead of being a central focus of the church's gathering, it becomes a peripheral ceremony largely devoid of any feeling or life.

Christ asked us to hold this service, 'in remembrance of me' (Luke 22:19), yet many churches today struggle to know how to hold the Lord's Supper in a deeply meaningful and spiritually enriching way that is a blessing and benefit to God's people. The answer to the problem of making the Lord's Supper heartfelt and meaningful, it is suggested, is to do it the way it seems they did it in the New Testament – as part of a participatory church gathering. In that way people are required to come along to the meeting spiritually prepared to worship, and with something to offer in thanks for Christ – a hymn or song, a reading from Scripture, a prayer of thanks, an insight into the person and work of Christ. A participatory Lord's Supper requires that God's people take responsibility for their own devotion to Christ.

Even if our love for Christ is low, it makes little sense to think about Him less often. It is hard to see how reducing the time spent worshipping Christ will deepen spirituality or draw out thankfulness for Him. Surely it is better to have a church meeting that acts as a spiritual thermometer and shows how spiritually cold we are than to play at church, covering up our spiritual shallowness.

Christianity has two ordinances, baptism and the Lord's Supper, but to participate in these two ordinances outwardly without inward spiritual feeling is a dangerous form of hypocrisy. As surely as baptism without true faith and repentance is a sham, so too is partaking of the Lord's Supper without heart-felt worship in spirit and in truth. Looking to the physical elements of the ordinance to convey some spiritual benefit is sacramentalism and superstition worthy of the Roman Catholic Church.

Participatory Church Gatherings without Teaching

In New Testament times, the church's main weekly gathering incorporated both the Lord's Supper and the exercise of spiritual gifts for edification. However, it is possible to so over-emphasise the Lord's Supper that the remembrance of Christ occupies the entire church gathering. The result is that the church does not receive sufficient encouraging teaching. There is nothing wrong with an occasional meeting that is entirely taken up with the person and work of Christ, if led by the Holy Spirit. But when a church pursues a policy that frowns on practical, edifying teaching and insists that everything must be about remembering Christ, the long-term consequences will be spiritual weakness and decline.

Our Lord Jesus Christ asked us to celebrate the Lord's Supper 'in remembrance of Me' (1 Cor. 11:24-25), but out of motives that seem only right and pure, it is possible to over-emphasise the devotional side of the church's gathering and by so doing to neglect the importance of general edification of God's people. The church gathering thus becomes spiritually unbalanced, and the participatory edification using spiritual gifts, as described in 1 Cor. 14:26-40, does not occur. 1 Corinthians 14 is as much a part of Scripture (and church life) as 1 Corinthians 11 and if the Lord's Supper is given to us by authoritative command, then participatory edification would appear to be equally so (1 Cor. 14:37).

1 Corinthians 14 presents the participatory edification time as something that happened at the main weekly gathering of the entire church, not as a separate special meeting of the church, scheduled for another time in the week. It appears that the early church had a main weekly gathering which included ample opportunity for open ministry. General edification using spiritual gifts is a necessary element in the church's gathering, and it is vital for the church's spiritual growth.

When the author was in his teens, his church had a week or two of evangelistic meetings. We advertised these meetings by various means, but few outsiders attended. However, one man started attending, recently converted from a staunch Roman Catholic background through the minister of another church. He was encouraged to hear the gospel message being clearly preached and came every night. After the evangelistic meetings finished, he started coming along to the Lord's Supper on Sunday morning. The Lord's Supper was participatory, and maybe this order of service seemed strange to the visitor. However, there was also very little time or opportunity for encouragement or teaching. After two weeks of attending the Lord's Supper, he went back to the church of the minister who had led him to Christ. He was a new convert and knew he needed feeding and teaching to establish him in his new-found faith. However, it is not just new converts who need to be fed, taught, encouraged and challenged from God's Word. All believers need to be fed from the Word of God every week.

G. H. Lang describes the problem of not allowing sufficient time for edifying teaching. He first summarises the subjects that Christ taught

His disciples at the institution of the Lord's Supper in John 13-16 (the need for a clean walk symbolised by washed feet, the lowliness of a humble servant-attitude, the hope of the Lord's return, the person and work of the Holy Spirit, abiding in Christ, the power of prayer, etc.), and then writes: 'These are some of the profound and exalted topics with which the Lord Jesus occupied the hearts of His followers as they conversed at the table that memorable night. He was preparing them for the tasks and ordeals that awaited them without the support of His visible presence. No one will or can be equal to these tasks and tests unless these mighty truths are the energy of the soul. Therefore it is a necessity of Satan to prevent the Christian from being saturated with those invigorating truths, and one of his subtlest devices is seen in such suggestions as that "we meet to break bread", "we meet to remember the Lord", not to hear addresses; or that there should be no ministry before the bread has been broken; or, at any rate ministry should only be occupied only with Calvary. So far have these injurious ideas been pressed that in one circle of Christians no ministry of the Word is permitted at the breaking of bread. The practical result is general starvation, with the resultant spiritual sickness and weakness of the famished. And one of the alarming symptoms is that the under-fed dream they are well-nourished, and know not that they manifest to all the ill health of their spirits in feelings and actions sadly unlike Christ. On the facts presented it is evident that much of the Lord's instruction that night was concerned with the spiritual state of His followers. This is ever a paramount necessity…'[223].

Instead of having the participatory time of teaching during a main weekly meeting, some churches have their main teaching in a midweek meeting. On Sunday, these churches instead concentrate upon worship or evangelism in their main services. The main problem that results from this is that the Christians do not get properly fed from God's Word during the main church meetings on the Sunday. As a result, some of the Christians do not get fed and taught at all during the week, either

---

[223] G. H. Lang, *The Churches of God*, London: The Paternoster Press, 1959, 77-78

because they find it difficult to come out to a midweek meeting (for example, a wife whose husband is not a believer, a shift worker who has to work nights, or a mother with young children), or because they are so spiritually weak that they have no desire to come and be fed. These believers become spiritually malnourished, sick, impoverished and discouraged – because they rarely ever get fed. Spiritually-sick believers become super-sensitive, criticize and grumble, fall into sin, squabble and fight over perceived slights, or fall out with each other (or the church) over some minor matter.

Another problem that results from relegating teaching to some other time is that the church develops two circles of fellowship. Some Christians come out to teaching whenever it is scheduled during the week – they are the inner circle of keen, committed and involved Christians. But the second group of Christians who do not come out to teaching times remain on the fringes of the church's fellowship. Sometimes, the response of the church's leaders or the 'inner circle' of keen Christians is to bemoan the lack of spirituality of these fringe, or 'outer-circle' Christians. Eventually, these 'outer-circle' Christians find that they have closer friends among Christians in another church than those in their own fellowship, so they leave and go to that other church.

Instead of worrying about the low numbers attending midweek teaching meetings, true shepherds need to show concern for the sheep who are not being fed. Sadly, the 'carrot and stick' approach is often used – alternately encouraging the Christians to come out to the extra midweek meeting, and then warning people that they are missing out on spiritually helpful teaching. Sometimes, the spiritually malnourished are quietly 'written-off' as second-class Christians for whom nothing can be done. Instead of being like sheepdogs who bite and criticize members who do not attend special midweek meetings, true shepherds need to feed the flock. Those with a true shepherd-heart should make every effort to go to where the malnourished and sick sheep are and feed them. The shepherd who truly cares for his sheep will not stand upon a high hill calling the starving sheep to rise up and climb the hill to get some food, but will instead go to where they are. It is the shepherd's job to provide health-promoting food and teaching during the times when these spiritually needy and even sick Christians are present – during the main weekly meeting when almost everybody is present.

Now, please understand: there is a place for midweek Bible teaching, and it can be a source of blessing and growth. It is usually a time when the keen and spiritual Christians attend, and the preaching can deal with more advanced subjects. But it is not usually the time for getting down to the level of the youngest or weakest believer and providing encouraging, helpful, pastorally-appropriate teaching. If only a few turn out to hear it, and the preacher does not put as much effort into his preparation, the preaching can become dry, academic and irrelevant. The result is that even when the spiritually-malnourished turn up, they do not find the teaching as helpful as it could have been.

Ultimately, by relegating teaching to another time (other than a main service), the church is sending out the message that teaching (and the healthy spiritual growth that results from being fed upon God's Word) is a secondary priority in the church. If it was a priority, would it not be given first place in the church's life? Would it not be given time on Sunday when the church meets together for its main meeting – like they did in the New Testament?

W. E. Vine, commenting on Christ's words, 'Feed my sheep' (John 21:15-17), writes, 'The lesson to be learnt … is that, in the spiritual care of God's children, the "feeding" of the flock from the Word of God is the constant and regular necessity; it is to have the foremost place'[224].

G. H. Lang argues the same point from the long hours which Paul spent teaching the church at Troas at the Lord's Supper (Lang holds to a midnight Lord's Supper at Troas in Acts 20 which we argued against in the previous chapter, but irrespective, his main point still stands): 'Acts 20 shows clearly that long hours were occupied with such conversation and instruction before the bread was broken, and that afterward the dialogue continued till dawn, forbidding the idea that ministry ought not to precede. These facts stare at us out of the pages of Scripture, yet in disregard of them believers will give the hour to many hymns, to long pauses, wearisome prayers, a formal partaking of the bread and cup, and

---

[224] W. E. Vine, "Feed, Fed", *An Expository Dictionary of New Testament Words*, Nashville, TN: Nelson, 1985

they depart as empty of grace as they came. It is feeding that they need; yet in one such assembly where there lived a well-known teacher his brethren complained that he would give at the Lord's Table general instruction, and they did not want it. The assembly paid the price by being underfed and weak'[225].

Participatory Church Gatherings with a Picked Speaker for Teaching

Some churches have a participatory Lord's Supper, lasting perhaps for an hour, followed by a picked speaker who gives some Bible teaching upon a pre-arranged subject or passage. However, this is back to front: there is plenty of New Testament evidence for participatory Bible teaching, but no direct evidence for 'open worship', a participatory Lord's Supper. As we saw in the previous chapter on the Lord's Supper, this does not mean that we cannot have a participatory Lord's Supper; indeed, we saw good reasons for doing this. However, the biblical evidence *implies* a participatory Lord's Supper; there is no *direct* New Testament evidence of a participatory worship time at the Lord's Supper. The New Testament does not explicitly teach or describe a time of 'open worship'. In fact, it is from the evidence for participatory edification in 1 Cor. 14 that we imply a participatory Lord's Supper. Therefore, a meeting with a participatory Lord's Supper but non-participatory edification is the reverse of what the New Testament evidence presents.

From a practical point of view, having a picked speaker after the Lord's Supper tends to result in any time for participatory edification being more limited. The more time that is left for a picked speaker, the less time there is for others to contribute. Another problem is that if a picked speaker is going to teach on a set topic at the end of the participatory church gathering, it discourages others from giving serious in-depth teaching; they will leave that for the 'teaching time'. By having a set 'teaching time', the message is (perhaps unconsciously) being sent out that serious teaching is best left for the person appointed to give it,

---

[225] G. H. Lang, *The Churches of God*, London: The Paternoster Press, 1959, pp78-9

and that ordinary contributions should not involve sustained exposition during the open participation time. The result is that the participatory edification time becomes filled with short, shallow and insubstantial contributions which do not really produce much food for God's people. Thus, the effect of having a set speaker is to squeeze and limit participatory edification, so that there is not the genuine freedom for God's Spirit to work as we see it in 1 Cor. 14.

It hardly needs stating that there is much blessing to be gained from inviting a particular speaker to teach on a set passage or topic or to give a series of messages. The reasons for doing so are too numerous to mention here. But in the New Testament, such teaching was separate from the ordinary, weekly church gathering; for example, Paul's daily teaching in the school of Tyrannus in Ephesus (Acts 19:9) was a different thing to what the New Testament shows happening in the central weekly church gathering which incorporated the Lord's Supper (Acts 20:7). In this author's opinion, 'set teaching' by picked speakers is best kept separate from a participatory church service, and scheduled at a different time that does not limit the opportunity for participatory edification. Hold one service on Sunday morning and the other in the evening, or separate the two services with a break or meal for fellowship. Or, if the quality of teaching in the participatory church gathering is good enough, dispense with the teaching service altogether.

The benefits of having an open time for edification where multiple speakers can minister as they are led by the Holy Spirit are two-fold. Firstly, not only are God's people fed by edifying, practical, encouraging teaching, but secondly, God's people also exercise their different spiritual gifts and thereby grow. Church life is a two-way street, involving give and take. Sitting and listening is not the only thing happening in church life according to the New Testament, nor is it conducive to growth. Participation is far more effective if we are truly desiring to see people grow. The New Testament shows that church members were actively involved in using their spiritual gifts in the church gathering, not just sitting as sermon fodder.

Stephen Short writes of the benefits of every-member ministry as follows: 'in churches, by contrast, where there is no one man appointed to do nearly all the preaching, the various members develop a sense of personal responsibility with regard to this matter. An exercise of heart is felt in relation to it; and it becomes implemented; and as time goes by, a very slight ability in handling the Word of truth becomes quite a fair ability in so doing, sometimes indeed a very considerable ability. Thus is gift raised up from within the church – not imported from two hundred miles away, but brought to fruition out of a church's own inner life'[226].

Participatory Church Gatherings with only a Token Time for Edification

Some churches that practise a participatory Lord's Supper, aware of the need for God's people to be fed and built up, leave a short space of time for a word of exhortation after the Lord's Supper. This is an improvement upon no time for edification whatsoever, but it neither corresponds with the New Testament pattern as seen in passages like 1 Cor. 14 where multiple members of the church use a variety of spiritual gifts for edification, nor will it be very spiritually beneficial in the long term. In fact, it is again the very opposite of the picture that we find in the New Testament where the time for edification was far longer than the time devoted to the Lord's Supper (cf. John 13-16, Acts 20).

A short period of time left for edification usually means that only one brother will be able to give a short word. If there are a number of gifted teachers in a church, there may be competition for this short opportunity to speak, and with such competition, the most forward will tend to dominate, discouraging those who are more reserved. The end-result is sometimes almost a 'closed-shop' where the more prominent teachers take it in turns. Sometimes, this situation almost results in a one-man ministry, as those who are less prominent or less gifted become discouraged at missing out on opportunities to speak (even when they have a message they feel led to give), and eventually stop attempting to do so.

---

[226] Stephen S. Short, "The Ministry of the Word", *The Witness*, pp47-8, Feb 1965

The old saying applies here: nothing grows under tall trees. If the time for open exercise of gift is short, and is dominated by a few people, the result is to limit the spiritual development of others. By contrast, 1 Cor. 14 allows time and opportunity for *multiple* messages – not just one – from a variety of brothers with different gifts.

Another problem that sometimes develops with a token time of ministry after the Lord's Supper is that the quality of the preaching is affected. Sometimes, because time is brief, all that is offered is the outline of a message and a few brief thoughts. The exposition of Scripture is short and shallow rather than extended. Someone has described this type of message as a 'sausage sermon', containing a few spiritual scraps swept up and held together, perhaps by an alliterative outline. Sometimes, the short amount of time is taken up with nothing more than the reading of a familiar passage without comment. Whatever the case, the end result is only limited edification of God's people.

Sermonettes produce Christianettes. God's people grow through sustained, serious, in-depth study of God's Word, both privately and in public preaching. Only when a church is receiving good solid healthy teaching will it grow strong, and this requires that people work hard in preparation for the church gathering. By contrast, if all the contributions are prayers, short 'thoughts', or hymns, not only are we encouraging lazy and shallow preparation, but the flock is not going to get fed. God's people need meat, not just milk (1 Cor. 3:1-2, Heb. 5:12-14).

There was once a family who left a church in which there was only a short token time for teaching after the Lord's Supper with the words, "All we ever get is ice-cream". The effect of limiting the time for edification results in 'the brother with a little word' which is not conducive to healthy church growth. Because the short time for ministry has been tacked onto the very end of the meeting – and Sunday dinner is maybe waiting at home – no one will complain (and some will even be pleased) with these half-hearted attempts at edification. The result of such ministry is, sadly, not the spiritual building-up of God's people. If, by contrast, there were more time allowed (as 1 Cor. 14 pictures), those with a care for God's people would rise to the occasion and work hard in preparation to meet their spiritual needs.

One of the purposes of the open opportunity for participation described in 1 Cor. 14 is that spiritual gift will develop and grow. Allowing only a very limited amount of time for exhortation after the breaking of bread neither reflects the freedom we find in 1 Cor. 14, nor does it allow for the gift-development that attends true participatory edification.

Participatory Church Gatherings on Special Occasions

Another way not to do participatory church gatherings is to think that every sort of Christian gathering must be participatory, or that certain special Christian gatherings must be participatory.

The author once heard of a particular church where every activity of the church was participatory. The result, on one particular Sunday, was that the Christians gathered for an evangelistic meeting, and then sat waiting for someone to speak, until after an hour of silence, they sung a hymn and went home. At least the participatory format exposed the spiritual poverty of the Christians. But while the story is merely embarrassing, it would be nothing short of a disgrace if there had been an unconverted person present seeking the Lord.

The author grew up attending various annual church conferences where the Bible teaching ministry was 'open-platform', i.e. participatory. Much of the teaching at these annual meetings was edifying while some was not so. It all depended on the quality of the Bible teachers who attended. Sadly, there were some speakers who majored on minors, some who (in the words of my grandfather) had buckets of words but thimbles of thoughts, and some who preached legalistic ideas not in Scripture. Yes, some people manifestly unable and unsuited to teach the Word of God presumed to do so, possibly overcome by the desire for public prominence and the temptation to be in the spotlight. The results were not always edifying.

Some people who have experienced such conference meetings might argue against the concept of participatory church gatherings based on their experiences. However, there were a number of differences between these conferences and the picture of participatory church gatherings we find in the New Testament. Thus, most of the conference speakers were 'big names' from other places, not the members of the local body interacting and growing together, nor was there much opportunity for 'grass-roots' gift development in such meetings. Nor was there opportunity for public questions or comments after preaching, which might have challenged some of the unedifying and legalistic teaching. Some might argue that it were perhaps better to have picked speakers at such conferences to ensure high-quality teaching. However, from a purely biblical point of view, the real question is not whether conferences in the Bible were picked-speaker or 'open-platform', but whether there were annual conferences in the New Testament at all.

The pressing need in a local church is not a yearly conference. The pressing need is rather to have weekly, edifying teaching that feeds and builds up the local church. This is what is supposed to happen at the main weekly gathering of the church. Every Sunday should be a conference, a spiritual feast, a three course meal. The saints should not only be fed from God's Word, but study God's Word themselves in preparation for the meeting, and grow through exercising their spiritual gifts. They should grow not only in knowledge but in love, through their mutual spiritual interaction with one another.

The problem with these annual conferences was not the fact that they were participatory; it was that attending annual conferences became a substitute for edifying teaching in the normal local church gathering every week. If there had been such local weekly teaching, addressing the pastoral needs of the local flock, perhaps these churches might not have declined, as many of them did. While these conferences provided encouraging fellowship for sometimes isolated believers, the large number of visitors attending an annual conference from other churches masked the dwindling numbers of people attending every week.

There is nothing wrong with having an annual conference, whether the speakers are invited or the platform is left 'open', just as there is nothing wrong with inviting a speaker to preach the gospel at an evangelistic meeting, or inviting a gifted teacher to give a series of expository or doctrinal messages on a particular topic or book of the Bible. What is wrong is a church where the flock is not fed from God's Word when they meet together every week.

Participatory Church Gatherings without Opportunity for Questions and Discussion

One of the problems of participatory church gatherings is that they can result in some contributions that are less than spiritually helpful, or even things being taught that are not scripturally true. It is for reasons like these that it is essential that there is opportunity for discussion and comments after someone has shared something from God's Word. Thus, in a participatory church gathering, there will be a number of Bible messages, interspersed by comments and discussion (1 Cor. 14:29), hymns and prayers. One of the benefits of this is that Christians learn to evaluate preaching by comparing what is being taught against the page of Scripture itself. For Paul in 1 Corinthians 14, preaching without evaluation was as unacceptable as tongues without interpretation.

If someone says something that is biblically true but nevertheless unbalanced, the time for questions and discussion gives opportunity for the truth to be put into proper perspective. It is not the job of someone preaching a message from the Bible to qualify everything they say with innumerable caveats, like a lawyer covering every eventuality. Sometimes, however, questions will result in clarifications that help younger believers to get the whole biblical picture. On the other hand, if someone says something that is not just unbalanced, but contrary to sound doctrine and the teaching of Scripture, it is important that the speaker is held to account by others in the congregation who can point out what the scriptures teach and set the speaker straight. This means that speakers will be more careful about what they say, knowing that they are going to be questioned afterwards. The fact that the speaker does not have the last word, but rather will be held to account publicly for what he has said means that he has to be far more careful than if there were no opportunity for comments.

The author used to be involved in a weekly bible study in a local prison, and it was interesting to see the development of conversational skills among the inmates the longer they were in the group and the more they started to grow in their understanding of Scripture. When a new inmate joined the group, there was a tendency to be quite blunt or rude towards others if there were disagreements. But, over a period of time, they would settle into the group, make friends and feel more comfortable in the conversation. In addition to realizing that rude comments produced an unpleasant atmosphere, the prisoners also seemed to observe and copy the courteous and diplomatic way that more mature believers in the group presented differing viewpoints. Instead of bluntly stating their opinions, participants would ask questions that opened up new angles on an issue. Or, more mature believers gently challenged unbalanced viewpoints by saying, 'I agree with you about what you said about [such and such]... but what do you think about the words in verse 10'? The prisoners themselves would start to choose their words more carefully, so that their comments were not taken as personal attacks upon others, but as attempts to help their fellow-believers to grow. In a setting where everybody has the opportunity to learn together in a participatory way, the reality is that people develop a far more sensitive and diplomatic way of conversing.

Thus, instead of comments and questions breeding disputes and personal attacks, discussion of what has been preached can actually produce the opposite, if it is led by godly and spiritual Christians. A question and comment time after preaching is itself a powerful method of helping believers to 'speak the truth in love' to each other. Allowing believers to develop the skills of conversational diplomacy and to share scriptural insights are important parts of spiritual growth. Preventing such discussion because of the perceived 'immaturity' of some believers is like stopping a child riding a bike because of the danger of falling off.

Small Group Bible Studies

Another sort of meeting that should not be confused with participatory church gatherings is the Bible class, the home group, or small group Bible study.

Home bible study groups have seen remarkable growth in the modern church scene. Beginning in the 1970s, they have largely replaced the weekly church prayer meeting and the adult Bible class. While Scripture neither mandates or describes any official system of home Bible study groups (nor does it discourage people discussing the Bible in homes or other small group settings), the vast majority of Western evangelical churches now have these mid-week gatherings for fellowship and spiritual growth.

Why have they proved so popular? Reasons for this include the fact that large churches are so impersonal that fellowship is required in a smaller unit, and that midweek church prayer meetings are so poorly attended. On the other hand, small bible study groups are testament to the fact that people learn best when they discover things for themselves. Rather than sitting and silently listening to someone giving a monologue, people are free to ask questions, share their own discoveries, and talk about the practical application of God's Word in the real world. A large reason for the success of the Methodist movement was the weekly 'class system' set up by John Wesley for the encouragement of his converts. By contrast, Wesley's fellow preacher George Whitefield complained that his converts and followers were 'a rope of sand'. Home groups have greatly increased the numbers of Christians participating in midweek spiritual activities, which can only be a good thing.

The Bible class, home group or small group teaches us the same lessons that we learn elsewhere: whenever God's Word is studied and shared there will be a benefit and a blessing, but what a person puts into the gathering will largely determine what that person gets out of it. Some home Bible study groups are effective, because the people attending put in serious preparation and grow as a result, while others have been aptly described as little more than a 'pooling of ignorance' or 'the blind leading the blind'. With the widespread use of published Bible study questions, the need for hard work through individual study preparation is nowadays lessened, and so too is the resultant spiritual growth.

The real attraction of the home bible study group is its social function, allowing fellowship at a deeper level than talking about family, weather and politics after church. However, it is quite possible for home groups to meet for friendship reasons rather than because of a desire to know Christ better. Once upon a time, the social dimension in church life was met through hospitality (a biblical command, Rom. 12:13, 1 Pet. 4:9, etc.), which involved a lot of work preparing an entire meal, where more extended personal conversation ensued, and where appreciation for the kindness shown resulted in an even deeper level of fellowship being experienced. Nowadays, some home groups (which tend to lack these elements) are mirroring more and more the shallowness of Western consumer convenience Christianity. By and large, they have not greatly arrested or reversed the declining standards of discipleship.

It is important not to confuse a home fellowship group with a church gathering. Although many churches met in homes in the New Testament (Rom. 16:5, Col. 4:15, etc.) and both settings allowed discussion and questions, the New Testament maintains a distinction between the two. Thus, women were allowed to ask questions in a home setting but not in church (1 Cor. 14:34-35), the Corinthians were told to eat at home rather than when the church came together (1 Cor. 11:22, 34) and a special 'place of the unlearned' (1 Cor. 14:16) surely only applied in a church setting, not at home. Participatory church gatherings also require hard work in study and preparation so that there is solid and helpful teaching. If we want God's people to be fed, built-up and prepared for the spiritual battles they are facing, it will require substantial, scriptural, Spirit-filled, prayerfully-prepared contributions. We must not allow the church meeting to be filled up with lots of little, shallow remarks – like some home Bible study group comments.

Because a participatory church gathering is a whole-church activity occurring at its main weekly gathering, there is much more need for the meeting to be spiritually edifying. The church comes together for a more serious purpose and with a less casual tone than the very informal nature of a home group. However, participatory church gatherings bring the same principles of spiritual discovery, personal interaction and real-life application into the church gatherings, where the Bible says they belonged all along.

In the early 1970s, Robert Girard wrote the book, *Brethren, Hang Loose*[227]. In it he described the journey of his program-driven evangelical Wesleyan church in Scottsdale, Arizona, to something more like a church patterned on the New Testament. Reading Watchman Nee's

---

[227] Robert C. Girard, *Brethren, Hang Loose, Or What's Happening to My Church?* Grand Rapids, MI: Zondervan, 1972

book *What Shall this Man Do?* and comparing it against the Bible, Girard learnt that the church is a body in which every member is meant to be functioning by using its spiritual gifts, not just receiving but also giving, with Christ operating as the Head of the body (not Pastor Rob).

Girard's church underwent many changes, guided by a number of important principles: 1. Depend on the Holy Spirit instead of the flesh. 2. Concentrate on the maturing of Christians. 3. Recognize the priesthood of all believers. 4. Build the fellowship around Christ. 5. Release church life from the confines of the church building. 6. Recognize our place in the total Body of Christ. Lastly, 7. Build church unity on the basis of love. However, in addition to these biblical principles, it also adopted a number of new practices. At the very centre of its program of renewal were home groups.

There is much to commend in the book. Exciting things were happening in the church and in the lives of the believers. But what was the end of the story? The book doesn't tell where it all led, but by 1979 the church had surrendered its buildings to the Wesleyan denomination and become a number of loosely-affiliated home groups or, in the words of its new mission statement, a 'network of relationships'. What started as church renewal became church dissolution. The church hung so loose that it eventually fell apart.

The lesson that *Brethren, Hang Loose* teaches is that it is possible to take the idea of small groups to extremes that result in church fragmentation, spiritual individualism or even anarchy, just like in Corinth. While every-member ministry is a biblical truth, Paul balanced it by emphasizing the need for edifying participatory teaching when the whole church came together (1 Corinthians 14), not in smaller sub-units and small-groups. Individuality is balanced by church unity and godly, spiritual leadership. Make no mistake: if participatory church gatherings are going to be spiritually beneficial, they require good leadership. Elders need to be foremost in feeding the flock so that congregational freedom is balanced and directed by godly leadership.

Paul deals with the disorders at Corinth by insisting that ministry needs to be motivated by love. Instead of speaking in church because we like to hear the sound of our own voice, we need to be seeking the well-being of others and striving to build them up. Ministry needs to be focused on the Christ-centred truths of the faith. He says the same thing to Timothy in Ephesus. Sound doctrine (i.e. healthy teaching) produces a stable church as opposed to a church full of disputes fuelled by individualism; it results in godly administration, love from a pure heart, a good conscience and sincere faith (1 Tim. 1:4-5).

Again, it must be clearly acknowledged that there are spiritual benefits to be gained from a small group Bible study, or a Bible class, or a home Bible study group – depending on the effort put into the study by the group. They can help new and immature Christians to learn God's truth and grow, as well as playing a role in helping shy Christians to open their mouths and start to participate. Similarly, the benefits of evangelistic small groups cannot be ignored. However, we should not confuse these small groups with the biblical picture of church gatherings, or think that we have fulfilled the New Testament model of church life by adding a small group Bible study to the list of a church's weekly activities. Participatory church gatherings are meant to be more than a handful of Christians making a few 'off the cuff' remarks. In the New Testament, participatory church gatherings were the central unifying gathering for the edification of the church.

Sharing Groups

In the same year that Robert Girard wrote *Brethren, Hang Loose*, 1972, Ray Stedman wrote his influential book, *Body Life*[228]. This book highlighted the same New Testament principles: the church is a body, all God's children have gifts, the Holy Spirit is the source of spiritual power, the need for unity, and the 'one-another' commands of Scripture. It, too, was based on the experience of a church, Peninsula Bible Church in Palo Alto, California. Listen to the description of a typical Sunday evening 'Body Life' service, from the May 21, 1971 issue of *Christianity Today*:

'It happens every Sunday night. Eight hundred or more people pack into a church auditorium designed to seat comfortably only 750. Seventy

---

[228] Ray C. Stedman, *Body Life*, Grand Rapids, MI: Discovery House Publishers, 1972, Revised Edition, 1995

per cent are under twenty-five, but adults of all ages, even into the eighties, are mingled with the youth, and people of widely varying cultural backgrounds all sit, sing, and pray together. A leader stands at the center front, a microphone around his neck. "This is the family," he says. "This is the body of Christ. We need each other. You have spiritual gifts that I need, and I have some that you need. Let's share with each other." When a hand goes up toward the back of the center section a red-haired youth runs down the center aisle with a wireless microphone. It is passed down the pew to the young man, who stands waiting to speak. "Man, I don't know how to start," he says, his shoulder-length hair shining as he turns from side to side. "All I know is that I've tried the sex trip and the drug trip and all the rest but it was strictly nowhere. But last week I made the Jesus trip – or I guess I should say that He found me – and man, this is where it's at!" A wave of delight sweeps the auditorium, and everyone claps and smiles as the leader says, "Welcome to the family. What's your name?"

Space prevents us quoting in full the report of all the other people who shared that evening: a single mother wanting to thank God for providing food that week, a girl whose brother was on drugs wanting prayer, a college-boy sharing something the Lord showed him that week from First John (the crowd laughing with delight at his application of the passage), a youth asking for prayer to be able to buy a car cheaply, a middle-aged housewife offering the keys to a car she doesn't need, an offering being announced (people in need can take ten dollars *out* of the plate as it goes past), a young man singing a folk song with a guitar as the offering plate goes round, someone calling out a hymn number for everyone to sing, and then the appointed teacher for the evening speaking for twenty-five minutes. A few hands go up to ask questions of the teacher, then a closing prayer. Everyone joins hands across the aisles and sing softly, "We are one in the Spirit, we are one in the Lord." After the meeting, people stay to talk, pray, sing or share with each other.

Again, just as Robert Girard's church ceased to exist, so the Sunday evening 'Body Life' services ceased after the 70s and 80s. Some people who read the original *Body Life* book and visit Peninsula Bible Church today are surprised to hear that the church no longer holds them.

But again, such services should not be confused with participatory church gatherings, even though there are many points of similarity. The basic starting point for the Body Life services at PBC was the question: 'Where are you hurting?' The primary purpose of the evening was to share needs and gifts. Guiding verses were 'bear one another's burdens' (Gal. 6:2), 'confess your faults one to another, and pray for one another' (James 5:16).

Now, again, there is no doubt that the sort of 'sharing' that went on in these 'body life' services is something that Christians should be doing. But it is also doubtful that some of the things included in the 'sharing' were meant to be done in the main church gathering. It is possible, for example, to confess our faults to one another in a more private setting that still fulfils the biblical mandate. Some Christians today are involved in accountability groups where they do the things described in the 'body life' service, but in a confidential, small group setting.

The main difference between the sort of sharing session we have been describing and participatory church gatherings is that the focus in a sharing session is me and my 'felt needs', whereas in the sort of church gathering described in the New Testament, the emphasis rests upon edification of others (1 Cor. 14:26).

The Church Business Meeting

Business meetings in some churches, particularly Baptist churches, usually take the form of a special congregational gathering. Such meetings deal with issues like the 'calling' of a 'minister', or the appointment of elders or deacons, or the direction church ministries and missions should take, the discipline of sinning members, financial matters or other questions. Believing in the autonomy of the local church, and claiming the priesthood and ministry of all believers, as well as the presence of Christ, these meetings involve all the believers seeking the mind and will of God, and taking decisions, usually by voting upon them. In other words, these meetings are participatory: anyone can speak. They occur infrequently: from monthly to yearly meetings, depending on the church.

Again, it is perfectly natural and proper that a church should have some sort of meeting to deal with its affairs. However, the idea that it is at some obscure, special business meeting that the truth of the priesthood of all believers, spiritual gifting and every-member ministry is most visibly demonstrated in the life of the church is a misunderstanding of what these biblical ideas involve and a far cry from what the Bible teaches about church life. In the New Testament, it is instead at the normal, weekly main Sunday gathering of the church that every-member ministry takes place using spiritual gifts. Business meetings at which sometimes fractious debates and votes over matters of church policy dominate the agenda are a strange way to display what it means for every member of a church to minister using their spiritual gifts.

Conclusion

The secret to a healthy church is given by Paul in letters like 1 Corinthians and the Pastoral epistles: edifying teaching that feeds the flock. Church meetings which are instead overly devotional (by allowing the Lord's Supper to dominate and squeeze out time for anything else), or full of shallow sermonettes, or simply 'sharing and caring' sessions, or business meetings, are not going to produce growing, healthy churches. Some might argue that because edifying teaching is the priority, we should appoint a minister or pick gifted speakers to do it for the church. However, this neglects what the New Testament says about the way that real spiritual growth occurs: through every member of the body exercising their spiritual gifts. It also neglects the benefit that comes from having a time for questions and evaluation of messages preached. Nor will it do to have the participation occurring in small groups, for the New Testament presents participatory church gatherings as occurring at the central weekly church gathering, balancing individual freedom with body membership – the interaction producing a unifying force in church life.

CHAPTER 14

Practical Objections, Problems, and Questions

Here are twelve objections, questions and problems:

Wouldn't it be Easier to Organize Church than to Wait and See who was going to speak?

In the introductory chapter, we mentioned the objection of a particular Pastor to the idea of participatory church gatherings: "surely some organization is preferable; aren't things going to degenerate into chaos?"

Modern Western evangelical Christians think of church in terms of an organised, scripted, pre-arranged performance, and indeed, there is a place for organised services, either for evangelism or discipleship or consecutive teaching. These are services for non-Christians, or new disciples, or continuing Christian education, where we explain the Bible's message. But the New Testament also shows us a different picture of church, where God is in charge, and His Spirit leads. These New Testament-style meetings are not primarily for outsiders, but 'in-house' family gatherings, for the church. There is preparation required here, too, as individuals come to the meeting ready to use their spiritual gifts.

Jim Cymbala uses an illustration that explains why organisation is out of place in some situations. Imagine if you were invited over to a person's house for a meal, but when you arrived at the door, you were given a sheet of paper with the outline of the evening's events. The first seven minutes were to involve light socializing about the traffic, the weather, and the family. Then for the next four minutes, you were to be given a quick tour of the house and garden. Following that, there are twenty-two minutes for the meal. Your name is down on the sheet for giving thanks to God for the food. The hostess' name is down too – she is responsible for passing the food around. And so it goes on, to the end of the evening.

Cymbala writes, 'You would say to yourself, *This is weird! Why all the regimen? Can't we just relax and get to know one another? What if somebody has an idea or wants to talk about something that's not on the agenda?*'

He concludes, 'Too often a church service, which is meant to draw us toward God, is not all that much different. Spontaneity and the leading of the Spirit have been thrown out in the name of keeping things on schedule. However, there has never been a revival of religion so long as the order of service has been strictly followed'[229].

What the New Testament says about participatory church meetings seems very foreign to our way of organizing things, while what seems natural to us (organization) is not mentioned in Scripture at all. But this is because what is true of other Christian doctrines (like the Trinity or salvation) is also true of church: '"My thoughts are not your thoughts, nor are your ways My ways", says the Lord' (Isaiah 55:8). In practical terms, it might be 'easier' to organize church services rather than waiting upon God in faith. But there are many examples in the Bible of people taking the easier option rather than following what God had said. Think of King Saul who took matters into his own hands and offered sacrifices instead of waiting upon the prophet Samuel (1 Sam. 13).

When King Jereboam set up his system of man-made worship in opposition to the true worship of God at Jerusalem, he deliberately made it easier. He 'made two calves of gold, and said to the people, "It is too much for you to go up to Jerusalem. Here are your gods, O Israel, which brought you up from the land of Egypt!"' (1 Kings 13:28). Jereboam set up two alternative places of false-worship to the only true place of worship in Jerusalem, telling the people they could choose to go to either Bethel or Dan. Why bother going all the way down south to Jerusalem any more – here are some more convenient locations!

---

[229] Jim Cymbala, *Fresh Wind, Fresh Fire*, p148

Likewise, when God set up the worship in the Tabernacle, He said all the items of furniture were to be carried on poles on the shoulders of the Levites. It would have been easier if the furniture could have been transported on wagons and indeed, when David tried to bring the Ark of the Covenant up to Jerusalem (2 Samuel 6), he made a new cart (copying the Philistines' method of transport in 1 Samuel 6). However, God struck down Uzzah dead for reaching out and steadying the Ark when the oxen stumbled. It was not until David called for the Levites to carry the Ark on their shoulders that it was safely transported to Jerusalem.

We could look at other examples of disobedience and false-worship (the Bible is full of them), but the lesson is that we need to follow God's instructions for how to worship Him, not our own humanly-devised or cleverly organised ideas. Some humanly-contrived religious ideas seem to be more convenient to follow than God's commands, and others involve something more complicated than God's simple instructions. For example, it could be argued that carrying the ark on the Levites' shoulders was simpler than building and maintaining special sacred carts for their transport. God's commandments are not burdensome (1 John 5:3) – it is actually humanly-devised religious ideas that end up becoming more complicated.

God had His reasons for wanting Jerusalem to be the only place of worship, and for the ark to be carried on the shoulders of Levites. These reasons had less to do with convenience, it is true, than with the lessons that Israel needed to learn about the One True God and about the sacredness of His Temple and its worship. But Israel never seemed to learn these lessons – they continually turned to the right hand or to the left, every man doing what was right in his own eyes (Judges 17:6).

Whether we in our human wisdom think that a certain way of 'doing church' is easier or not, just because a form of worship seems more convenient is no reason for abandoning or ignoring what the New Testament says about how the church should gather.

"I Don't Get it"

Due to the unfamiliarity of most Christians with the New Testament picture of church worship, one common reaction upon coming into such a meeting is "I don't get it". Others ask: "what is going on?", "why do you do things this way?" Someone once came into such a meeting and asked, "Has the minister missed his bus?" Many Christians are used to coming to church to be ministered to, or to be entertained, or to socialize, and they are confused when they encounter participatory church life. Even godly Christians who have never been taught about the biblical picture of participatory church gatherings find it unusual until it is explained from the Scriptures. Some Christians are confused by such meetings, but out of courtesy say nothing and simply decide not to come again. Everything is so different to the traditional forms of Christianity, or the seeker-sensitive, consumer Christianity they consider normal.

What can a church do to minimise the culture shock, so that Christians who are open to what the Word of God teaches and who come into a church which is attempting to follow the practices of the New Testament are not put off by first appearances? What can a church do to prevent discouragement of the church members who see visitors quickly leaving after the meeting and never coming back again?

There are numerous things that can be done in the information-age we live in:

- put up a page on a church website explaining what visitors should expect if they attend, and the biblical reasons behind the gathering,
- prepare a little booklet to give to visitors explaining why the church gathers the way it does,
- or make a short announcement at the commencement of the meeting (if new visitors are present) giving a brief introduction to what is about to happen.

These, surely, are the sorts of simple courtesies that any visitor should expect to receive to minimise confusion or embarrassment, and to start them on the pathway to learning about participatory church gatherings with an open mind and heart.

In fact, it might be best not to make a participatory church gathering the 'shopfront' service of a church (forgive the consumer metaphor) – the service to which we invite new visitors. That is, it might not be the best meeting to invite visitors if they are Christians long-used to the staid and traditional or 'seeker-sensitive' consumer models of Christianity. New Christians are perhaps different; they are open to what the Word of God teaches about church life – they only need to be told that this is how Christians met in Bible times. Instead, it is probably better to invite visitors to a service which is either evangelistic or, if they are already Christians, to a service devoted to the systematic exposition of God's Word. During an evangelistic or teaching service, they will hear announcements (or read in a bulletin) about the 'church meeting' held at another time. Be sure to tell visitors, maybe to their surprise, that the event they are attending is not the actual church gathering, but is just an outreach service for friends in the community. (It is good to keep the 'entryway' evangelistic/teaching service short and sharp – just some songs and a message, nothing much more than an hour – so that it leaves keen and hungry Christians longing for more). As visitors become more regular in attendance, they can start to learn about the 'church gathering', and begin to find out about why it happens the way it does. Or, Christians can be invited to a class that explains participatory church gatherings (among other things), so that if or when they join the church they understand and are ready to start participating intelligently in the church meeting.

Once upon a time, most evangelical churches had more than one different type of service on a Sunday, with a special service dedicated to evangelism or teaching or the needs of young Christians. Nowadays, for a variety of reasons, many churches only have one Sunday service which tries to meet all the needs: worship, teaching, discipleship, evangelism, and fellowship. Most of these services fail to be all things to all people, and some services fail to do most of them very well. The reason is that some of these activities are so different that they almost require a different gathering. There is therefore plenty of room on Sunday for an extra, separate meeting for participatory church gatherings that meets some of these different needs, perhaps in the evening like the early church did in the New Testament.

Whatever our approach, it is only sensible that we try to bridge the gap between the ignorance and confusion of modern Christians and what the New Testament teaches about church gatherings – and that we help people cross this bridge at a pace they are able to handle. The reason is simple: unless and until we have shown people from the Bible why we do participatory church gatherings, most Christians are not going to 'get it'.

The Danger of Adding Man-made Traditions

Genuine Christianity is always confronted with the twin dangers of the false-teachings of the Sadducees and the Pharisees. The Sadducees deny Scripture, while the Pharisees try to add to it. Some people today deny what the Bible teaches about church life and 'do church' their own way, but equally, some zealous and devoted believers try to add all sorts of rules and traditions to what Scripture teaches to 'protect' the church from abuses. Just as it is possible to ignore what Scripture teaches, so it is possible to over-emphasise biblical truths or to add man-made traditions to what the Bible says.

Because there is a great deal of freedom under the Holy Spirit in participatory church gatherings, it is possible to add many man-made rules and traditions. For example, here is one case of a man-made rule added to the Word of God: we should not have any Bible readings at the Lord's Supper. This is justified on the basis that we should have done our Bible-reading at home beforehand, or perhaps because prayers of thanksgiving are more real and heartfelt expressions of worship. The problem with this rule is that while singing the words of uninspired hymns is allowed, we are forbidden to read the inspired Word of God. There is something seriously wrong when we cannot read the Bible in church. Thus, under the guise of 'spirituality', we can add unbiblical rules to Scripture. The author has heard quite a number of man-made rules, unwritten but enshrined in collective example, particularly relating to the Lord's Supper:

- we should have a theme for our worship (i.e. everyone should share something along the same lines)
- a brother ministering should not use notes (it must be extempore)
- we should not have anything before the Lord's Supper on a Sunday morning ('worship before service')
- the same brother must break the bread and pour the wine

- the same brother cannot dispense the emblems and also minister afterwards (such would be taking too much honour unto oneself)
- ladies should not wear perfume to the meeting (the only fragrance should be that of Christ).

Unbiblical traditions like these not only add to Scripture, but they also bring in a critical spirit – anyone who doesn't keep these unbiblical rules is frowned on and so instead of a spirit of encouragement and love, there is criticism and pulling other people down.

The author has heard of many such little rules. However, there is one central man-made rule, or tradition, about participatory church gatherings that governs many of these other rules. This is the tradition that we come to the church meeting just to remember the Lord. Listen to some of the slogans that are used to convey this idea: 'we're not here to talk about our blessings', or 'we're not here to talk about our experiences'. They all come back to this rule: we're just here to worship.

However, in the New Testament, we do not read of a meeting solely devoted to remembering the Lord. The early church had one main weekly gathering which included the Lord's Supper but also had open opportunity for the exercise of spiritual gifts. We see this, not only in 1 Corinthians, but also in Acts 20 at Troas: not only did they break bread, but Paul dialogued with the believers, teaching them till midnight. We see the same thing at the institution of the Lord's Supper in the gospels: the Lord broke bread with the disciples, but he also dialogued with them, teaching them for four chapters – John 13-16. In all three cases, there is the Lord's Supper plus interactive teaching.

There is no such thing in the New Testament as a meeting devoted solely to remembrance. At the institution of the Lord's Supper, Christ did not ask each of the disciples to offer a prayer of thanksgiving or a hymn in his honour. There was no quiet hour of thanksgiving and remembrance, what we might call 'open worship'. Nor is such a meeting described or recorded in Acts 2 or Acts 20 or 1 Cor. 11. The breaking of bread was part of a larger meeting that included multiple speakers using a variety of different gifts to build up the saints. It was a spiritual feast, a three-course meal, a conference. In the New Testament, the church gathering had two purposes: to remember the Lord, but also to encourage, feed and teach each other. In 1 Cor. 14:26, Paul writes, 'let all things be done for edification'; do we have the right to change God's Word to read 'remembrance' instead of 'edification'?

Look at three sad results of ignoring the biblical picture of church gatherings and having a remembrance-only meeting:

1. **God's people are not fed**. The church exists for the mutual encouragement, feeding and teaching of its members, as well as Christ-centred worship. So, one problem with the worship-only rule is that, if perpetuated, it causes spiritual famine – there is no feeding. Only the most spiritually strong and healthy survive. Instead of growing, some of God's people wither and shrivel, or they fight and squabble. Either way, they eventually leave and go to other churches.
2. **Gifts are not developed**. Participatory church gatherings allow for a wide variety of gifts to be developed, not just suggesting a hymn or praying a prayer or reading a short passage. When we introduce new rules which forbid certain types of spiritual gifts being exercised, we hinder the development of gift. The author was visiting a church one Sunday morning in a particular city, and in this participatory church gathering, two 15-16 year old boys got up and shared (for 5-10 minutes each) two words of encouragement. One of them spoke from 1 John about how we should love one another. In some places these boys would have been criticised because their contributions weren't directed to the remembrance of Christ. But the word of encouragement is a valuable gift, a gift that is almost forbidden in many churches today, and the church gathering is where gift should be developed. The author was thrilled to see evidence of the Holy Spirit working in the lives of these growing young Christians as they shared God's Word.
3. **God's Spirit is quenched**. 2 Cor. 3:17 says, 'Where the Spirit of the Lord is, there is liberty'. Liberty is a characteristic of the Spirit, and freedom is a characteristic of churches where He is leading. Sadly, we can set up our own rules that restrict and stifle God's Spirit. In some worship-only meetings, there is no freedom for God to speak

through one of His servants: everything must be about remembering Christ. If we insist on a one-track meeting, week after week, we quench the Spirit. As a result, in some meetings, there are long silences, repetitive prayers, the same old bible readings and stale worship; instead of meetings full of joy, the church gathering resembles a funeral.

Now, please, don't misunderstand. Of course, we should be worshipping and remembering Christ when we come together. Worship is the Christian's highest occupation. We want to have a growing appreciation for our Lord Jesus; we want to have our hearts melted as we think of His death for us. We do not want a shallow, token remembrance. But we need to be biblically balanced – by allowing both open remembrance and edification. This is the church meeting, New Testament-style.

Some man-made rules and traditions show a certain amount of wisdom, and some are destructive. But none are found in the Bible. Beware of adding to God's Word. 'Every word of God is pure; He is a shield to those who put their trust in Him. Do not add to His words, lest He rebuke you, and you be found a liar' (Proverbs 30:5-6).

"I Don't Get Anything out of It!"

There has been more than one person who has said about participatory church gatherings, 'I don't get anything out of it'. Sometimes this statement reflects a negative spiritual attitude on the part of the person complaining. If we have a positive spiritual attitude we can get a blessing from any church service. However, often this comment is the result of the person's spiritual needs not being met in the gathering, week after week. This is usually the result of the Spirit being quenched by man-made rules or stifling arrangements that prevent encouraging and edifying ministry being given.

The author once received a letter, in a church which he had recently joined, from an elderly member distressed about the fact that the church was unable to keep members. Mature Christians were leaving and new members were not staying. As a result, the church was dwindling and declining. What was the cause? To quote from the letter, 'we do not get enough spiritual food ... 52 Sundays a year available and every week it is the same theme – the Cross – REPETITION'.

Needy Christians who are struggling in a godless, materialistic, pleasure-loving, sensual society are under continual spiritual attack and pressure. The purpose of the church's meeting is to help, strengthen and encourage them. Failure to ensure that the flock is fed leads to spiritual weakness. Shepherds must feed the flock. The meeting should be truly open to the Spirit of God to meet the spiritual needs of God's people.

The response to the complaint, "I don't get anything out of it" has sometimes been to say, "we're not here to get, we're here to give". However, this is not quite true: we are here to get as well as to give – the church gathering has both purposes. Further, we can only give something to God from what we first receive. We cannot worship if we are not first being fed, challenged, corrected, and encouraged. Christians who are spiritually struggling and starving, malnourished and dried up inside, don't 'get' very much out of other peoples' worship. If the church does not encourage and help them spiritually, they will eventually go to another church where they get fed and encouraged.

What about Strangers coming in and throwing Meetings into Confusion?

Another (quite legitimate) objection to participatory church gatherings is that they might allow opportunity for people from various pseudo-Christian cults (like the Jehovah's Witnesses) to come in and spread false-teaching. Or they might encourage modern-day Judaizers (like Seventh-Day Adventists) to come in and unsettle the souls of God's people, as they did in the book of Acts (see 15:24). Or they might allow any madman to walk in off the street and disrupt the meeting with bizarre interruptions, causing confusion.

However, in the New Testament, we are provided with a simple precaution for how to deal with this problem. In 1 Corinthians 14:16, Paul mentions that there was a special place for the unconverted or for the untaught to sit during the church gatherings: the place of the unlearned. He writes, 'Otherwise, if you bless with the spirit, how will he who occupies the place of the uninformed say "Amen" at your giving of thanks, since he does not understand what you say?' The KJV translates this as the 'room of the unlearned', the ESV has the 'position of the outsider', while the NIV uses 'position of an inquirer'. When we come further down the passage to verses 24 and 25, we read more about who this person is: 'But if all prophesy, and an unbeliever or an uninformed person comes in, he is convinced by all, he is convicted by all, and thus the secrets of his heart are revealed; and so, falling down on his face, he will worship God and report that God is truly among you'. It seems that the person in these verses is (a) someone who comes in, that is, off the street, an outsider, not a normal member of the church, (b) who is not yet converted, but (c) becomes a Christian under the preaching.

There was obviously a special place for those who were not members of the congregation, but were either unbelievers or 'seekers'. They were not granted full membership privileges, but had to sit and listen to what happened in church. The 'place of the unlearned' was an observers' gallery. It would appear that they were not allowed to participate in what happened, but only to observe.

In addition to adopting this biblical precaution God has provided, it is possible for a church to have a separate service for evangelistic or teaching purposes where such outsiders could be invited to come and learn more about Christianity.

Aren't Participatory Church Gatherings a Case of Majoring on Minors?

Another objection says that whatever form of church worship (or government) we adopt is less important than the fact that we are actively worshipping and serving Christ. The sort of church that pleases God is one which wins sinners from wickedness to God and which turns them into devoted disciples of Christ. "The world is perishing", say such people; "why waste time debating doctrinal fine-points?" A more theological way of stating this objection is that faith is important, forms are not.

The argument is a powerful one. The whole purpose of the church is to be Christ's missionary organisation on earth. The church does not exist for its own sake. It does not exist to point to itself; it must point others to Christ. It would be a very strange version of Christianity that was more obsessed with the Holy Spirit's role in leading church gatherings than in His role in the larger task of spreading of the gospel.

Furthermore, as we are often reminded, and as the New Testament itself shows, it was a characteristic of the Pharisees that they majored on minors. However, notice what the Lord said to the Pharisees: "Woe to you, scribes and Pharisees, hypocrites! For you pay tithe of mint and anise and cummin, and have neglected the weightier matters of the law: justice and mercy and faith. These you ought to have done, *without leaving the others undone*" (Matt. 23:23). Read the last line carefully and you will see that the Lord said we should major on justice, mercy and faith, *without* leaving the minor matters undone. Christ told us it is our responsibility to major on majors but also to be obedient in minor matters as well. He was not saying that they should ignore small things; He was saying to make sure they *also* did the big things.

Here is the problem with this objection: it tries to make a virtue of ignoring God's Word, in this case in relation to what it says about church gatherings. The objection thus becomes a front, a smokescreen, for not doing what God tells us to do. It is a mark of fake-spirituality to disobey what God says in His Word, whether something is (or is not) the highest-priority of the Christian. Furthermore, people usually tend to make this objection (that church government or worship is unimportant) because they belong to church organisations which are plainly indefensible on biblical grounds or because they practice church worship in ways that are sometimes blatantly disobedient to scripture.

Another problem with this objection is that, while we may have every sympathy with the argument that the only church order that is of any value is one which promotes evangelism, love, godliness, worship and growth, it would appear that it is precisely because of these concerns that God gives us directions for how we should run our church gatherings.

The missionary Ken Fleming put it like this in a powerful little couplet: 'the mission of the church is mission, the mission of mission is the church'[230]. That is, the purpose of the church is to evangelise the world. But the end-purpose of evangelism is to see new believers gathered together in churches which turn them into spiritually-mature disciples, so that they evangelise and the whole cycle continues. Therefore the argument that church organisation is unimportant is unsustainable.

While this objection therefore contains some truth, and anyone who is more concerned about participatory church gatherings than preaching Christ's gospel may be suspected of lacking either spirituality or sanity, it also presents us with a dangerous false-dichotomy. We are not asked to choose between mission and the church; following Christ means obeying all things which He has commanded.

The Danger of Division

Another similar objection is that focusing on church worship and organisation is bound to lead to differences of opinions and even division among Christians who should be working together for the spread of the gospel and the growth of the Church. There are already enough matters over which Christians are divided without adding another to the list. Do we want to see more churches divided and destroyed over secondary matters? It is all very well to have Christians using their spiritual gifts in church like 1 Corinthians 14 teaches, but if we forget the lesson of 1 Corinthians 13 – love – then we have missed the most important thing of all.

Again, this objection carries great force, and warns us of a great danger. Thinking that participatory church gatherings are the be-all and end–all of church life is wrong. In fact, such an attitude is the result of knowledge that puffs up with pride (1 Cor. 8:1) instead of love that builds up. Because such pride is not loving, it can actually destroy (by division) the church that we profess to care so much about. Beware of holding truth in pride, not love, with a harsh and haughty spirit.

---

[230] Kenneth Fleming, *Essentials of Missionary Service*, Carlisle: OM Publishing, 2000, p38

T. Austin-Sparks wrote: 'It is possible to have the most perfect New Testament order and framework, and a most devoted adherence to the letter of the Word, but to be almost totally devoid of life and unction. ... Truth without life is fatal, as is righteousness without love. Prejudice and suspicion are fruits of bondage to some religious thing and not of the Spirit'[231].

Jon Zens, writing about eldership, warns against three dangers that also apply to participatory church gatherings: (1) we must not idolize this subject, (2) we must not polarize over this subject, and (3) we must not minimize this subject. He writes, 'As men grow in the truth it is quite often the case that a newly-found Biblical concept can be magnified out of proportion ... It is possible to have the eldership doctrine straight, and somewhat implemented on the local level, and still be far from the overall New Testament pattern for church order. It is shameful if a church blessed with elders manifests a superior attitude and looks down their nose at other churches who are not "straight" in this area'[232].

The problem at the root of any division is ultimately pride (and often personalities too), not participatory church gatherings or any other biblical truth. The proverbs remind us that 'By pride comes nothing but strife, but with the well-advised is wisdom' and 'He who is of a proud heart stirs up strife, but he who trusts in the LORD will be prospered' (Proverbs 13:10, 28:25). The Bible nowhere tells us to give up divine truth because of the danger of division. Instead, the proverb tells us to 'buy the truth, and do not sell it' (Prov. 23:23). The solution, as the New Testament teaches, is that we should be characterised by 'truth and love' (2 John 3), that we should be 'speaking the truth in love' (Eph. 4:15) and that we should imitate Christ who was 'full of grace and truth' (John 1:14, 17).

Instead of causing division over the matter of participatory church gatherings, we need to wait patiently for God's people to grasp His truth. Instead of using political methods and power struggles to force God's

---

[231] T. Austin-Sparks, *The Centrality and Universality of the Cross*, Ch. 2, http://www.austin-sparks.net/english/books/000740.html

[232] Jon Zens, "The Major Concepts of Eldership in the New Testament", *Baptist Reformation Review 7* (Summer, 1978) p26

wisdom upon others, we need to use spiritual methods: teaching what God's Word says and waiting upon the Holy Spirit to reveal the truth to others and convince them in His own time and way. Paul says, 'a servant of the Lord must not quarrel but be gentle to all, able to teach, patient, in humility correcting those who are in opposition, if God perhaps will grant them repentance, so that they may know the truth' (2 Tim. 2:24, 25). Church divisions which dishonour God's name can be avoided if we remember that 'love is patient' (1 Cor. 13:4).

Indeed, it would be a strange irony if we believed in the leading of the Spirit in relation to church meetings, yet tried to introduce such gatherings, not by praying and depending upon the Holy Spirit, but by using 'the arm of flesh' to accomplish such goals.

The Problem of How to get Quiet People to Speak

'Public speaking is listed as Americans' number one fear, before death at number five and loneliness at number seven. Guess that means that most of us are less afraid of dying alone than of making a fool of ourselves in front of others' (Anne Cooper[233]).

In most churches, there will be some people who never publicly participate in the church gatherings – particularly some men who like to think of themselves as 'strong and silent' types. In fact, there will be some people who do very little for the church at all. Encouraging these people to take a more active role in the church is not easy. But there are certain ways that this can start to happen.

One of the most important principles we need to remember is that we all have different spiritual gifts. Therefore, we need to try to encourage people to discover and use their own spiritual gifts. In his book, *Everybody Communicates, Few Connect*, John Maxwell stresses the importance of participation. Under the heading of 'Connecting in a Group', he writes, 'The key to making others feel valued in a group or on a team is to invite participation. The smartest person in the room is never

---

[233] Anne Cooper Ready, *Off the Cuff: What to Say at a Moment's Notice*, Franklin Lakes, NJ: Career Press, 2004, p19

as smart as all the people in the room. Input creates synergy, buy-in and connection'[234].

Maxwell suggests that to connect with people in a group setting it is important to:

- Discover and identify the strength of each person
- Acknowledge the value of each person's strength and potential contribution
- Invite input and allow people to lead in their area of strength

Maxwell is talking here about groups of all kinds, not just Christian groups, but some of his principles are clearly derived from the New Testament, and Maxwell's suggestions are easily translated to the church setting. Instead of talking about people's 'strengths', we simply need to substitute the more biblical expression 'spiritual gifts', and his prescription is immediately applicable.

The lesson is obvious: we need to make sure we are not trying to get someone to participate in the church gathering in a way that they are not gifted to contribute. Instead, we need to help such people discover their spiritual gifts and use them. Some Christians, for example, have an incredible knack or ability to suggest the right hymn at exactly the right time. Others will find that a question-time after a message allows them opportunity to start making comments. As a result of their increasing participation, they will start to become more spiritually 'switched-on'.

Those who are shepherds among God's people need to be encouraging the quieter and less-forward members of the church to consider contributing. This is particularly important with new and young Christians. If they are not encouraged to participate when they are young, they will find it harder to start when they get old. Maybe they can be encouraged to suggest a hymn to sing, or to share something from God's Word that has been a help to them. Once they have taken this first step and broken the ice, they need to be encouraged by more mature

---

[234] John Maxwell, *Everybody Communicates, Few Connect*, Nashville, TN: Nelson, 2010, p45

believers and told to keep on participating. As they grow, they will perhaps develop and use their gifts in other areas.

Another way to encourage participation is for those who are regular contributors to keep their mouths closed sometimes. Or, if a certain regular contributor is not going to be present, he could let some others know of his absence, and encourage them to take part in the meeting in his absence. It is amazing how many people who are normally silent will start to take part when certain people are absent.

Some people never seem to want to take part, however much encouragement they are given. Sometimes, the reason is that their spiritual life is not in a healthy state. They are not involved in any service for the Lord or evangelistic outreach and they are not in the habit of regularly reading God's Word, or hearing God speak through it, let alone studying it systematically. Shepherds need to try to meet up with these Christians, maybe every week over a cup of coffee, making a regular time to pray and read God's Word together. These Christians need to be encouraged to get involved in some service for the Lord. It is only when our private spiritual life is healthy and active that we are going to be of any help in the church meeting. The fundamental need in these peoples' lives is not to participate in the church gathering – it is spiritual health. Participating in church is part of a spiritually healthy life, but spiritual health starts with private fellowship in God's presence, develops through service, and flowers in the church gathering.

The Problem of Silences

In participatory church meetings, there will sometimes be silences. Occasionally these may be the result of the congregation being overwhelmed at God's glory. But, more commonly, they are the result of spiritual barrenness, the church having sunk to a low level of spiritual life. Apart from being embarrassing, however, silences are a helpful flag of the spiritual sickness of God's people. Elders should take these silences as a sign that the flock needs more feeding and encouragement. Participatory church gatherings thus become a barometer of spirituality – they show us when our spiritual life is getting dangerously low and empty. Long silences can also result from the quenching of the Spirit, when man-made rules have been brought in, adding to what the Scriptures teach and limiting the contributions of God's people to just one or two types. If we insist on one-track meetings all the time, we should not be surprised if they become stale and empty.

The Problem of Poor Quality preaching

At the other end of the spectrum, there are those who are keen to speak and teach but who are not very gifted. We have examples of this in the Pastoral Epistles, where Paul speaks of those who are given to 'idle talk', ('vain jangling', KJV, 1 Tim. 1:6, 6:20, Titus 1:10). What can be done about poor quality ministry?

Paul's solution in 1 Corinthians is a time of evaluation after preaching, so that the quality of what was said can be sifted. Some young men have been crushed by criticism of their first, faltering attempts to preach, vowing never to open their mouths in church again. We must be sensitive and restrained in our feedback, giving encouragement where it is due, not descending to personal attacks.

Paul's solution in the Pastoral Letters is three-fold. Firstly, those like Timothy who are gifted and capable teachers should be more actively involved in teaching, setting a good example and feeding the flock. 'Preach the word! Be ready in season and out of season. Convince, rebuke, exhort, with all longsuffering and teaching' (2 Tim. 4:2). Secondly, Timothy was to train the most faithful and promising brothers (2 Tim. 2:2), by committing the great truths of the faith to them so they could pass them on to others. Not only would this involve doctrinal instruction but also training in communicating the truth to others. Thirdly, warnings against unprofitable ministry and false teaching were to be made publicly so that the saints were aware of the high standards expected. Still, today, it is worthwhile listing all the sorts of unprofitable preaching that Paul lists in the Pastoral letters and publicly reading out, and explaining, the list in church.

For example, Paul speaks against 'profane and idle babblings' (2 Tim. 2:16), which refers to people talking about empty, worldly matters. In the church, sometimes there are those who think that the solution to a long pause or to a boring meeting is to stand up and crack a few jokes about their recent camping trip. The solution to dry meetings is the Living Water that Christ gives (John 7:37-39), not the water from this world's leaking cisterns (Jer. 2:13).

Edward Groves suggested a few other ways to deal with unprofitable ministry: 'I do not think anything would surprise you more than to hear the difference of judgment expressed by those whose opinion you might ask concerning ministry you found hard to listen to with patience. Some admire and profit by that which others lightly esteem ... I have been told by brethren of large experience of a more excellent way of dealing with unedifying ministry than that of raising a protest against it. It is for those who feel tried by the frequency or quality of any brother's ministry to meet regularly to pray about it; and the Lord has either increased his gift or shut his mouth. It seems to me that if we were fitly joined together as a spiritual family we ought to be able to tell a brother that we do not understand the drift of his remarks, or suggest to him something that would improve his ministry'[235].

Of course, there are other types of problem preaching. Some, including false-teaching and divisive tendencies, require rebukes and admonition (Titus 1:13, 2:15, 3:10).

The Problem of Meetings becoming Stale

Churches which have participatory meetings will inevitably fall into routines, even ruts. The same person will get up and pray the same predictable prayer every week. Or the same people will get up and share a word from the Scriptures every week. Or the same people will sit silently and contribute nothing every week. The result is a staleness in the meetings that is deadening. Remember: the only difference between a rut and a grave is the depth. How is this problem to be dealt with?

Staleness is not a characteristic of the Holy Spirit. A brother needs to be careful that he is not running ahead of the Holy Spirit by contributing in the way that he has become accustomed to doing. Some people are too

---

[235] Quoted by R. B. Dann, *Father of Faith Missions, The Life and Times of Anthony Norris Groves*, Waynesboro, GA: Authentic Media, 2004, endnote 65, p410

forward in their participation, perhaps because they fear that the meeting might suffer if they do not contribute. These Mr. Too Quicks need to be careful that they do not hinder others participating. They need to leave a few moments' space before they jump up – maybe even half a minute! If they are used to contributing in the same way each week, they need to perhaps think about contributing in a different way. Thus if they are always sharing some thoughts from a passage of Scripture every week, maybe one week they might instead simply pray or suggest a hymn to sing. This will leave room for others to exercise their gifts. Sometimes it is possible to stand up and share something even though we do not feel the leading and prompting of the Holy Spirit to do so. We need to stay seated on such an occasion, even if it results in a period of silence.

Those who regularly contribute in the same way every week need to realise that their repetitive contributions have a negative effect upon others. They need to spend more time in God's presence making sure that they are in tune with God. They need to be more sensitive to the Holy Spirit in the actual meeting. They also need to think of ways that freshen up their participation so that it captures the attention of those about to switch off at the sound of their voice. Thus, instead of sharing their regular lengthy exposition, maybe they might simply share a brief testimony in response to someone else's word, showing how the Word of God has made a difference in real life, or give a word of wisdom, or simply ask a practical question after someone has spoken.

Others who are slow to contribute, and have perhaps got into the habit of not participating in the meeting, need to be sensitive to the leading of the Holy Spirit in their lives during the week, so that if they have been blessed by a particular truth from Scripture, they should feel bold enough to share what they have learned, even if it is not their usual practice to speak in church.

One of the characteristics of the church gathering in 1 Corinthians is the variety of different contributions. A church that is characterised by repetitive and stale meetings has a problem that needs to be addressed. Such is not a characteristic of a meeting in which the Holy Spirit is actively working.

The Problem of What to do in a Big Church

Some people ask whether it is possible to have participatory church gatherings in big churches. The answer is: not very easily or profitably.

It is hard to put a number on how big is too big. But if we are wanting to give believers the opportunity to participate on a regular basis, there probably needs to be less than two hundred people in fellowship. If a brother cannot use his gift more than once every few months – because there are so many others who are able and active in participating – then he is not going to grow and develop very much. If a large church is spiritually thriving and healthy, it is probably time to start thinking about planting a new daughter church. When the church at Jerusalem grew too big, the Lord sent persecution which scattered the believers throughout Judea and further afield. As Acts 11 tells us, the scattered disciples went as far as Antioch, and this lead to the great mission to the Gentiles in Acts 13.

Alternatively, another solution is to have a large gathering for systematic teaching or evangelism, where people just come to sit and listen, and then have the church split into smaller groups for participatory church gatherings. This is presumably the way that the Jerusalem church in the book of Acts had its meetings after their numbers exceeded 3,000 – meeting for apostolic teaching in the temple courts and meeting in 'upper rooms' or homes for the Lord's Supper and participatory spiritual edification and fellowship.

However, there are dangers here: small groups can be more social than spiritual, leading to a superficial approach to Christian edification, teaching and growth. The participation time may be taken less seriously than if it was the whole church gathering together, and result in shallow and unedifying contributions. Unless there is considerable preparation for any meeting, there is usually little spiritual benefit. Perhaps it would be better to treat such groups as incipient church plants from the beginning, meeting together with a view to eventually starting an autonomous daughter church.

CHAPTER 15

STEPS TO IMPLEMENTING PARTICIPATORY CHURCH GATHERINGS

A church that is not used to participatory church gatherings will probably not be able to start having such meetings without a transition period. Here are suggestions for transitioning to Participatory Church Gatherings:

1. Recently I was in a congregation where we sang the hymn, *I stand amazed in the presence of Jesus the Nazarene*. When we came to the chorus, there was a change in the words. Instead of the normal, *How marvellous, how wonderful*, the words read, *Oh how marvellous, Oh how wonderful*. There was only one word inserted (twice), and the difference was meaningless. But I felt a strange resentment to this small change in a familiar hymn. Maybe I am just becoming a grumpy old man prematurely, but I don't handle change so easily as I get older. Even in daily life, I sometimes struggle when sudden changes are made to a plan. If you are someone who doesn't struggle with change, please understand that there are many Christians who do. The lesson is this: we need to be very patient and prayerful with others if we are wanting to introduce participatory church gatherings. Remember: this is a big change that some people will not immediately understand. In fact, they might think the idea is a little bit crazy. We need to look to God in believing prayer to soften peoples' hearts. Therefore, the very first and most important step in implementing participatory church gatherings is dependent, earnest,

persistent prayer, and then a patient waiting upon God for Him to help others to be open to what the Word of God says.

2. A second important requirement for participatory church gatherings is to encourage the people in your church to read God's Word and pray every day. Part of the reason for participatory church gatherings is to develop discipleship, but one of the requirements for participatory church gatherings is the involvement of disciples who are already growing through reading God's Word. Christians who are not growing through reading God's Word in their daily lives are not going to be of any use in helping others to grow. The Bible says that we should meditate in the Word of God day and night (Joshua 1:8, Psalm 1:2). This means reading it morning and evening. If we are instead spending our mornings and evenings listening to the radio, watching TV or on the internet, we are going to be spiritually empty – with nothing to give in church. Colossians 3:16 says, 'Let the word of Christ dwell in you richly in all wisdom, teaching and admonishing one another …'. We cannot be useful participants in church unless the Word of Christ is dwelling in us richly. Notice also that this passage in Colossians 3 corresponds in a remarkable way with a similar passage in its sister epistle, Ephesians 5. Both speak of singing psalms and hymns and spiritual songs, giving thanks to God the Father and submitting in various situations. However, one interesting difference between the two passages is that whereas Colossians 3:16 says, 'Let the word of Christ dwell in you richly', Ephesians 5:19 says, 'Be filled with the Spirit'. It is almost as if being filled with the Spirit corresponds with letting the word of Christ dwell in you richly. If we are letting God's Word dwell in our hearts richly, we will be learning more of the Lord every day, rejoicing in Him, giving thanks and acting in ways that are more pleasing to the Lord – not a bad description of being filled with the Spirit! Personal spiritual growth through spending personal daily time with the Lord in prayer and meditating on His Word needs to be encouraged in a church – otherwise all is vain.

3. Another important way to teach the church to love God's Word is through good expository preaching. Expose them to God's Word, chapter by chapter and book by book, so that they feel its power and come to love and trust it. Good expository preaching helps God's people to see how the Bible is coherent, logical, divinely powerful and applicable to our lives. If God's people's 'blood is bibline' (Spurgeon), then there will be much more likelihood that they will be receptive to what God's Word teaches about participatory church gatherings.

4. Another good idea for helping people with reading the Bible is to meet up with a number of individuals weekly and have one-on-one Bible reading times, so that people are mentored and pastorally encouraged to read the Bible and to learn lessons from it. The two people simply read a passage of scripture together, consecutively reading through a book that is appropriate for the stage of development of the person needing encouragement. After reading, any questions arising can be discussed, and truths that the passage teaches can be summarized, and any lessons for how we should live can be prayed over. This way, people struggling to spend time in God's Word privately every day are helped and encouraged, so they grow in their love for God.

5. Another idea that is particularly helpful for new Christians who are not very familiar with the Bible or not very confident in expressing themselves is to have a weekly small group Bible reading session. In this setting, there are maybe three or four people involved, and the advantage of a few more people is that each of the people will at least make one or two comments without having to hold up one end of the discussion. A shy person or a new Christian without much Bible familiarity will be able to contribute without having a very advanced knowledge of the Bible. These people will remember things that they have learned and shared in the group, partly because they were the person who noticed a particular truth, and partly because they found it more challenging to speak to the group. The truths that they shared will therefore be more clearly etched on their minds.

Steps to Implementing Participatory Church Gatherings

6. Get people involved in speaking in church by asking them to give testimonies, share devotions, pray publicly or lead a meeting. Get people involved in studying the Bible and presenting their findings by asking them to lead a Bible study or take a Sunday School lesson, where preparation is required. These 'baby steps' in using spiritual gifts enable people to grow and develop.

7. Have multiple preachers involved in the teaching program of the church – not just one. Try and encourage other Christians from within the congregation to preach, not just visitors from outside the church. In that way, people will learn that it is not just the best preachers who are fit to stand before God's people, but even preachers without a big reputation or outstanding gift.

8. Leave 10-15 minutes for questions and discussion after sermons. If members of the congregation do not have questions, provide some for them to respond to and discuss publicly. Leave some issues from the message for the question time rather than preaching about them during the message. Try to provide a variety of questions – some at the level of observation, some at the level of interpretation, and some at the level of application.

9. Teach the biblical basis for participatory church gatherings, by looking at a passage like 1 Corinthians 14, comparing this passage with others like 1 Thessalonians 5 and Ephesians 4. Teach about the subject over a period of three or four weeks – do not try to do it all in one session. Or, set the subject within a series that perhaps begins with spiritual gifts in Romans 12, then look at some of the principles behind participatory church gatherings like the 'one anothers' of the NT, then thirdly teach through 1 Corinthians 14, and finally follow it up with a final message on some of the other passages like 1 Thessalonians 5, Ephesians 4, 1 Peter 4:10-11 and Timothy 1. By teaching the subject over four weeks you will demonstrate that the idea has a solid biblical basis, and is weighty enough to force consideration of implementation in the church.

10. Follow up the public teaching on the subject of participatory church gatherings with small group studies for the church members in a mid-week setting, so they can interact and wrestle with the Word of God for themselves.

11. Once a church has come to a united conviction about the matter of participatory church gatherings, hold a special church meeting to discuss moving towards having participatory church gatherings. Give a brief overview of the biblical basis and reasons for them, and allow time for questions and objections. If there is not church unity on the matter, continue to pray for the Lord's time and leading. If there are people who are obstinate for reasons of tradition or personal preference, meet with them to discuss their concerns, and pray together. Wait until there is consensus in the matter. Remember: consensus doesn't mean that everyone totally agrees with the idea – it means that they give consent to the church to act in the matter.

12. At some point, you need to step out in faith and start having participatory church gatherings. There will never be a perfect time – no church is so mature that an interactive format for church gatherings will ever be without difficulties. You need to trust God and start growing through doing what the Bible says about church gatherings, depending on the Holy Spirit's help. You also need to make it a weekly occurrence – not just a once-in-a-while novelty. Participatory church gatherings are a spiritual discipline that produces fruit over time. Almost any church can get itself sufficiently excited about a concept to make a good job of it once in a while, but the personal preparation and individual spiritual input required to continue to hold participatory church gatherings every week is more difficult, and it is this spiritual discipline that produces growth in the individual members of the congregation.

13. Those who are leaders need to make sure that they put their best effort into their contributions, so that if some other peoples' contributions are not of the highest standard, the flock is still fed. Encourage those who have participated, even if their contributions

were not stellar. Persevere, because there will be ups and downs, and spiritual growth and gift development takes time.

14. Train and mentor the most spiritually promising younger men in the congregation to be involved in preaching and teaching God's word. Take them aside as a group, like Timothy was encouraged to do in 2 Timothy 2:2 and spend time training them, teaching them about Christian doctrines as well as doing book studies. Get them to practice preaching on these subjects and passages. It will take a few years but you will develop a production line of preachers. Be sure to encourage these younger men when they publicly participate in the church gatherings – point out the things they did well, and encourage them to keep on doing it. Don't be negative and critical even if their contributions were not perfect. If there are doctrinal problems that need to be discussed, use the question and discussion time as a learning opportunity to explore what the Bible says about the matter.

15. Remind people periodically about the need for good teaching in the church (in the same way that Timothy was charged to by Paul). Talk about the sorts of poor-quality contributions that should be avoided as well as the sorts of contributions that provide 'sound teaching'. It is easy for us to get off track in the way we do things, so that bad habits develop or we get into ruts. Every now and again we need a wake-up call about the important need for edification through the best sorts of teaching and other spiritual contributions in church.

16. Make an explanation of participatory church gatherings part of membership preparation class for people wanting to join your church. Do not assume that new members are already familiar with participatory church gatherings. Assume they know nothing about them and need to be taught from the scriptures why the church worships the way it does.

17. Every year or so, give some teaching on the subject of participatory church gatherings. This will help remind, clarify and solidify people's

understanding of the subject. It is good to 'go round the foundations' every now and again, to check that everything is sound.

18. Don't be embarrassed or apologetic about participatory church gatherings – they are what God's Word teaches we should be doing. They are not the be-all and end-all of Christianity or of church life – they should not be a source of pride or a reason to despise others who do not practice them. We should stand up for them in the same way we defend any other part of the 'whole counsel of God' (Acts 20:27).

19. Be prepared to be criticized and mocked for putting participatory church gatherings into practice. Some Christians who are not aware of what the Bible teaches about church life, or do not wish to submit to Scripture, or look at it with an open mind, will perhaps say negative things. Many Christians are content with tradition and custom and will feel uncomfortable with what the Scripture teaches. Pragmatists who think that human cleverness will build the church, and political fixers who suggest that if only we were 'practical' and 'level-headed' we would not have so many problems in the church, may make sarcastic comments. Do not let the criticisms, mockery and insults cause you to respond in the same way. Do not become bitter and censorious, or continually harp on about how unscriptural other forms of church worship are. Instead pray that God will open their minds and hearts to God's way of working.

20. The essential requirement for implementing participatory church gatherings is conviction, a conviction that this is what the Bible teaches, a conviction that seeks to prayerfully, patiently, and lovingly put God's Word into practice. If we are bold enough to believe God's Word and show what it says about church meetings to other Christians, those who also love God's Word will be open to considering the truth, and following what it says. Confidence is contagious. On the other hand, it is possible for us to have an ecclesiastical inferiority complex: we are embarrassed to defend biblical church practices because they are so counter-cultural, so different to the way most modern churches are run, particularly some

contemporary pragmatic churches that seem to be successful. Conviction is also needed to continue with participatory church gatherings even though the results will sometimes be discouraging and at best variable (particularly at first). Conviction is necessary for the hard work of personal spiritual discipline and preparation that makes any church ministry profitable. Conviction is needed because participatory church gatherings require patience, that people need to be continually encouraged, and because spiritual growth, both individually and corporately, takes time. In the final analysis, whether a church moves towards participatory church gatherings comes down to this question: do we have a firm conviction that results in a 'will to implement' this form of church meeting? Do we have a firm conviction that will weather the storm when difficulties arise and discouragements come? There will always be people who are negative, people who are doubters, people who will sit on the sidelines and do nothing, people who will discourage and people who will mock. Doing anything for God requires that we step out in faith, that obstacles and opposition will arise, and that nothing will ever be perfect on earth. Conviction is required for all who wish to do the will of God in their own generation (Acts 13:36).

God's words to Joshua still apply to us, despite our different situation today: *'Only be strong and very courageous, that you may observe to do according to all the law which Moses My servant commanded you; do not turn from it to the right hand or to the left, that you may prosper wherever you go. This Book of the Law shall not depart from your mouth, but you shall meditate in it day and night, that you may observe to do according to all that is written in it. For then you will make your way prosperous, and then you will have good success. Have I not commanded you? Be strong and of good courage; do not be afraid, nor be dismayed, for the LORD your God is with you wherever you go'* (Joshua 1:7-9).

INDEX

Abbott, T K......................108
Alford, H......54, 114, 225, 231
Austin-Sparks, T..............294
Banks, R & J..........................38
Barclay, W.........47, 48, 70, 71
Barker, H P.....................141
Barna, G....15, 16, 19, 204, 207, 211, 212, 213
Barnes, A........................232
Barnett, P.....30, 31, 45, 46, 94, 233
Barnhouse, D G................146
Barrett, C K....32, 41, 188, 245, 246, 252
Belleville, L.................... 256
Bengel, J A................. 14, 232
Bishops... 69-75, 144, 154, 160, 188, 196
Blomberg, C......................30
Blum, E..................... 89, 90
Bounds, E M...................142
Bowen, G...................... 145
Bruce, F F.... 35, 37, 39, 51-54, 60, 102, 176, 231, 250
Calvin, J...............93, 94, 107
Carson, D A.................200, 201
Carson, T.................. 95, 102
Chapman, R C................,26, 27
Chrysostom......... 54, 114, 231
Church Government
    Congregationalism..........154-157, 188, 189, 195
    Episcopalian.......... 154, 155
    Presbyterian....154, 155, 157, 188, 189
Clarke, A........................231
Clowney, E...................93, 94
Cole, A.................... 146, 147
Cooper, A......................295
Croft, B......................... 15
Croucher, R....................215
Cymbala, J............201, 281, 282
Darby, J N............... 163, 249
Deacons....6, 70, 72, 85, 93, 94, 154, 156, 160, 195, 251, 279
Denney, J...5, 55, 57, 58, 59, 61, 177, 178
Discipleship.........17, 19-22, 87, 137, 206, 207, 275, 285, 303
Drane, J........................... 4
Elders.. 6, 14, 30, 33, 64-66, 69-75, 81-85, 87, 93, 94, 101, 119, 129, 130, 132, 133, 135, 141, 147-149, 154-157, 172, 188, 189, 193, 195-197, 234, 251, 279, 294
Ellicott, C.................114, 231
Ellison, H......................179
Erickson, M 167, 168, 170, 187, 188
ESOP...........................219
Fee, G D.... 31, 39, 40, 45, 125, 153, 191, 247
Fleming, K....................292
Frame, J A.................54, 55
Gallup, G.................. 19, 207

Index

Garland, D............... 171, 174
Geisler, N....................... 172
Gill, J............................ 231
Gilley, G.......................203
Girard, R.................. 275-278
Gooding D W.... 246, 247, 249
Griffith-Thomas, W H..... 152, 154, 155
Groeschel, C...................214
Groves, E......................299
Grudem, W...... 176, 182, 183, 190-192
Hammond, T C.......... 152, 153
Havner, V....................... 112
Hawkins, G.............. 210, 211
Hendricks, W...................207
Henry, M............. 93, 94, 231
Hodge, C..........107, 108, 175
Holmes, F............................ 26
Honeysett, M........... 214, 215
Horlock, M.................... 250
Horton, M........................19
Howlett, B..................... 168
Howley, G C D............... 117
Hybels, B........... 209-212, 214
Inrig, G.. 10, 11, 31, 32, 34, 104
Ironside, H...................... 64
Jackson, A......................214
Jamieson, Fausset and Brown......................231
Jennings, G....................185
Johnson, S L.................29, 33
Kelly, W....... 90, 100, 101, 166
Kierkegaard, S........... 198, 199
Küng, H....................... 143

Lang, G H...128, 137, 138, 141, 145, 262, 263, 265, 266
Leafblad, B..........................189
Learning Triangle.... 17, 18, 216
Lenski, R C H.................249
Lewis, R........................ 215
Lightfoot, J B.................. 154
Lindsay, T M......29-31, 34, 35
Lloyd-Jones, D M................ 9
Lord's Supper   vi, 2, 21, 33, 34, 138, 139, 161, 175, 221-243, 259-263, 265-269, 280, 286, 287, 301
Macarthur Study-Bible........ 69
Macarthur, J.......... 50, 69, 183
MacDonald, W 4, 5, 37, 59, 60, 96, 97, 177, 206, 249
Mackintosh, C H............. 194
Marshall, I H.. 5, 35, 37, 50, 53, 226, 227, 234, 250
Martin, R P...................... 52
Maxwell, J....219, 220, 295, 296
McRae, W...... 11, 12, 237, 238
Michaels, J R......... 92-96, 177
Morgan, G C.................... 86
Morris, L........4, 29, 32, 45, 50
Moule, H.......................147
Nee, W.....22, 23, 236, 237, 275
Packer, J I...................... 176
Parry, R St. J....................31
Pastors... 13, 27, 69, 72-75, 103, 105, 107, 108, 111, 113, 118, 144, 154, 160, 189, 215
Phillips, J B....................255
Piper, J...............16, 103, 104

Prophecy 24-26, 39, 41, 43, 46, 52, 55, 57, 59, 60, 72, 90, 93, 96, 108, 131, 147, 167, 175-183, 240, 247, 250
Rendall, F......................114
Renwick, A N.............. 57, 58
Richards, L......................153
Robinson, A....................111
Robinson, H....................205
Ryle, J C..........................194
Samarin, W.................... 186
Schweizer, E...................202
Short, A R.................48, 141
Short, S...65, 66, 72, 75-77, 90, 102, 148, 149, 267, 268
Smith, C..........................209
Southern, R....................204
Speaking in tongues..24, 26, 38-40, 46, 54, 57, 166, 175, 181-187, 191, 233, 240
Spiritual gifts 1, 2, 9, 11, 12, 21-25, 28-32, 34-36, 38, 40-42, 46, 47, 49, 50, 54, 56, 58, 60, 85, 89, 91, 92, 99, 104-106, 109, 115, 116, 120, 143-147, 157-159, 161, 169, 170, 172, 176, 181, 189, 191, 202, 224, 228, 229, 233, 236, 240-242, 261, 262, 267, 268, 271, 276, 278, 280, 287, 288, 293, 295, 296, 305
Spurgeon, C H.........18, 26, 304
Stedman, R..109-111, 149, 160, 277

Stott, J......8, 9, 51-53, 59, 111, 177, 231, 232
Streeter, B H...... 188, 189, 195
Studd, C T...................... 142
Taylor, J..........................141
Thirty-Nine Articles......... 154
Thiselton, A C..32, 36, 41, 124, 125, 171, 173, 174, 176, 177
Towner, P..................85, 255
Tozer, A W.................7, 19, 162
Tregelles, S P...................128
Trueblood, E............ 150, 151
Turner, M............... 112, 113
Vine, W E.......... 60, 96, 144, 165, 196, 197, 249, 265
Viola, F...20, 208, 209, 215, 216
Wallace, D......................115
Wallis, A.................. 142, 143
Warfield, B B..................122
Warner, R................190, 191
Watson, J B..............25, 41, 117
Weber, E...........................18
Wells, D.............. 19, 20, 205
Welmes, W..................... 186
Wesley, J........................7, 274
Westminster Confession of Faith...................... 154
Whitefield, G................. 274
Wigram, G V..................128
Wolfe, A.........................201
Women...... 30, 43, 44, 87, 168, 172, 180, 191, 244-257
Zens, J........................ 294

www.ingramcontent.com/pod-product-compliance
Lightning Source LLC
Chambersburg PA
CBHW050528300426

44113CB00012B/1998